HARVARD EAST ASIAN MONOGRAPHS

55

LAO SHE AND THE CHINESE REVOLUTION

LAO SHE AND THE CHINESE REVOLUTION

by
Ranbir Vohra

Published by
East Asian Research Center
Harvard University

Distributed by
Harvard University Press
Cambridge, Mass.
1974

The East Asian Research Center at Harvard University
administers research projects designed to further
scholarly understanding of China, Japan, Korea,
Vietnam, and adjacent areas. These studies have been
assisted by grants from the Ford Foundation.

Library of Congress No. 73-82346
SBN 674-51075-5

To my parents

CONTENTS

ACKNOWLEDGMENTS

This monograph began as a seminar paper which I wrote for Professor John K. Fairbank during my graduate year, and which developed into my doctoral thesis at Harvard. I am deeply indebted to Professor Fairbank for the constant encouragement and patience with which he guided every phase of my research and writing. I also gained much from Professor Benjamin I. Schwartz, whose philosophic insights often provided a framework for my own thinking.

During the course of writing this book I visited Japan, Hong Kong, and Taiwan in search of materials and to meet some of Lao She's old friends. My visits were brief and would not have been successful had it not been for the generous and kind help given to me by Mr. Sydney Liu, and Professors Peter Golas, Chang Tsun-wu, Wen Chung-yi, and Chuzo Ichiko.

I should like to thank Mrs. Wilma Fairbank, and Professors David Arkush, Fred Drake, Andrew Nathan and Ezra Vogel who read the earlier drafts and gave many useful suggestions. I am also grateful to Edward (Chung-man) Ch'an who helped me read some of the more difficult Chinese texts and to Mrs. Olive Holmes for her scholarly editing of the book.

Last, but not least, I am indebted to my wife who saw me through many difficult times with tolerance and understanding.

INTRODUCTION

LAO SHE AND MODERN CHINESE LITERATURE

Political history generally needs the flesh of social and intellectual history to cover its bones. The study of creative literature is one approach to the latter for it presents a kind of complex truth about society. Though literature lacks "hard" facts, it is nevertheless an indispensable source for the understanding of *Zeitgeist*. If this is true of literature in the West, it is even more true of Chinese literature.

Modern Chinese literature has certain unique characteristics that differentiate it from the literature of other countries. Having been consciously created by patriotic Chinese intellectuals who were motivated by a compelling desire to help renovate the nation and to provide a substitute for the inheritance of the past, which stood in the way of China's modernization, modern Chinese literature perhaps has a closer and more dramatic connection with revolution than any other literature in the world.

To achieve their end the promoters of the "literary revolution" (circa 1917) discarded the classical Chinese language in favor of the vernacular and adopted new literary forms from the West. This was a revolutionary act of as great significance as the elimination of the gentry class from the body politic of China. It must be remembered that the writers who were behind this revolution were trained in classical Chinese and did not find it easy or natural to make the adjustment. Indeed the vernacular used in the first instance was based on the local dialect of the writer's home province and was not a well-defined language.

Modern Chinese writing, therefore, has certain political connotations and reflects the deep concern of the writers for their country and its people. This seriousness of purpose made it impossible for writers to withdraw from society, to get overly involved with introspective and psychological themes, or to produce such "frivolous" literature as the detective novel.

The Chinese writer as an artist and an intellectual has, however, played more than one role. As a self-conscious leader of change he has tried to bring "enlightenment" to China; as an inheritor of the traditional scholar's role of censor he felt committed to attack the political abuses of the times; as a perceptive and sensitive artist he mirrored in his works the confusion and bewilderment that the breakdown of traditional culture and institutions brought to the lives of the common people.

The writings of modern Chinese writers, and their lives, therefore, provide an extremely important source for our comprehension of Chinese nationalism

1

and revolution. This study of Lao She, which focuses primarily on the content of his works and not on their literary quality, has been made within this context.

Lao She, whose high place in the field of modern literature is universally recognized, was born in a Manchu family of limited means in 1898 and is reported to have committed suicide in 1966 because of the humiliations he suffered at the hands of the Red Guards. He belongs to the generation of intellectuals who witnessed several political revolutions and many radical social and cultural changes, and for whom the tragic and humiliating overtones of Chinese history until the founding of the People's Republic was not a backdrop but a living experience.

It is hoped that the examination of Lao She's little-known personal life, the manner in which he was alienated from traditional, social, cultural, and political patterns, the changes in his ideas and values, and his comprehension of the problems involving Chinese society in the throes of change, will add, however slightly, to our understanding of the nature of the change itself.

The poverty of his childhood and the fact that these were also the years when the dynasty was collapsing and the Manchus were becoming a target of increasingly bitter attacks left a deep shadow on Lao She's impressionable mind and later kept him from personal participation in political activities. But his alienation strengthened his sense of patriotism and made his need to identify with China even more acute.

Lao She received a "modern" education and on graduating from Peking Normal School became a teacher by profession. In 1924 at the age of 26 he went to England to teach Chinese language at the London School of Oriental and African Studies. During his stay abroad, which lasted six years, Lao She began to write fiction and became established as a popular writer with the publication of his very first novel.

He had witnessed and been deeply impressed with the possibilities of the literary revolution and so when he began his literary career he, too, looked around him for Western forms and styles of literature to borrow from. It was Charles Dickens who provided him with the inspiration for his first novel and so Lao She became China's first great humorous writer. His humor and his non-participation in the politico-literary polemics that mark the world of Chinese literature in the 1920s led many to feel that his works were less than adequately serious. Such a label does great injustice to Lao She, for his writings not only reflect the author's deep sense of commitment to China but also have a strong undercurrent of pessimism and tragedy.

The polarization in the field of letters which resulted in the founding of the League of Left-Wing Writers in 1930 put a pressure on all writers claiming to be "serious" to join the League. Most of them who did so then had to show special respect for Communist ideology. That Lao She accepted no ready-made ideology on which to hang his tales in no way makes him a less sensitive social analyst or less concerned for the fate of his country.

Lao She is one of those great writers who have a genuine love and understanding of the suffering down-trodden little man in China. When he describes life in the over-crowded *tsa-yuan,* the courtyards where hunger, death, and disease inhabit the shabby tenements, he does so not with the objectivity of an ideologue denouncing the rich but with that sensitive tenderness which comes from deep fellow-feeling. By and large Lao She writes about the middle and lower urban classes and his main characters are students, teachers, petty officials, rickshaw pullers, peddlers, and small shopkeepers.

If writing about the underprivileged and the exploited elements in society and emphasizing the need for a radical change in state and society constitutes "leftism," then Lao She can be said to be a leftist writer without having aligned himself with any leftist group. He was by inclination a leftist who was groping for a suitable ideology, and in the forty-two years of his prolifically creative life he never did discover one.

By 1937 Lao She had not only won himself a place among the great Chinese writers, he had also earned the healthy respect of the left and right wings for his nonpartisan stand. Because of this he was chosen to be the de facto chairman of the All China Association of Writers and Artists against Aggression. In this capacity he tried to unite the writers and gear their literary work to the war effort. His activities did not make him popular with the Nationalist government which suspected him of being a Communist agent.

Tradition makes it possible for the Chinese writer in his role of elite intellectual to be an ally of the government in power if both sides are bound by the same ideology. Otherwise the writer as critic feels justified to form an opposition. This explains why the Nationalist government, until its collapse in 1949, was increasingly harsh toward the writers who in turn kept up a relentless attack on the Chungking regime.

That they had denounced the ways of the Nationalist government and suffered at its hands may have led many writers to believe that they would be automatically welcome in the People's Republic of China. They failed to realize that the Communist government did not want the writers as allies but as followers. The writers who could not accept this new role wholeheartedly suffered even more oppression under Mao Tse-tung than they had under Chiang Kai-shek. Lao She belonged to this unhappy group.

This study concentrates on Lao She's pre-1949 writings but a last chapter has been added to complete the story of his life and to show how he fared under the Communist regime. It appears that after his death Lao She's works were withdrawn from the market in mainland China. Since he was looked upon as a Communist writer by the authorities in Taiwan his works could not be purchased there at all. It is hoped that one day not only will this great writer be rehabilitated but that his works will receive the appreciation worthy of his unique genius.

I

GROWING UP, 1898–1924

Childhood

Shu Ch'ing-ch'un (*Tzu:* She-yü)—better known, inside and outside China, by his pen-name, Lao She—was born in a Manchu family in Peking or some place in Shantung in the year 1898.[1] Since Lao She's father was a palace guard,[2] and since we know that Lao She was educated and brought up in Peking, we can consider him a *"pei-ching jen"*—a person from Peking—regardless of his place of birth. Lao She always thought of Peking as his home, and his fondness for this city is repeatedly expressed in his writings.

Lao She's father was killed in 1900 in the fighting in Peking when the armies of foreign imperialist powers entered the city to protect the legations from Boxer excesses. The family, never very well off in any case, was now impoverished.[3] There was no doubt a meager pension for the widow, but it was hardly sufficient to cover the needs of mother and son; it appears that there were no other children in the family.

In 1909, at the age of 11, after having received private schooling of some type, Lao She entered the Two Grade Elementary School on Hsi-chih men Street. Since the Northern or so-called Tartar City was not officially opened to non-Manchus until 1911, it is likely that the school was mostly for Manchu children. At this school Lao She became friendly with a classmate, Lo Ch'ang-p'ei, who was also a Manchu and was later to achieve great renown as a philologist. The friendship lasted a lifetime and, perhaps, Lo Ch'ang-p'ei was Lao She's only really intimate friend; it is, at any rate, from him that we get an insight into Lao She's childhood and youth.[4] It is also significant that Lao She, compelled no doubt by a strong emotion, talks frankly of his school days, for the only time during his entire life, in an article eulogizing Lo after his death.[5]

Lo Ch'ang-p'ei's description of Lao She as a school boy gives us a picture of a vital lad who is naturally free and easy on the one hand, and highly restrained (where his emotions are concerned) and stubborn on the other. Lo, himself given to crying very easily, talks with admiration about Lao She's refusal to weep a single tear or utter a sound even when the teacher broke the cane beating him. Lao She was not particularly brilliant in school and it was only later when he entered Peking Normal School that he began to show his scholarly talents. One of the things Lao She and Lo Ch'ang-p'ei particularly loved to do after school was to go to some tea house and hear the storyteller recite or sing popular folk tales. Later Lao She was to use this art form to propagate national unity for resistance against Japan during the war. Since Lao She never had any money, Lo paid for the entertainment.[6]

After finishing elementary school, which took three years, Lao She and Lo Ch'ang-p'ei both entered the Third Middle School on Tsu-chia hu-t'ung. After half a year in the Middle School, the classmates parted company, for Lao She shifted to Peking Normal School from which he was graduated in 1917. While Lao She was still in his teens and completing his elementary school education, China as a whole was undergoing a traumatic experience of revolt and upheaval and a profound change was taking place in political and social outlook. The very foundations of Chinese civilization and institutions were being shaken. The upheaval which culminated in the successful 1911 Revolution was essentially a Han revolt led by Han revolutionary thinkers against the Manchu government.

Relationship Between the Manchus and the Han

Ironically enough, 1898, the year of Lao She's birth, was the last time radical Han reformers attempted to work within the framework of the Manchu imperial systems. With the flight of K'ang Yu-wei and Liang Ch'i-ch'ao—Chinese scholar-officials with ideas of fundamental reform—a rift was created between Han radical thinkers and the establishment. Many Han reformer-intellectuals, who before 1898 would have been satisfied to pass imperial examinations and accept government positions, hoping to influence policy from within, now became extremely "racist." Ideas of revolution and hatred for the Manchus seemed to go hand in hand.

After 1898, many Han intellectuals shifted their thinking from reform to revolution, and Chinese communities overseas, particularly in Japan, became centers of revolutionary activity. Basically, there was a difference in approach between K'ang Yu-wei and Sun Yat-sen. The K'ang Yu-wei group believed in monarchical republicanism, and Sun Yat-sen's followers in revolution to overthrow the Manchus and establish a republic. In actual fact, however, K'ang and Liang could not control the growing sentiment for revolution even among their students. In 1901 Ch'in Li-shan, a student of Liang Ch'i-ch'ao published an article which is said to have been the first public call for a revolution in China, and in the following year, a pupil of K'ang wrote that since the Manchus preferred to capitulate to foreigners rather than yield to the Chinese he could see no alternative but for the people to seek independence by making good use of newspapers, schools, and secret societies.[7]

Between 1900 and 1906, the number of Chinese students in Japan rose from 100 to 15,000. Having imbibed strong doses of revolutionary ideas there, they often returned to the mainland secretly to start uprisings which though mostly in vain produced martyrs and heroes[8] because the government promptly beheaded the rebels and young revolutionaries. Their activities captured the imagination of other youth and made the Manchus the target for increasingly bitter attacks.

The concession areas in the treaty ports also became havens from which the revolutionaries could publish newspapers and otherwise propagate their ideas. The Manchus were now openly described as "bandits" and the Dowager Empress was referred to with epithets like "the lecherous Yehonala."[9]

A few examples indicate how widely anti-Manchu sentiment was spreading. In 1903, a book by Tsou Jung called *Ko-ming chün* (The revolutionary army) was published by the editors of the newspaper, *Su-pao,* in Shanghai. In this book the author declared: "The Manchus, who are like animals, should all be killed. . . how wonderful and glorious is revolution!" and "Let us revolt and revolt! There is no justification for having a Manchu ruler. The Manchus are only about fifty thousand in number. Many of their princes and high officials are illiterate and amateur opera singers."[10] This book became a best seller and had a strong impact on youth.

In 1905, when the T'ung-meng hui was founded by Sun Yat-sen, the members swore to drive out the Manchu barbarians and restore China to the Chinese.

Even a comparatively liberal thinker like Liang Ch'i-ch'ao, who was against violent revolution and for a constitutional monarchy even if the monarch was a Manchu, wrote: "Several years ago I advocated anti-Manchuism; even though my teacher and friends reprimanded me every day, I refused to change my mind, and even today my feeling is still the same . . . If there is a way which can save the nation and at the same time help us to take revenge against the Manchus, I would certainly be delighted to follow it."[11]

In his last will and testament, Ch'en T'ien-hua wrote: "The Manchus and Chinese can never stand together on the earth . . . the only way is . . . govern the people with Chinese alone."[12]

There had always been some racial hatred in the country and many secret societies had propagated anti-Manchu sentiments, but in the first decade of the twentieth century this hatred became universal and intense. Han officials, upholders of the Confucian imperial system who would not have dared harbor a disparaging thought against the august person of the Son of Heaven, now believed with Liang Ch'i-ch'ao that "in free political competition whoever has superior ability must occupy the superior position. Since the political ability of the Chinese is far greater than that of the Manchus, there will be no problem whether the Manchus or the Chinese will have the predominant position under a constitutional government."[13] The Manchus were inferior beings and the Manchu Emperor was the "little comic figure." Great Han chauvinism and anti-Manchuism became nationalism in the narrow sense, and the motive for many to join the revolution.

On the other hand, the Manchus themselves, and very rightly, were increasingly afraid that if ever the Han were given more power, the Manchus would be massacred. Rumors to this effect were circulating freely, creating in the hearts of all classes of Manchus a feeling of fear and hatred for the Han. As a reaction, the Manchus became more belligerent. "In the offices the Manchus are very domineering and arrogant toward their Chinese associates, and the latter can only bear their insults in silence. Outside the office, the resounding anti-Chinese talk fills the people's ears." [14] This was particularly true in Peking, where the Manchus were still in command, and which was still far away from the centers of rebellion and riots.

From 1906 to 1908, seven attempts were made to overthrow the Manchu government, but all at a great distance from Peking—three in Kwangtung, one each in Yunnan, Kwangsi, Anhwei, and Hunan. With every one of these uprisings there was a natural hardening of attitudes between the two communities. In any case such incidents were not likely to draw a sympathetic response from the Manchus. In 1907, government decrees had been issued to prohibit students from participating in politics, and to ban public speeches and meetings in Peking, and an uneasy sense of superficial tranquillity prevailed in the capital.

Ultimately, the revolutionaries were successful and the Wuchang uprising proved to be not a local riot, but a turning point in the history of China. News of the defeat of the imperial troops did not, perhaps, strike terror in the hearts of the Manchu residents of Peking as much as the reports of wholesale massacres of Manchu residents in every town that was taken over by the revolutionaries. At Wuchang, "the revolutionaries, with their blood aroused, were in no mood to spare Manchu man, woman or child. The word had gone forth to wipe out the hated race . . . The soldiery . . . had tasted blood and were already engaged in the fierce Manchu hunt which formed such a blot on the revolutionary cause." [15] The Proclamation prepared by the revolutionary committee and issued by an unnamed general of the People's Army stated: "I am to dispel the Manchu government, and to revive the rights of the Han people." [16]

In reviving the rights of the sons of Han, whole families of Manchus were ruthlessly hunted out and put to the sword. At Sian-fu "no humane sentiments of pity could stay [the Manchus'] dreadful fate; lust only, in the case of women could stay [the soldiers'] thirst for blood. The Manchurian city— the northeast quarter of the actual city—is a grave[yard]. Shot down, sabred,

. . . burned alive, fled to be butchered elsewhere, with the exception of the women survivors, after a week's slaughter, a population estimated between 20,000 to 30,000 has disappeared." [17] Similar stories of how the Manchus were slaughtered in Hankow, Hanyang, and other cities came in quick succession.

The proclamations issued by the "Republican government," established at Shanghai in November, were obviously not intended to allay any Manchu fears for they stated that "all are unanimous in their sentiment of hostility to the Manchu race," and that "five millions of a nomadic tribe" were being supported by "four hundred millions of the descendants of the Holy Han." [18]

Peking, however, the undisputed stronghold of the Manchus with the imperial household and the residences of the princes, still had thousands of bannermen ready to take up arms. There was a strong desire to avenge the merciless killing of the Manchus in other cities, and word went around that the Han in Peking would be exterminated. There began an exodus from the capital but the situation was saved from deteriorating further by the abdication of the emperor and the coming to power of Yuan Shih-k'ai. Though Yuan Shih-k'ai may have been motivated by personal ambition, it was his manipulation of the situation that saved the Manchus in the north.

Manchus had been saved, but at the cost of their identity. Suddenly, they were no longer the ruling race, they had no guarantee of jobs or pensions, they could not live in separate sections of the city, they had no homeland, they had no protectors, they were nobody. They had "great difficulty in getting jobs unless they pretended to be of the Han nationality." Not to mention the plight of the lower ranks, even the members of the imperial clan took on "surnames like Chin, Chao or Lo." [19] In 1923, Liang Ch'i-ch'ao, reviewing China's progress, could say with a certain amount of racist pride that "during the last fifty years, the assimilation of the Manchus has advanced full speed, until the [1911] revolution, after which every Manchu was capped with a Chinese name. *Hereafter there will really be no Manchus in the world*." [20]

As we shall see, Lao She, like the other Manchus, submerged his identity in the vast Chinese population but he never forgave or forgot all that transpired with his people in 1911. Near the end of his creative life he managed to refer to this period and write in defense of the Manchus.

1912–1924

The 1911 Revolution brought many currents of change into Peking but, on the whole, life in the capital city did not undergo any violent disruption. There was no break in Lao She's studies. In 1912, when he was fourteen he entered the Third Middle School on Tsu-chia hu-t'ung. He had been there only half a year when he competed successfully in the entrance examination for the Peking Normal School. The reason for this shift was that the Normal School provided free tuition and free uniforms as well as books. It must be remembered that Manchus, not of the imperial clan, stopped receiving government pensions after 1911. This must have been a serious blow, and further explains why such a school would naturally have had a very great attraction for Lao She.

This one act of changing schools was to govern Lao She's future life—he was now well set on the path which would lead him into the world of education and make a teacher out of him. Whether he wanted to be a teacher or not had nothing to do with it. Years later, referring to his teaching days at Nan-k'ai Middle School, he said: "If I were to speak relying on my conscience [I would say] I taught Chinese only because it provided me with bread." [21] Money, or the lack of it, was a ruthless force that determined the relationship between a person and his environment, and Lao She was never to forget this. In many of his stories, we will find him wrestling with the basic question: "Does man live by bread alone?" And in the answer, we discover Lao She's attitude toward life.

Lao She seems to have grasped the important fact that, as a poor Manchu, his future depended entirely on his own hard work. We find that he was now exceedingly diligent at his studies. According to Lo Ch'ang-p'ei, Lao She shone as a brilliant student at the Normal School. He was very good not only in the field of literature but also in every other discipline and an impressive debater besides. The principal of the school was exceedingly well satisfied with him and, no doubt, this helped Lao She acquire the job of headmaster in a municipal elementary school, immediately after his graduation. At the same time he entered the National Higher Normal College of Peking and did particularly well in the Triennial Examination held in 1918. Thereupon he was appointed by the Bureau of Education to go on an "educational inspection tour" to Kiangsu and Chekiang. He apparently did a satisfactory job, for on his return he was promoted to the post of supervisor of the Northern Educational Section. (*pei-chiao ch'uan-hsueh-yuan*) This was the year 1919, and Lao She was 21 years old.[22]

Lao She was not yet sure what he wanted to do with himself but he was definitely sure what he did not want to do. He did not want to continue in a job which, however lucrative, called upon him to become friendly with "hobgoblins and devils," [23] the corrupt officials who depended on nepotism and bribery. Though poverty was revolting, he was ready to suffer it rather than flatter others in order to keep his job. He wanted to live a life of independence.

So in 1921, he gave up his job and joined Mr. Ku Meng-yü's Peking

Education Society as a secretary, and at the same time worked for two hours a day teaching Chinese at the Number One Middle School. His total earnings now were only forty yuan a month—less than one-third of what he had been drawing in his previous post. Though it was hard for him to manage within this amount—to look after himself and his mother and to attend extension courses at Yenching University—he turned down many tempting offers which would have brought him in contact with what he saw as corruption.

Lo says that one day when he was visiting with him Lao She told him "with tears in his eyes" that, "yesterday I sold my fur coat to provide my mother with winter clothing and rations." Since it was the season of freezing cold and bitter north winds, as only those who have lived in Peking can fully realize, Lo Ch'ang-p'ei suggested that he could help with money. Lao She's response was indicative of his strong and resolute character. He said: "The cold winds will strengthen my bones further. I hope that when I cannot stand it at all, you will help me." [24]

During this trying time, Lao She fell in love. He was distraught and wrote agonized love poems. Lo was ready to act as the go-between and arrange the marriage, but when he made actual inquiries, he found that the girl's father had become a monk and the girl a nun. Years later in the story *Wei-shen* (Vision), Lao She gives us a description of this first love of his, and we find it is a typical example of love-from-a-distance, old-style love with the couple hardly ever speaking a sentence to each other, but sighing deeply in the privacy of their chambers and undergoing tortures or feeling ecstatic:

> We had one glorious time together, only one. Everything conspired to be perfect that day. The crabapple tree in her courtyard was one mass of blossoms like a pinky-white snow-drift, the delicate bamboo by the wall was putting out fresh shoots, the sky was a delicate blue, her parents were out and the big white cat was sound asleep under the flowers. When she heard me come, she darted out like a swallow from under the eaves, not stopping to change her shoes, and her green slippers were like soft green leaves. She was radiant as the morning sun, her cheeks were much rosier than usual . . .
>
> From time to time she glanced outside to make sure no one was coming . . . At last she threw me a searching glance and said with most palpable reluctance: "You'd better go" . . . Slowly at last I tore myself away and there were tears in her eyes as she saw me outside the screen . . .
>
> Another chance like that never came.

On another occasion when he came nearly as close to her was during a funeral at the girl's house:

We were so close, each could almost hear the other's blood racing, as you hear young grain growing after rain. I uttered some brief commonplaces —a movement of the lips and tongue, that was all—our thoughts were far away.

Although we were 22, this was before the May Fourth Movement. Segregation of the sexes was still the rule. After graduation, they made me head of a primary school and that was the proudest day of my life, because she wrote me a letter of congratulation. The letter . . . had a postscript: "Don't reply." Nor did I dare . . .

To propose to her was out of the question. Too many senseless and yet insuperable obstacles stood between us, fierce and powerful as tigers.[25]

It is fairly obvious from this excerpt that Lao She is talking about himself, and one can feel how deeply he was in love with a girl whom he knew only from a distance.

In the fall of 1922 he left for Tientsin to teach in Nan-k'ai Middle School. We know very little about his stay in Tientsin except that there he did write his first short story, which was published in the school magazine. According to him it was nothing but a "space filler" which could not even justify his saying, with any pride, that "of course a teacher of Chinese language can write."[26]

Sometime in the summer of 1924, at the age of 26, Lao She left for England. He had an appointment as Lecturer in Mandarin and Classical Chinese for five years, August 1, 1924 to July 31, 1929, at the School of Oriental Studies, University of London.

We do not know how Lao She managed to get this job or what arrangements he made for his mother. It appears that Lao She was not in very good health when he left China and some of his friends told his mother: "Lao She will never return, he is so frail."[27] No doubt the implication was that he would not be able to stand the rigors of staying outside China and might die abroad. In actual fact he returned physically in much better condition than when he left.

Lao She is said to have been converted to Christianity some time before he left for England. There is even a suggestion that this act not only helped strengthen Lao She at a time when he was in a deep depression and had lost faith in everything, but also that his missionary contacts led to the opportunity to go abroad. In the novel *Lao Chang ti che-hsueh* (The philosophy of Lao Chang), one of the characters, Li Ying, who reflects some of the author's own character, becomes a Christian, and the reason for the act is described in the following statement: "He is basically a sincere and guileless person, but he suffered from oppressive circumstances, and so he lost some self confidence.

Furthermore, he had no faith in anything in society and so was attracted to religion."[28]

Some doubt remains about the exact time of Lao She's conversion to Christianity but it is certain that he did become a Christian at one time or another. From the facts available it seems more likely that it was before, rather than after, his visit abroad. From all that has been said earlier in this chapter, Lao She's life seems to have been extremely difficult before 1924. He gave up a job and was not able to marry the girl he loved; he was poor and his work was taxing. He could easily have lost faith in the new Republican China, which took away much more than the Manchu pension from his mother. It had taken away Lao She's identity. He had to search for a new value system; and the self-denying Christian faith, which provided ultimate hope to its followers, may have proved the spar that saved him from drowning.

1912–1924: New Politics and New Culture

As far as a common citizen of Peking was concerned, the 1911 Revolution was a matter of military trouble and revolt in distant provinces, most of them south of the Yangtze; it was the culmination of a spate of rumors and counter-rumors enlarging upon items of news which were increasingly terrifying to the Manchus and heartening to the Han; it was finally political maneuvering between Yuan Shih-k'ai, the Imperial Court and the Republicans, which led to the abdication of the Manchus in February 1912 and the establishment of the Republic with Yuan as president in the following month. The city of Peking, retained as the capital, was not ravaged and the Manchus living in it were not massacred, as had happened in many southern cities. The emperor was allowed to stay on in the Imperial Palaces in Peking, to retain his titles, and to receive an enormous annual subsidy for the maintenance of his court and other expenses, under the "Articles of Favorable Treatment."[29]

The presence in Peking of both the Ch'ing Emperor (who had abdicated but had not been dethroned and who resided in the Forbidden City and maintained his "little court") and the President of the Republic; the promonarchical and pro-Republican sentiments among the leading officials of the Republic; the attempt at an imperial restoration in 1917, following close on the heels of Yuan Shih-k'ai's failure to establish a dynasty, and the repeated rumors thereafter of an impending restoration—all were matters of direct concern to the Manchu nobility and the court princes. To the Manchus of a more lowly rank, their reduced social status after 1911, the arrogance of their Han neighbors, the difficulties of eking out an existence without government support were matters which had a greater bearing on their lives.

There were three occasions between 1912 and 1924 that may have had a heartening effect on the middle and lower-class Manchus in Peking. The first was in 1913 when Yuan Shih-k'ai declared a national mourning at the death of the Empress Dowager Lung Yu, the second in 1917 when Chang Hsun tried to restore power to Emperor Hsuan T'ung, and the last in 1923 when Hsu Shih-ch'ang presided over the "Grand Nuptials"—the wedding of the emperor. On all these occasions Ch'ing court dress reappeared in the streets of Peking and briefly, like the sun bursting out from dark clouds, there was an atmosphere of the "good old days." However, any small hope that the Manchus may have nourished in the privacy of their hearts was finally and completely dissipated when the emperor was forced to flee for protection to the Japanese Legation in 1924—the year Lao She left for England.

Any educated Manchu, who grew up in this period and who was sensitive to his surroundings, would have readily understood that politics was now a game which only the Han could play and that even the so-called monarchists were in favor of the revival of monarchy but not for the restoration of the Manchus. Politics, in any case, was a dirty word, and even the Han intellectuals felt frustrated and impotent in view of the fact that power had shifted into the hands of the militarists.

One aspect of the new politics, especially after the death of Yuan Shih-k'ai, was the infighting between the warlords. In this era, in the words of Professor Ch'ien Tuan-sheng, "multitudinous alliances, counteralliances, struggles and open wars among the factions ravaged China, year in and year out, almost without interruption. No fixed principles and no unchanging loyalties marked the factions. An ally of yesterday could be an enemy of today and the enemy of today could again turn to be a comrade of tomorrow . . . The only interest of each faction was to maintain itself in power, preferably at the seat of government, or, if that were not possible, at least in certain provinces."[30]

In these circumstances what type of political participation can one envisage for a middle-class Manchu intellectual? Can anyone really conceive of the possibility of a Manchu intellectual being motivated to join one of the political parties or factions, which had been founded by Han intellectuals for the sole purpose of rejecting the Manchus from China's body politic and restoring power to the Han race? We can understand why Lao She did not participate even in the May Fourth Movement, though he was very much a part of the world of education in 1919.

Writing a commemorative article on the death of his Manchu friend Lo Ch'ang-p'ei in 1955, Lao She repeatedly emphasizes that both he and Lo in their early days (that is, the period we are writing about) had only one desire and that was to be able to lead an "independent" life with no need to "toady or flatter" others or to be anybody's "running dog."[31] He adds that they "hated the reactionary forces" and were "patriotic" but "looked lightly upon politics" and did not care for it. It is not difficult to comprehend why Lao She and Lo Ch'ang-p'ei had no interest in politics.

In 1935, when Lao She was already a well-known author, he wrote a series of essays in which he gave his comments on the novels he had already published. Lao She had been criticized for showing in some of his works that the students of the May Fourth period were destructive and had little sense of positive revolution. In an apologetic vein he explains that he had only been a bystander at the time of the May Fourth Movement and had missed the Kuomintang Revolution of 1926–1927 because he was in England at that time.[32] Here we must reckon with the fact that Lao She always wrote about himself and his works with a certain defensive self-deprecation.

Lao She may have *avoided* politics but he was keenly conscious of the political and cultural revolution taking place around him. He missed nothing, but he had no desire to participate. With hindsight gained from his novels, we can locate broadly the strains of new thought that appealed to him.

It is not possible to draw a sharp line dividing culture from politics in the China of the 1910s and 1920s. The spirit that fired the pioneers of the Literary Revolution and fed the May Fourth Movement, which in turn dovetailed into the New Culture Movement, was closely associated with the spirit of political revolution. The aim was to revolutionize and modernize China. Modern Chinese literature, one of the products of these movements, was looked upon as a means to a sociopolitical end.

Liang Ch'i-ch'ao, who started a magazine called *Hsin hsiao-shuo* (New novels) in 1902 while he was in Japan, was one of the first to speak of this need for new literature and its potential for propaganda: "To establish a new morality, we must first create new novels. To found a new religion, we first need new novels. To have a better government, we must first have new novels. To have new science and technology, we must first create new novels."[33] Even Lu Hsun turned from medicine to writing, because he suddenly realized that it was not the diseased bodies but the ailing souls of his countrymen that needed attention. "It is not necessarily deplorable, no matter how many of them die of illness," he wrote. "The most important thing . . . is to change their spirit . . . I felt that literature was *the best means to this end,* I determined to promote a literary movement."[34]

When political change from monarchy to republicanism failed to make the nation more progressive, the floodgates of attack on the entire Confucian tradition were opened. From 1917 onward the reformer-scholars brought together at Peking National University by its liberal-minded chancellor, Ts'ai Yuan-p'ei, created a unique intellectual ferment. Intellectuals like Ch'en Tu-hsiu,

Hu Shih, and Li Ta-chao introduced such new ideas as realism, utilitarianism, pragmatism, liberalism, individualism, socialism, anarchism, Darwinism, and materialism, through the columns of *Hsin ch'ing-nien* (also called *La Jeunesse* or *New Youth*) and offered them as substitutes for Confucianism.

In 1917, Hu Shih published an article on the need for literary reform in *New Youth*.[35] With the backing of Ch'en Tu-hsiu, he urged writing in the vernacular instead of classical Chinese and won over many of the younger intellectuals. In the May 1918 issue of *New Youth,* Lu Hsun published his first story in *pai-hua* (vernacular)—"The Diary of a Madman." It was a sensation. In the April issue, Hu Shih had published his famous article on "Constructive Literary Revolution: A Literature of National Speech—A National Speech of Literary Quality," in which he emphasized the need for using "plain speech" to produce living literature based on real life experiences and dealing with the lives of the common people.[36]

Lao She appears to have been strongly impressed by Hu Shih and to have accepted practically all of his advice. One of Lao She's best novels, well-known in the English-speaking world in the translation, *Rickshaw Boy,*[37] relates the life of a rickshaw puller. He also weaves his plots around the clash between old and new in such fields as marriage, education, and women's rights. Even more telling, Lao She repeatedly emphasizes the fact that, however improbable his stories may be, they reflect actual observation and personal experience.

The proposal for literary reform aroused considerable opposition but the famous May Fourth Movement[38] helped the reformists win. It brought a new force—students and professors—into the political arena and resulted in a sudden proliferation of student magazines in the vernacular, which provided a platform for intellectual debate and expression. Lastly, it brought one type of unity to the whole country, even though the political division between the governments at Canton and Peking and the incessant wars among the warlords persisted: in 1920 the Peking government ordered the introduction of textbooks for the first two grades in *kuo-yü* (national language, which was the official name given to *pai-hua* demanded by the reformers).

Most of the writers had themselves been educated in the classical language. Now when they turned their hand to writing in *pai-hua,* they did so out of a conviction that it was good for the country and not because it provided the best medium of expression. For a long time they experimented with the new medium and wrote in a peculiar half-classical, half-vernacular style, until they evolved a *pai-hua* rich enough to produce good literature and yet not too far above the common man's level of understanding. Here Lao She excelled all others. He was a native of Peking, and the Peking dialect was the basis of the new "national language."

Although Lu Hsun had already published stories in the new genre, 1920 can be considered a starting point of "modern" Chinese literature. Of the many literary societies established at this time, the two most important were the Society for Literary Studies, or Literary Research Society (Wen-hsueh yen-chiu-hui), and The Creation Society (Ch'uang-tsao she) both of which were founded in 1921. The first, which propagated "art for life's sake" and emphasized humanism and realism, took over *Hsiao-shuo yueh-pao* (The short story magazine) published by the Commercial Press in Shanghai. From 1921 to 1931 this magazine helped discover literary talent, and its high standard made it one of the most prestigious publications in China. Among those associated with The Society for Literary Studies were Mao Tun, Chou Tso-jen, Yeh Shao-chün, and Cheng Chen-to.[39]

The Creation Society, guided by the principle of "art for art's sake," was founded by a group of Japan-returned students led by Kuo Mo-jo. From May 1922 they began publishing a literary quarterly called *Ch'uang-tsao chi-k'an* (Creation) and for some time this provided them with a platform for expressing their ideology of romanticism and individualism in the manner of Shelley, whom they greatly admired and translated into Chinese. Like Shelley, these young Chinese writers soon established a link between romanticism and politics. In 1924, the year Lao She left for England, Kuo Mo-jo translated a work by the Japanese Marxist, Kawakami Hajime, entitled *Social Organization and Social Revolution.* From then on, the society advocated socialism and revolutionary proletarian literature. The most important writers connected with the group were Kuo Mo-jo, Chang Tzu-p'ing, Yü Ta-fa, and T'ien Han. The magazine ceased publication when it was banned by the government in 1929.

One negative aspect of the May Fourth Movement was the students' frequent misuse of the liberty they had won. They often went on strike without sufficient reason, and caused much destruction of property. Both the Kuomintang (which was reorganized on the Russian model between 1919 and 1924) and the Chinese Communist Party (which was founded in 1921) often guided, or misguided, the students to revolt in order to hurt the Peking government. The mystique of revolution had caught on, and intellectuals like Ch'en Tu-hsiu and Li Ta-chao turned as avidly to communism as they had to democracy earlier for a quick solution to China's problems. By 1920, however, the Peking government had managed to re-establish its repressive controls and the period of free debate and intellectual liberty was over. A split also developed in the original group, some turning to communism and revolution, and others to democracy and gradualism.

Those in the country who upheld the pragmatic and gradualist approach, such as Sun Yat-sen in the 1920s[40] and Hu Shih, would have liked the students to study harder so that they could help with the reconstruction of the country. Lao She, too, in practically all his writings, particularly those of the early period, was rather cynical about student participation in politics, and he condemns those students who went around demonstrating.

When Lao She left China, the process of political polarization had hardly begun. It was to crystallize during his absence when Chiang Kai-shek rose to power, and not only broke with the Chinese Communist Party, but tried to eliminate the influence of the leftist thinkers by ruthlessly destroying them. The spirit which had led alienated Han intellectuals to work for a republican revolution in the last years of the Manchu era showed up again in the late 1920s and led the young writers and artists to identify themselves with Communist ideology and to help achieve a Communist revolution. Lao She, an alienated Manchu intellectual, watched the new infighting from London with the same objectivity with which he had witnessed the fighting among the warlords, and the happenings of the May Fourth Movement. Lao She's need to identify himself with China was great, but he still had to find the niche in the new Chinese edifice where he could stand securely and with dignity. Luckily, even if it was inadvertent, he found his place when he tried his hand at writing and became one of China's leading novelists and short story writers.

II

THE FIRST NOVELS, 1924–1929

The excitement of traveling abroad and settling down in a strange new world soon wore off and within half a year, Lao She started feeling lonely and nostalgic for home. He says that since he had not lived with his family since the age of 14, he was actually remembering all that he knew of China when he thought of home. Often when he sat down with a book of fiction, his mind would wander and he would see scenes of things past. His memory was so vivid that he finally decided to put down on paper what he saw in the mind's eye.

He had never written before, except the one piece for the Nan-k'ai Middle School magazine, and he was not even aware that there were books dealing with the art of writing. He had read Chinese traditional novels but he did not want to use this form for his own writings. Now that he was so far removed from the centers of literary debate, he must have tried to understand and review all the ideas like "art for art's sake," and "literature for humanity" which had been bandied about in the last few years in China, seeking, no doubt, a pattern which would suit his own thinking. All attention in the field of letters in China was turned to Western and other non-Chinese literary forms and Lao She, not immune to the currents of the New Culture Movement, decided to use the European structure of the novel although his knowledge of Western literary models was "very superficial." And, of course, his models had to be drawn from the literature of social criticism.

Just before settling down to write his first work of fiction, *Lao Chang ti che-hsueh* (The philosophy of Lao Chang), probably the first novel written in modern Chinese literature, Lao She had finished reading two of Dickens's novels—*Nicholas Nickleby,* and *The Pickwick Papers.*[1] He used these novels as a model, and so it is no surprise to find that *The Philosophy of Lao Chang* is episodic and loosely structured. Wang Yao thinks that Lao She was still under the influence of the Chinese traditional novels,[2] which are also episodic and do not have well-knit plots. However that may be, Lao She gradually improved the unity of his stories, and we find that the second novel, *Chao Tzu-yueh,* and his third and last production while in England, *Erh Ma* (Mr. Ma and Master Ma), are far more successful in this direction.

Lao She's first novel, and to a lesser extent his second novel, also suffer from the fact that they are written in a language which is half vernacular (*pai-hua*) and half classical (*wen-yen*).[3] In each new work Lao She increased the content of the vernacular in his mix and by the time he wrote the fourth novel we can consider him, more or less, a writer of true *pai-hua.*

19

In spite of the obvious experimental nature of the London-period novels, and their weaknesses, they were very popular and were repeatedly reprinted until 1949.[4]

Lao Chang ti che-hsueh (*The Philosophy of Lao Chang*)

Reminiscing in 1935 about how he wrote *The Philosophy of Lao Chang*, Lao She said there was no central theme in the novel, and that like one "with a new camera, taking pictures at random everywhere" he had set down "characters and incidents as they came to [his] mind."[5] Add to this note on the contents of *Lao Chang*, Lao She's remark that it lacked form because it was structured on the model of *Nicholas Nickleby*, and *The Pickwick Papers*, and we have the author's defense against critics who had attacked his work on the basis, obviously, of Jamesian criteria of thematic unity and total form. Lao She is, no doubt, aware of the Jamesian criteria, but like Dickens he can never really get away from the episodic form and in spite of his apology for the first novel, he finds it hard to restrain himself from introducing some "unnecessary" episodes even in his best works.

If he had written *Lao Chang* entirely on the basis of emotion, Lao She says:

> It is possible I may have written a comparatively powerful tragedy, but I didn't go all the way. On the one hand, I used emotions to taste the flavor of life, on the other, I restrained my emotions and did not entirely judge matters on the basis of my loves and hates. This contradiction is born of my character and environment. From my childhood I have been poor, and my character has been strongly influenced by my mother—she was a woman who would rather have starved than to have been willing to beseech help. And yet, at the same time, she had a great sense of righteousness and public spiritedness (*i-ch'i*). Poverty made it easy for me to curse the world, willfulness made it easy for me to judge others on the basis of my own emotions, but, *i-ch'i* made me sympathetic to other people . . . [because of this] I lost satire and gained humor . . . I hate a bad person, but he also has his good points; I love a good man, but he also has his bad points.[6]

He could have added, if he had realized this himself and had the courage to speak forth openly, that he was a Manchu, an alienated outsider who could look upon things with the cold critical eye of an outsider, and yet, because of his tremendous need to identify himself with the country of his birth, he longed to be accepted as an insider. It is interesting that Lo Ch'ang-p'ei's analysis of Lao She contradicts Lao She in some ways. Lo says that: "because of poverty in childhood [Lao She] had been injured emotionally and that he, with a critical eye, always divided people into categories of good and bad—hating the bad with an indignation one feels for an enemy, and, with a similar passion, ready to sacrifice his life for a good man."[7] The clash between these contradictory but interconnected emotions of which both Lao She and Lo Ch'ang-p'ei speak, produced the tension between the pure creative comic spirit and the satirical intent, or the didactic purpose which underlies the overall pattern of Lao She's writings. He wavers between the two and it is in fusing creativity and social significance in the thematic structure that he ultimately produces the powerful novel *Lo-t'o Hsiang-tzu* (Camel Hsiang-tzu).

Lao Chang deals with the author's experience of his country and his countrymen during his maturer years, that is, from about 1916 (when he was 18) onward. Lao She is more interested in the people he knew than in the country as a whole, and it is through the people that he tries to reveal the country. So we find that for the characters in *Lao Chang,* the northwest corner of Peking is Peking, indeed it is China and so the whole world. The novel is set in the period 1919–1924, but one would seek in vain any references to student demonstrations, or warlords or any of the other stirring events connected with nationalism and modernization with which political histories are full.

The plot is rather simple. Chang, an extremely miserly person, owns and runs a primary school in the northwestern suburb of Peking. He also owns a shop, and is the local moneylender. Though a reprehensible character, Chang is very clever and in his machinations to get on to the "local autonomy committee" and thus gain greater power and authority, he uses his wealthy but stupid friend Sun Pa, who is a member of the local gentry. Chang feels that to be successful in the world of politics one has to keep up with the modern times and in practice, this means that one has to acquire a concubine who has been to a new type school and received a modern education. He wins over Sun Pa, who too has political ambitions, to this point of view and arranges that Sun Pa and he "marry" educated concubines on the same day. The girls, Li Ching and Lung Feng come from respectable families and have a decent schooling, but are forced into being sold because their families owe money to Chang. Li Ching, who is an orphan, is acquired by Chang against a loan which is owed him by her uncle. Lung Feng is the daughter of Lung Shu-ku, an officer in the Salvation Army. Chang forces him to sell her to Sun Pa, thereby not only getting the money he had loaned Lung Shu-ku, but also forcing him to resign from the local autonomy committee (due to loss of face) and hand over his post of chairman to Chang.

At this point it is necessary to shift our attention to another skein of the story. Li Ching has a brother, Li Ying, who is a student in Chang's school.

One day Li Ying and a classmate of his, Wang Te, stop Chang from beating his wife and in the process Li Ying gives Chang a thrashing. For the unpardonable offense of having laid hands on their teacher they have to leave school and go to the city in search of work. In the city, Wang Te falls in love with Li Ching, as does Li Ying with Lung Feng. They are, however, thwarted in their love by Chang's action. As the day for the "marriage" approaches Li Ying runs away from Peking because he finds himself in no position to either help his sister or fulfill his own desire. Wang Te is driven out of his mind at the tragic developments, and armed with a knife comes to the marriage hall to destroy Chang, but is overpowered. At this stage the rich, good-hearted Captain Sun, Sun Pa's uncle, arrives on the scene and saves Li Ching by paying off her uncle's debt. He also helps out Lung Shu-ku by making Sun Pa consider the money paid for Lung Feng as a loan to her father.

The true lovers are, however, not united. Wang Te is married by his parents to some village girl while he is still sick and mentally unbalanced. When he comes to, he becomes reconciled to his arranged marriage, and Li Ching wastes away and dies. Lung Feng moves to Feng-tien with her father, and the author tells us that she later married a rich husband. Nothing is known of what happened to Li Ying.

Chang, the evil genius, does not suffer in any way. On the contrary, he becomes a provincial commissioner of education in some southern province and acquires two concubines.

Most of the characters in *Lao Chang* come from the educated, or at least the literate, middle class, but only a very few among them have the finances and the leisure to think of anything more than the struggle for existence. As for the lower classes, they are far removed from concepts like nationalism, and even in matters like elections to offices in the local government their understanding is that "after all persons like the local gentry and teachers have watches which they can wear, so can become watch-wearers."[8] Lao She makes it sound comic, but it is not beyond imagination to conceive of an ignorant, unlettered laborer or peasant mistaking the word *tai-piao* which means representative or delegate, for *tai* meaning to carry or wear, and *piao* meaning a watch.

On this subject, Lao She says:

> People from the countryside pay no attention whatsoever to the imperial flag or the republican flag or the Japanese flag flying in the city; they do not take notice of the emperor, the president, or the empress taking over authority. The people in the city are vastly different . . . while walking down a street, sitting in a teahouse, sleeping at home they feel as if they

have acquired some sort of political power or authority. Those who have had schooling sit with a newspaper on a bamboo seat in the park, read a few lines and have no trouble recognizing themselves as venerable masters of the country. It is not necessary to mention that . . . the "masters of the country," after all, have an opportunity to gain wealth and office—an opportunity to gain more wealth if they already are wealthy, and to acquire more offices if they already have an office. Rice has become more expensive, the number of soldiers have increased, taxes have become heavier, but what do they care . . . this is a matter which concerns only the people from the country.[9]

When he says "people from the city" Lao She is, no doubt, referring to the more affluent section of the community, persons like Sun Pa and Lao Chang, who are self-seeking and corrupt and manipulate politics to gain personal ends. When Lao She resigned his post in the Bureau of Education in 1921, it was because of such wily and deceitful persons. Their corruption was too much for Lao She to bear because the only way he could survive under these circumstances was to become like one of them and to toady to those above him while squeezing those below him. He saw through all these "patriotic" and "nationalistic" new masters of China and would have no part of them. But they had authority and power and wealth and in China during this period, only those who had could acquire more.

In the novel, even before the elections to the local autonomy committee are held it is known who would hold the offices. The only thing not known is who would be elected to which office, and it appears that this too could be manipulated. As Lao Chang explains to Sun Pa, the autonomy committee is organized by us, the members of the committee have been appointed by us, only the person we call upon to act as chairman can do so. He amplifies the statement a little later by saying: "Sun Pa you are too honest. It is indeed not easy for honest persons to manage civilized matters. Aren't the members of the committee appointed by us to come and applaud? If you use a little money to buy some sweets for them to eat, can they dare not listen to your orders?"[10] To make the reader even more keenly conscious of the farcical and undemocratic nature of the local autonomy committee Lao She with biting sarcasm makes the policeman drive away the crowd of common folk that had gathered outside the meeting place of the committee with the admonition "of what concern is the meeting of the local autonomy committee to you? Disperse, disperse."[11]

There are no laws that can control or fight this parasitic class. Law courts are inefficient and take years to settle a case, and this naturally, gives the lawyers a greater chance to fleece their clients. "Go to law? Is this something the Chinese can manage? Are we talking of law courts? Chinese law courts! Are they devised to settle law suits? . . . That's a joke!"[12] And as for the police, "Peking policemen are most obedient to the people's will. If you wear a long gown and can produce a printed namecard giving your official title, you can order them around . . . If you have authority you can telephone the police station and inform them of the time you will go to excrete in the middle of the road, and sure enough, a policeman will be ordered to clean the road for you."[13] Lao She views with great indignation the failure of these new, "modern" government institutions to provide an effective substitute for the controls which Confucian ethics and imperial bureaucracy had maintained. Nor does he find any hope that the so-called independent press will expose their doings. Wang Te, who had joined a newspaper after leaving school, is morally aghast when the editor not only puts him on the mat for writing an eyewitness story of how the vice-minister of education had run over and killed an old woman, but ends all further argument by saying: "I do not want you to write the truth."[14]

So these are the people in authority, not nationalists and nation builders sacrificing themselves for the common weal, but self-seeking, nepotist parasites, whose only connection with the common people at large is one of cynical exploitation. They are the peculiar product of the "new age" when Confucianism has lost its political content and an attempt is being made to fill the vacuum with "democracy," "local elections," "liberalism," "individualism," and so on. Lao She had been in England only a few months before he began to write this novel, but even a few months were long enough for him to be able to make a comparison between the confusion which marked Chinese society, the lack of law and order, and the absence of moral and social values in China, and the orderliness, sobriety, and social consciousness which were the attributes of the proud, independent-minded and freedom-loving Englishmen. Before he left England, Lao She was to use his experiences of British society in his novel *Mr. Ma and Master Ma*.

Though Lao She is deeply concerned with the corruption and immorality of men in power, he is not interested in making a political analysis of the source of ultimate authority—the government. He views society in a more traditional way, seeing the web of relationships which locally affect a person's life—the neighborhood as a microcosm—as of primary importance. In traditional China, the magistrate and, to a greater extent, the local gentry were an immediate reality, and the emperor in a manner of speaking, only a myth. So also in *Lao Chang* we notice that although the story is laid in the 1920s, Sun Pa and Captain Sun, who are unhesitatingly defined by Lao She as the local gentry, are the most important personages on the scene. This approach of

Lao She is to be found not only in his first novel, but in practically all his writings. It is the state of society that Lao She depicts and not the causes that produced that state; and if his characters act in a confused way, it is because the common man in this era of transition was confused. In this Lao She is far more like the early Lu Hsun than any other writer of this period.

Perhaps the best way to comprehend Lao She's conception of the social situation in *Lao Chang* is not to read the novel from the point of view of the main character Mr. Chang, but to see things through the eyes of Li Ying and Wang Te. These two young men, both nineteen years of age, have a naive quality and Lao She makes them faceless for they are also without any blemish and devoid of any evil. As they move through the story they find that a good, honest person has no place in society. An upright and sincere official like Li's uncle is dismissed and allowed to die slowly in poverty and isolation; a public-spirited man like Chao Ssu, who desires to use his wealth and energy to help mankind, is driven to the outer fringes of society where he survives by becoming a rickshaw-puller, scorned and laughed at;[15] Li's paternal aunt and uncle are "good" people, full of kind feelings for their orphaned niece and nephew, but they are tolerated because their Confucian values only make them helpful pawns in the game of those in power—Li's aunt who really loves Li Ching as if she were her own daughter, finds it more honorable to let Li Ching become Chang's concubine than to see that she marries a man of her own choice.

So Li Ying and Wang Te are caught between the old and the new, and inappropriately enough for them, all the worthwhile values are still the old ones or at least it is only among those who still hold on to the old that any ethical or moral values are to be found. On the other hand, these "good" people are the very ones who by their helplessness prove that they represent something that is dying and in no way can provide inspiration to youth. Since the new offers no substitute values the young are bound to be confused.

Let us take education as an example. Here youth comes in direct contact with the "new." Lao She cleverly uses a visit by an inspector of schools to Chang's school to depict what was happening in the field of education. His humorous description of the inspector's visit reveals the extent to which the undying past refuses to give way to the forces of modernity. The very fact that Chang receives information about the impending "surprise" visit of the inspector from a "sworn brother" in the yamen shows how the protective local network of relationships still works against intrusion from the higher offices of government.

Though the time lag between the arrival of the panting informer and the arrival of the inspector is not much, it is still adequate for Chang to make the necessary preparations for the inspection. With admirable haste Chang orders the students to hide the classical texts from which they have, obviously, been studying and replace them with the *kuo-wen* (national language) textbook. That some students have not even brought this book to school shows how little use Chang makes of it! Chang also gets his wife to prepare tea and has his students sweep the ground under the apricot tree outside and lay out the tea things there.

Another most important act of preparation is to dispatch one of the students home to fetch his father. Sun Pa, the boy's father, is a member of the local gentry. Chang, in the spirit of tradition, knows that it would be most helpful to have Sun Pa on hand to receive the inspector, who in turn would feel honored by this act.

The inspector is no better representative of the new forces in education than Lao Chang. After he has inspected Chang teaching a class, he expresses his satisfaction with the manner in which Chang pronounces foreign words, adding his learned comment that "the principles governing Chinese and Western languages are the same."[16]

It is fairly obvious that Chang and the inspector are making a desperate effort to display their limited knowledge of new things, and that they are much more at ease only when the subject shifts to something traditional. Just as Lao Chang is more familiar with classical books and appears to actually teach them regularly in preference to modern subjects, so also the inspector, having made a superficial examination of Chang's teaching methods, comes around to a topic in which he seems much better versed:

> "Mr. Chang, there is one matter where I cannot help but point out your mistake . . . Why is your teaching dais on the west side of the room? It is a 'White Tiger Dais' and has an evil influence on the families of your students. How could you arrange it like this knowing that education is a noble and beneficial profession?" said the inspector emphasizing every word.
> "The honorable official before you said something about the classroom receiving light from the east, [replied Chang] so I built the dais on the western side. Actually I also comprehend a little bit about *feng-shui* and *yin-yang*, but I did not dare to disobey an order from my superior. Sir, please forgive me."[17]

Soon after the inspector's visit Li Ying and Wang Te have to leave the school because of the unfortunate affair between Mr. and Mrs. Chang in which they had interceded. Before going to the city to search for jobs both these boys have a talk with Li's uncle and it is from him that they learn of Chang's intention to buy Li's sister and make a concubine of her. This is their first real contact with the harsh reality of life. Li's uncle, who is an upright and a good man, who has himself suffered grievously from the corrupt and tainted society, gives the youth this advice:

> Wang Te and Li Ying please remember: If a good person does not hold on to right conduct and morality and does not war with the evil men, he is in that case, just a slave of the evil person. If a good heart is only weak, goodness is like arsenic which can destroy one . . . I myself have no hopes, but I do hope that you will be able to, in the future, strike off the heads of evil persons . . . As for money, please remember to be careful in making money and careful in spending it . . . In the past I advocated 'pay back injury with kindness' but now I say, 'pay back injury with justice.' In the past I advocated that money should be spent indiscriminately though I did not permit the obtaining of it by foul or illicit means; now I hold that money should neither be made illicitly nor should it be spent indiscriminately.[18]

Li's uncle represents traditional China and from this and other novels we feel that Lao She sympathizes with his philosophy of money, morality, and action. The morality appears to have close associations with Confucianism; action seems to spring from Lao She's admiration for the heroes of Chinese traditional novels like *Shui-hu chuan* (Water margin), who went forth to avenge foul play by destroying the perpetrator of evil—an isolated action unconnected with any political philosophy but heavily flavored with righteousness, a Confucian attribute; money seems to have acquired a new dimension, which is spelled out indirectly in some detail by the events in the novel.

But Lao She also realizes the impracticality of the advice being offered to Li Ying and Wang Te. Li's uncle does not appear to understand the nature of society outside the shadows of his little room, where he finds solace in classical texts and bides his time waiting patiently for death. The meaninglessness of his advice becomes apparent to the reader, as it does to Li Ying and Wang Te, when it is found that moral principles are fine as long as one does not try to live by them in society; that money is a rare commodity and difficult to come by because jobs are not easy to find; and that in a society full of evil people, one cannot go around cutting off heads unless one is ready to sacrifice one's own life for an action which, to say the least, has a debatable beneficial value to society.

Li Ying and Wang Te are honest, sincere, hardworking, but their moral fiber is weakened as they are forced to compromise at every step. At the end

of the story, Wang Te makes one last heroic effort to vindicate his individuality
—he tries to murder Chang. By making him unsuccessful in doing even this,
Lao She puts a finishing touch to the sense of total frustration which tragically
concludes the short love affairs of the youth. The reader gets a deep feeling
of pessimism. If youth is the new force in society, it seems to be a very weak
force, and there appears to be very little hope for it to be able to break
through the strong chains of reaction and to raise its head above the choking
atmosphere contaminated by foul corruption. Demoralized and desperate, Li
Ying becomes a Christian, hoping to find some spiritual and moral solace in
that religion.

But Christianity cannot instantly replace the traditional sense of morality
and so when Li Ying is faced with the proposition that he can marry Lung
Feng, his desire for individual self-satisfaction clashes with his sense of loyalty
to his relatives: "Firstly, I cannot marry because I am young and poor.
Secondly, I cannot only think about myself and forget my sister and uncle."[19]
At the end Li Ying comes to the conclusion: "There is only one way out . . .
die."[20] He doesn't die but runs away in a most cowardly fashion, unable to
face the situation.

If Wang Te had eloped with Li Ching then perhaps Li Ying's problems
could have been sorted out, but Lao She has not overlooked this possibility.
"If Li Ching were to elope with Wang Te," he says, "it is not necessary to
think twice, that neither she nor he would be able to survive in our ritualistic
society."[21] It was preferable to suffer being a concubine of Lao Chang than
to be ostracized and destroyed by society. Lao She observes cynically:

[Li Ching] has had schooling and understands . . . the "new principles"
. . . But she went to school in a ritualistic society and she studied national
language and geography, already a terribly frightening matter . . . If she
had come to appreciate the new ideas to the extent that she had the courage
to elope with Wang Te, then the death sentence condemning new education would have been pronounced long ago. There would not have
been any place where one could even study geography or national language.[22]

The so-called revolt of youth ends in a whimper. It is to be remembered that
Lao She is describing the society of the 1920s. "How is it that the 'new people' cannot root out the old forces? The revolutionaries who advocate 'anti-
filialism' can declare war against their parents, but weaken and are defenseless
before any entreaty made by their parents. Besides, there are times when you
cannot analyze or judge the love between parents and children on the basis of

reason."[23] And, there lies the crux of the matter. Lao She himself is not totally convinced that the destruction of filial piety is necessarily a good thing.

Lao She in this novel gives us a sense of the tragedy that faces youth in transition. Some of the happenings, for example, the incapacity of Li Ying to marry the woman he loved, the turning of Li Ying to Christianity for values which he found missing in his own society, have a bearing on the author's own youth. Lao She gives us a slice of life as it was found in Peking, and no doubt in other parts of China too, before 1924. He makes no attempt to analyze all the causes of the confusion and the contradictions which faced many people at this time, nor does he try to give any solutions. It is clear, however, that Lao She is not carried away by the mystique of revolution, and does not see an easy or quick solution to the problems facing Chinese society.[24]

After the novel had been published serially in *Hsiao-shuo yueh-pao* in 1926, it was printed as a single volume by the Society for Literary Studies. Lao She never came to know how it fared at the hands of the critics and although he asked his friends, he received no letters of critical appreciation.[25] It is understandable that Lao She, himself, was very pleased with the fact that he had gotten into print so easily, and in a magazine which had an exceedingly high standing in China. So, his next novel followed in the footsteps of the first, and he himself calls it the "tail" of *Lao Chang*.[26]

Chao Tzu-yueh

Chao Tzu-yueh is set in post-May Fourth Peking. Unlike *Lao Chang* it does not deal with a broad social theme, but limits itself to the activities of a group of college students. The group is composed of Chao Tzu-yueh, Ou-yang T'ien-feng, Wu Tuan, Mo Ta-nien, Chou Shao-lien and Li Ching-ch'un, who all attend the same college—Ming-cheng College—and live in the same boarding house. Chao, who comes from a wealthy landlord family, is supposed to be the leader of the group; Ou-yang has no family to help him—he lives by his wits, and is the villain of the piece; Wu-Tuan, who like Chao comes from an affluent family is the most Westernized of the lot; Mo Ta-nien who wants to be a banker, and Chou Shao-lien, who is a poetaster and always composing "modern" poetry, are minor characters; Li Ching-ch'un, who is the only student in the group who has an independent point of view, disassociates himself from the rest and, instead of strikes and demonstrations, advocates diligence and hard work.

The novel can be divided into two broad parts. The first section gives a picture of the free and easy life of the students, who seem to be a community drifting aimlessly in the void, cynical about China's heritage but not too sure of the path that would lead to new China, mistaking violent demonstrations for nationalism, and superficial Westernization for modernization. They are a confused and alienated lot who lack all sense of direction, are irresponsible, and are not motivated toward any constructive effort whatsoever. In the second section the author describes the students after they have left college—their search for jobs, their ambitions, hopes, and frustrations. The ties that had bound them together now dissolve, and these representatives of "new youth" become victims, to a greater or lesser extent, of the archaic forces of traditional China or of the corruption which engulfs the new social and political institutions. Only Li Ching-ch'un remains true to his ideals and it is in his arrest and execution—the result of his having made an unsuccessful attempt on the life of an evil warlord—that the members of the group, except Ou-yang T'ien-feng, find a source of inspiration to lead more serious lives which would benefit the nation.

In *Lao Chang,* Lao She depicted a class of youth so hemmed in that it can hardly think of rebellion; in *Chao Tzu-yueh,* he introduces us to the new order of youth, which is full of the ardor of revolution. They are the products of the May Fourth spirit and they know that they have acquired the right to revolt, but Lao She with much obvious irony reveals the bankruptcy of their thinking and appears to have little sympathy for the student mob. His description of the destructive rioting which they indulge in reveals the horror and distaste with which Lao She looked upon unbridled young passions. He saw no signs of a constructive revolution in such activities. Incidentally, his description of Ming-cheng College, after the strike was put down, has an almost contemporary ring and it is the irony of fate that Lao She should have been mauled by a Red Guard student mob so similar to the one he had described forty years earlier:

> Red, yellow, blue, green—various colored paper; black, white, gold, purple—various colored characters; orthodox, running hand, plain, seal—various styles of writing; long, short, classical, colloquial—various types of articles; bitter ridicule, searing curses . . . all kinds of abusive expressions . . . They were plastered from the main gate of Ming-cheng College to the back gate, from the bottom of the walls to the eaves . . .
>
> The main gate was in fragments, the signboard had been pulled down, glasspanes were shattered, windows had disappeared . . . Outside the principal's office lay a broken strand of rope: The principal had been tied up and beaten. In the hallway were five or six satin slippers: the teachers had escaped barefoot. Pinned against the frame of the door of an office by a three-inch long nail was an ear with the blood already congealed. It had been lopped off the head of a faithful, prudent [his crime!] supply clerk of twenty years' standing. On the green near the hothouse was a

patch of blood that had turned purple-black. It had poured forth from the nostrils of a gardener whose income was ten dollars per month.[27]

Lao She concludes this episode by adding a paragraph which puts the strike at Ming-cheng College squarely on the national plane, and by so doing the author makes sure that the reader gains the impression that this is no stray incident of some local importance only, but an example of what was going on in the whole of China:

> The newspapers reported the ferment in this college with three-inch large black characters. Desperately urgent telegrams went to all parts of the country, the main gate of the Ministry of Education was closed fast . . . educational organizations confusedly called for meetings to discuss the methods of relieving the situation."[28]

There is no denying that the students have become a force in society but the author does not see them as a constructive force of any sort. They have no positive goal, they have no definite ideology, they lack leadership and the only thing that unites them is the ardor of senseless destruction. "The 500-odd students [at Ming-cheng College] are split into 327 parties,"[29] and the only time they show any sign of unity is when they decide not to take an examination!

The new military and the new students symbolize the new revolutionary China but Lao She finds that both these classes lack the true spirit of self-sacrifice and the strength of character necessary to advance the cause of the nation.

> In the new society there are two great forces—the military and the students. The military, although it won't fight the foreigners, indiscriminately whips everybody. The students, although they won't fight the military, whip everybody else. So these two great forces march on together, giving the common people an experience of the "new militarism." If the soldiers, who don't fight the foreigners, did not insult the common man, they would have absolutely no qualification to be soldiers. If the students, who don't fight the soldiers, do not beat up the principals and professors, they cannot be considered courageous youth.[30]

The chief fault Lao She finds in the students is that they lack character. Not only the students but the whole nation lacks character. The Chinese like to perpetuate the myth, says Lao She, that they are a peace-loving people whereas they are quite the opposite. "Chinese people love peace very much, but it does not mean that they do not quarrel or fight. When people who love peace, quarrel, they seek out one weaker than themselves to beat. This is characteristic of the Chinese."[31]

There seems to be little doubt that it was Lao She's experience in England that made him so indignant about Chinese youth. He says that Chinese youth go around shouting "Down with imperialism," and if it was only a matter of raising slogans, imperialism would have disappeared long ago, but, "unfortunately, the big guns of the imperialists and the fact that every citizen [of the imperialist countries] knows how to use a rifle makes it impossible to frighten them into withdrawing by just shouting!"[32]

At this period in China, Lao She notices that there is a belief among many of the new youth, like Wu Tuan, that to renovate China and bring it up to the level of the Western powers it was sufficient to wear Western-style clothing and leather shoes. Wu Tuan with his foreign hat, foreign coat, hard collar, Indian tie, and leather shoes with rubber soles, also goes to Western-style restaurants in Peking where many young men believe "Western culture" lies hidden behind "the banners depicting a bleeding cut of roast beef and drunkard Frenchmen tippling away beer."[33] Lao She has nothing but derision for these new youth who think that a "presidential order directing the people to wear foreign dress, to eat foreign food and learn to dance in the Western fashion" would cause a social revolution in China.[34] Lao She sees a great danger in any feeling of progress that comes from borrowing Western symbols of modernization and says with biting sarcasm:

> The foreigners have invented the car—good, we can bring it here and sit in it. The foreigners have invented the gas lamp—good, we can buy it and light it up. In this way the foreigners have cars and gas lamps, we also have them—what have the foreigners to boast about? In this way whatever the foreigners invent, we shall receive; the foreigners toil bitterly day and night, we sit at the mahjong table and wait—doesn't this make the foreigners . . . our slaves?[35]

With all their lack of self-discipline and their misdirected energy, the students while in college have a healthy buoyancy of spirit and hopes for the future. Once, however, they leave college and face the cold reality of the world outside we find that they readily and willingly fall victims to the corruption in society. It is rather pathetic to note that Wu Tuan and Chao Tzu-yueh are as anxious to acquire official positions as their forebears had been in the decadent old Confucian society. They get themselves gowns which the officials wore, they give each other official names, they seek out all persons in power who can help them get a job and they give lavish dinners to influential persons. The worst humiliation comes when Chao is advised to learn to sing operatic songs so that he can perform before the Women's Association and thus get into the good books of the wives and concubines of high officials, who would, supposedly, then help him get a recommendation from their husbands. In spite of all this Chao is unsuccessful. Wu Tuan however, does manage to get a post in the local government.

In *Lao Chang,* Lao She was content to describe the state of society and to highlight its sickness without attempting to provide any solution. In *Chao Tzu-yueh,* the author not only reveals the shortcomings and the degeneracy in Chinese society, with particular reference to youth, but tries to furnish a solution. In the person and thoughts of Li Ching-ch'un Lao She reveals his ideal. Like the author himself, Li's father is dead and he has a very kind and understanding mother. Again, just as Lao She was not very strong physically when he was in school, Li is also a rather weak person. Other parallels are that Li is not very well off, Li is a hard-working and diligent student, Li avoids participating in student movements, and is generally an upright and an honest person with much self-discipline.

Though most of the other students admire Li, they also feel slightly afraid in his presence. This is particularly true of Chao Tzu-yueh who spends his time gambling or wining and dining, is active in organizing the strike, and is all that Li is not. When, however, Chao is with Li he cannot help but succumb to Li's stronger character, and listens to Li's advice with the humility of a disciple. Even before the trouble in the college, Li gives some good advice to Chao and for a moment it appears that Chao is going to turn over a new leaf and give up his life of decadence, but he is too weak to do so and within a few days is back to his old ways. Li's advice to him is that there are three kinds of positive action which Chao can follow:

> The first: select a subject [in college] and for four or five years work at it intensely hard. This is the most difficult . . . The second: your family has land . . . buy a few books on agriculture and modern agricultural implements, go back home, study the books and experiment . . . If you attain any success it will be of considerable benefit to the peasantry. The third: this is the most dangerous . . . If one's knowledge is not sufficient and one undertakes a job [for society], it is dangerous. If you have learning, and cannot find a job and die of starvation, it is still glorious, but to have no learning and to go around begging for a bowl of rice [a job] . . . that is like a rat which steals things to eat.[36]

Nearly at the end of the novel Li once again advises Chao and it becomes clear that he is also an advocate of direct action—assassination of evil officials:

> One road is to study hard and after finishing your studies to go among the people and work for them and gradually build up the national spirit; the other road, is to risk your life and assassinate the wicked people. I am an advocate of peace and I also know that it is not economical to lightly sacrifice the lives of youth, but, you cannot help but act in this manner when you are living in an age such as this.[37]

The first time Li gives Chao advice is when he wants to awaken Chao's conscience; but the second time, Li is more specific. Li has heard that Wu Tuan, in league with his fellow officials, is preparing to sell the Temple of Heaven to some foreigners. Li has come to Chao to seek his help in avoiding this calamity. He wants Chao to go to Wu Tuan and reason with their old friend not to perform such a nefarious act and if reason fails, to kill him. Loyalty to the nation is more important than loyalty to a friend:

> Perhaps you have doubts and think: why go to the extent of shedding blood and killing a person to protect an ancient monument? . . . every nation has a kind of pride in history and this pride is the motive force that unites popular sentiment—great historical monuments arouse such a sentiment. Our people do not have any national feelings, and therefore, when the Anglo-French Allied Armies burnt our Summer Palace (Yuan-ming yuan) and the Germans removed the scientific apparatus from the astronomical observatory (T'ien-wen t'ai) we paid not the slightest notice to it.[38]

Li is trying to provide Chao with a cause, a cause so great that even a friend can be killed to help further it. Lao She, living in England when the glory of the British empire had reached its apex, feels that the weakness of Chinese nationalism is partly due to the lack of pride in the past among his countrymen. How different it is with the British! In the words of Li: "Let me ask you, if the Chinese were to set fire to an ancient British monument, wouldn't the English people risk their lives [to protect it]? Not only England, but probably in the whole world, except for China, there is no second country that would bear such humiliations with patience!"[39] The most important matter of the day, according to Lao She is to create a "feeling of patriotism" and a "feeling of self-pride" because a "people who have no national sentiments are like a field of wild grass, which looks like an expanse of water but cannot produce any grain."[40]

Chao Tzu-yueh deals with China of the 1920s, the period of the warlords. Lao She sees in the militarists and the corrupt government cliques the two scourges that afflict China. Since, in many ways, the two are practically synonymous, his attacks on the military can also be taken to be his attack on the government. It appears that Lao She would like to root out the evil elements in China so that a cleaner, nationalist government, which would strengthen the nation, throw out the foreigners, and protect the poor, can come into existence. The only hope for this development is that the youth of the country may realize their grave responsibility and, discarding all personal ambitions, rise to the occasion.

The "two paths" of which Li talks to Chao are not the paths open only to Chao but to all Chinese youth. Lao She appears to lay great store by this philosophy of action which he propounds repeatedly in the novel. But Lao She is a "humanist" and he reconciles the acts of "assassination" with "humanism" with a logic similar to the one later used by Mao Tse-tung to reconcile "democracy for the people" with "dictatorship over the reactionaries."[41]

> I do not recognize the militarists as human beings at all, therefore, it is not necessary to talk of humanism. The question before us is whether the people or the militarists are to live; peace and humanity are most pleasant themes in literature . . . To save the people is humanity, and to assassinate the militarists is to save the people.[42]

It is also significant that, when discussing the path that leads to expertise, Lao She emphasizes the need for a more intimate knowledge of the West:

> For example if you like to study local government, fine, go and quickly prepare yourself by learning a foreign language. Thereafter go to a foreign country to study the subject, because this type of knowledge is not to be found in the *Five Classics* or *The Four Books,* nor can it be gained by reading just a few books [available locally]. Only after you have looked around in a foreign country and done research there, can you acquire real comprehension . . . we must attain, as early as possible, true knowledge; we must hope that in the future the government will set up institutions where specialist talent can be utilized . . . Let me put it plainly; [that unless this happens] the united protection of Boddhisatva, the Jade Emperor, Christ, and Mohammed, will not be able to help China.[43]

To follow either of these two paths youth, and by that Lao She means educated youth, must have self-discipline, and be capable of self-denial and self-sacrifice. "The starting point for anyone who wants to do revolutionary work for society or state is 'sacrifice'; his ultimate aim is 'reconstruction' and 'personal gain' does not figure in his calculations."[44] True self-sacrifice is, however, possible only when one is rational and understands the real value and significance of things. "Do you think that just by wearing Western clothes you can come to comprehend Western culture?" asks Li of Wu Tuan, "or is the wearing of a padded gown the protection of the national spirit?" Lao She then, through Li gives his answer:

> I believe that clothing, food, and housing are important to living, and one cannot but deliberate on which type would be most suitable and which most economical. If you think that Chinese clothes are not good you must ask the question: why is it so? . . . This is not a question of culture or the lack of culture, but a problem connected with making the body comfortable as economically as possible.[45]

Lao She finds that there is too much superficial aping of the West and too little real comprehension of the problems facing the Chinese people.

Of all the "freedoms" which Lao She condemns, the "freedom to fall in love" is one which he finds most irritating. Lao She, himself, did not marry the girl he had loved. Perhaps, he tried to rationalize that act, and came to look upon it as a deed of self-sacrifice for the larger ideal of working for the nation, or, it could be, that he genuinely distrusted the value of "romantic love" at a time when the nation demanded that all youthful energy be harnessed to the cause of reconstruction. Or it could mean that after reaching England he realized that Chinese youth did not fully grasp the fact that before romantic love could be meaningful the status of women had to be raised much higher and they must be made more secure economically. Once again Li who, is so obviously the spokesman for the author, says: "There are many things we have to do first which are more important than finding a wife."[68] At another place Lao She says that it is only in an age of political tranquillity that love has a meaning and that in warlord China a man or a woman who understood love was not likely to receive any special consideration from the militarists or the foreigners.[46]

A theme which has a close connection with the subject of love is Lao She's view of the position of women in Chinese society. In *Lao Chang*, Li Ching in spite of her great love for Wang Te seems to intuitively grasp the basic truth that in the Chinese society of the 1920s, women had no freedom of personal action, and she tells Wang Te: "Woman is a plaything for a man . . . if there is a man in the world [meaning China] who does not take a woman to be a toy, well, then, I can only say that she is a very lucky woman."[47] And the truth of this statement becomes clear when Li Ching and Lung Feng, the other female character in the novel are nearly sold to become the concubines of some rich local persons, and neither is married to the boy she loves. In *Chao Tzu-yueh* Lao She elaborates on this theme a little further. New ideas and modern education had supposedly raised the status of women, given them individual freedom and made them conscious of their rights. However, it was very much a man's world that women lived in and they could neither escape from being exploited by the "modern" men around them nor from the much-condemned but still-pervasive forces of traditional thought.

In *Lao Chang,* ambitious men like Chang and Sun Pa, wanting to make good in the changing times, needed educated wives. In spite of all their modern education, the fate of Li Ching and Lung Feng is clearly one of subordination. Miss Wang and Miss T'an in *Chao Tzu-yueh* highlight this tragic situation more dramatically. Both Miss Wang and Miss T'an defy tradition and try to exercise their right to find fulfilment in romantic love and seek a partner of their choice. Both leave their homes to exert their independence. Unfortunately the alliances they make end disastrously: Miss T'an's husband dies within a year and Miss Wang discovers to her misery that her young man is an utter scoundrel who squanders his allowance on drinking, gambling, and prostitutes. Neither Miss Wang nor Miss T'an can return to their families because their tradition-minded elders have barred the door to them. Luckily, Miss Wang is saved by an understanding and benevolent teacher in her college. Miss T'an is forced by circumstances into a life of prostitution.

According to Lao She, empty words are not likely to raise the standing of women in China. Comparing the situation with that in England, Lao She points out that, in England, it was only after World War I that the status of women rose. During the war educated women took over many of the jobs which only men were supposed to be able to do. Men could no longer look down upon them and they acquired for themselves a place of honor in society. Women must have economic independence to gain equality and status.[48]

From *Chao Tzu-yueh* the reader forms a strong impression that Lao She has nothing but total condemnation for the militarists who are courageous in suppressing civilians and cowardly when faced with the problem of stopping foreign aggression. Their officers, like the one who reduced Miss T'an to a life of prostitution, are without any feeling of compassion; they are corrupt and self-seeking, immoral and licentious. The warlords at the head of the new-style armies represent one aspect of the new China. The new students, who go to the new schools and receive a modern education, are another. The novel, as a whole, berates the students and what they stand for, and even goes to the extent of comparing them with the militarists; yet it is more than obvious that Lao She looks upon educated youth as a possible hope for China.

To be able to fulfill their role in society adequately and help in the great task of rebuilding and strengthening their motherland, the students need to practice high moral principles, be self-sacrificing, put the state above their personal desires, and dedicate themselves to the cause of the nation. As long as the country is poor and weak and suffers repeated humiliations at the hands of the foreigners, the students have no right to think in terms of love and marriage and an easy life.

Erh Ma (*Mr. Ma and Master Ma*)

The third and last novel, *Mr. Ma and Master Ma,* which Lao She wrote before he left England, was begun in 1928 and finished in 1929. Lao She had been in England for nearly four years and had had an opportunity to see at first hand the nation that had been an anathema to China for many decades. In London, which was still the hub of the most powerful empire on the face of the earth, Lao She not only met the intellectuals at London University where he was a teacher, but he also came in contact with the vast British business community, and common or garden variety Londoner, the ignorant landladies, the China-returned missionaries, and the traders who did business with China. And juxtaposed to this community of proud and arrogant Englishmen he also saw the state of perpetual humiliation in which the Chinese students and workers lived in London. Lao She occupied himself with the problem, which had concerned Chinese intellectuals from the 1840s onward, of seeking out the roots of British strength and Chinese weakness.

Mr. Ma and Master Ma is set in London and the action is contemporaneous with the author's stay in the metropolis. The story deals with Mr. Ma and his grown-up son, who have come to London to take over a curio shop which they have inherited from Mr. Ma's brother. By putting the Mas in the context of London, Lao She was able to compare British and Chinese national characteristics.[49] By making Mr. Ma a representative of the older generation of Chinese who still held on to traditional values, and Ma Wei (the son) a representative of the new youth, Lao She introduced the conflict which reflected Chinese society of the day.

When the Mas arrive in London, Mr. Evans, a missionary they knew in China, finds them a place to live with Mrs. Winter. The landlady, like so many British people, is afraid of "rat-eating" Chinese, and when with much hesitation she accepts the Mas as her boarders, she is ostracized by her friends and relatives. In due course, Mrs. Winter and her daughter Mary discover that there is, after all, nothing very weird about their Chinese lodgers and Mrs. Winter actually comes to like them. The father and son fall in love with the landlady and her daughter, but the affairs do not conclude in matrimony—in the case of Ma Wei because Mary does not love him, and in the case of Mr. Ma because the pressure of social prejudice is too strong for Mrs. Winter to take such an unconventional step.

At the end of the story Ma Wei, who is basically a filial son, finds it impossible to continue to live with his tradition-ridden father and leaves him. The novel was not supposed to end so abruptly, but Lao She was pressed for time—he was preparing to leave England—so he concluded it in this fashion.[50]

Lao She, it is obvious from the novel, deplores China's poor image in the West and feels that people are ignorant about the real China because schools in England do not include the history of China in their curriculum. The only source of information is the sensational articles in the press, and the highly biased stories in films and literature, which more often than not, have little relationship with truth. Slit-eyed, flat-faced, nose-less, pig-tailed, opium-smoking, yellow devils who shuffle around on legs that reminded one of the Peking dog, and who generally spend their time indulging in arson, rape, and looting—this is what the average Englishman thinks of the Chinese. The Chinese are depicted as wantonly barbaric and cruel. They decapitate prisoners and hang up their heads on telephone poles for crowds to stand around and watch for fun. At the same time, in the face of a stronger enemy, they are a cowardly lot and a single foreigner can destroy a whole host of them.

So it is quite understandable, says Lao She, that Chinatown in London attracts many visitors:

> During their stay in London, Germans, Frenchmen, and Americans, who do not have money to travel to the East, always pay a brief visit to Chinatown for the purpose of finding some material for writing a novel, a diary, or an item of news. There is actually nothing strange or exceptional about Chinatown, and nothing startling about the behavior of the workers who live there. But, because they are Chinese [the foreigners] want to have a look . . . if there are twenty Chinese living in Chinatown, in the [tourists'] notes the figure was bound to be 5,000. Moreover, these 5,000 yellow devils would all be smokers of opium, smugglers of ammunition, murderers who hid the dead bodies under their beds, rapists who pay no regard to the woman's age . . .[51]

So it is understandable why a decent hotel or a respectable landlady did not wish to put up any Chinese guests. Mr. Evans has a difficult time trying to find the Mas a place to live and though it is amusing to read his conversation with Mrs. Winter, who ultimately rents her rooms to the Mas, the same reaction would perhaps occur in many parts of the world:

> "But, pastor!" she took out a small handkerchief from her purse and wiped her mouth, although there was no need to do so at all, "you think that I can allow two Chinese to cook and eat rats in my house?"
> "Chinese don't . . ." He thought of saying that the Chinese didn't eat rats, but on further consideration felt that to talk like that would evidently upset her . . . he corrected himself, "I shall naturally enjoin them not to eat rats."
> "I hope they don't smoke opium either," Mrs. Winter said.[52]

There are only two types of Englishmen who have a personal knowledge of China: the missionaries and China traders. But in spite of their direct contact, they too have no good will toward China. Pastor Evans, who has spent twenty years in China, prays to God that He may quickly cause China to become a colony of England. With tears in his eyes he tells God: "If the Chinese do not get the English to look after them, these masses of yellow-faced blackhaired things would never be able to enter Heaven."[53] Mrs. Evans, who was with the pastor in China, kept aloof from the Chinese and did not allow her children to play with Chinese children. But, back in England, she considers herself to be an expert on Chinese culture. When the Evanses invite the Mas for dinner, Mrs. Evans forces fatty meat and rice pudding on her guests saying in a loud voice that she knew that all Chinese loved fatty meat and rice pudding. It is not unlikely that Lao She is relating one of his personal experiences.

One can also imagine how humiliated Ma Wei must have been when he goes to the room of Mr. Evans's son and finds on display such things as an opium pipe and slippers meant for ladies with bound feet! To most twentieth-century Chinese youth these objects were symbols of China's shame. One is reminded of Lu Hsun's anger when he saw how the Japanese customs officials examined with great curiosity a pair of "lotus feet" slippers, which they had found in the baggage of a Chinese student.[54]

Lao She uses Alexander, Mrs. Evans's brother, as an example of the China trader. Alexander has done business in China for such a long time that he has developed an "overbearing and rude character," having behaved with nothing but "disrespect and arrogance toward his Chinese employees."[55] All the stories he has to tell of China cast a poor light on that country. "I tell you, Peking is a poor place," says Alexander recounting one of his experiences. "There is not even one big shop, there is not even one factory; the roads are extremely filthy. Some people told me that Peking is beautiful, but I didn't discover any [beauty there]—filth and beauty don't go together." He then goes on to describe how an elderly Chinese at the hotel where Alexander stayed "followed (me) like an old dog" when invited for a drink. To Alexander's amusement it is the Chinese who ends up paying for the drinks, and it then becomes clear that the Chinese had behaved so abjectly only because he wants to find out how he can make bets at the Shanghai racecourse. "All you Chinese like to gamble! Isn't that so?" Alexander asked looking at Mr. Ma.[56]

With such a deep knowledge of China, Alexander is naturally an "expert" and so is called upon by a film company to help in writing the scenario for a film on China. The story is laid in Shanghai and the film contrasts the order, beauty, and cleanliness of the International Settlement with the dirt and disorganization in the Chinese sector of the town. "The story is about a Chinese girl and an Englishman, who fall in love. Her father wants to kill the Englishman but not knowing what to do, takes poison and dies. His family and friends seek revenge and so bury the girl alive. After doing that, they all go in search of the young Englishman. He, along with the British soldiers, gives them a severe trashing until they get down on their knees and beg for mercy."[57]

The Chinese workers who live in London, in this British atmosphere of insolence and intolerance, can be divided into two types. There is one type who has no self respect and will undertake any kind of job for money. For example, he would hire himself out to a film company to be beaten up. The other type, also illiterate, cannot speak English and has no technical skill, but truly loves his country and would rather starve than do anything that will make China lose face. "The knowledge of men in both these groups is equally limited, their behavior is equally unpolished, their living is equally pitiable. The difference between them is: one group only seeks food for the belly and does not care for anything else; the other group wants to make a living which is honorable." And yet both lend themselves to the derision of the foreigners for, when those who are "stupidly patriotic" meet those who are "stupidly unpatriotic" the only thing they can do is to start a fight.

Lao She similarly divides the students into two categories: those who have come from China proper, and those who belong to the overseas Chinese community. "They are all patriotic, except that they do not [really] comprehend the [true] state of the nation. The sons and grandsons of overseas Chinese, having been born abroad do not know much about national affairs [in any case]. Students from the mainland [who know better] want incessantly to explain things to the foreigners but what they do not realize is that, because of the weakness of China there is no way to make foreigners respect us. Relations between countries is between equals—a rat cannot have a friendship with a tiger."[58]

According to the author the reason for this degrading situation was entirely due to the fact that China was not a powerful country; its navy was not much of a navy, and its army did not amount to an army. Moreover, China did not produce one man in the field of science, literature, or sports, who had gained the respect of the outside world. Civilized and advanced countries could not help but have a contempt for China. If Chinese are mocked abroad, says Lao She, it is because the government of China cannot protect its nationals.

Lao She's exasperation at this state of affairs makes him intrude into the novel to appeal to his countrymen to bestir themselves to greater sacrifice and action:

> In the twentieth century, "people" are treated according to their "country": the people of a strong country are "people" and those of a weak country—dogs!
> China is a weak country, and the Chinese are therefore . . . !
> Chinese people! You must open your eyes and see [things as they are], the time has come when you must wake up; you must straighten your backs for the time has come when you must stand erect . . . unless you wish to be always treated as dogs![59]

To hammer home this point, Lao She compares the treatment meted out to the Japanese with that given to the Chinese. It is not that the Japanese are liked any more than the Chinese, but that, since Japan is a powerful nation, no Englishman dares to insult a Japanese to his face. Wherever there were Chinese abroad there one was sure to find Chinese restaurants and Chinese laundries, and that was about all the Chinese could boast of, but the Japanese ran shipping companies, had established well-known business houses and banking enterprises. The result was that the Japanese walked with their chests out and the Chinese shuffled around with their heads bent low.

The only Englishmen who seem sympathetic toward the Chinese are the members of the Socialist Party. These gentlemen frequent Chinese restaurants; they like to talk to the Chinese and say things which sound favorable to China. Things like: "The Chinese discovered tea for the whole world and they really know how to drink it. If it was not for the Chinese we would be unable to think of drinking tea, of wearing silks, of printing books. Chinese civilization! Chinese civilization is beyond description!"[60] The Chinese of the older generation like Mr. Ma are greatly pleased to hear this kind of patronizing talk and respond by offering these gentlemen drinks and dinners. Even the Socialist Party members, however, forget all their talk of equality and justice when they witness Ma Wei beat Paul (Mr. Evans's son) in a fair fight which is started by Paul and not by the Chinese boy. If it had been a fight between two English boys, says Lao She, nobody would have cared, but no Englishman, not even the members of the Socialist Party can tolerate the idea of seeing a "chink" fight one of their countrymen and win.

When Mrs. Evans hears about the fight she makes the classic comment: "Twenty years ago when you saw a foreigner you trembled and now you have the insolence to start a fight! . . . This is not China where you can be lawless and ruthlessly slaughter people and create a disorder—England has laws." The lady is not angry because her son is hurt, but because he has been beaten by a Chinese.[61] This is intolerable.

Lao She explains that "when an Englishman opens his or her eyes, he or she sees the whole world under foot—Hong Kong, India, Egypt, Africa, and so on—all are his or her colonial possessions. The Englishman is not only proud of himself but he also wants peoples [of other countries] to recognize the fact that they are many times lower in status."[62]

Though Lao She is acutely conscious of the vast ignorance regarding China in the West, and the many prejudices which Westerners have against the Chinese, he does not try to attribute all Chinese ills to foreigners and foreign aggression. He tries to analyze, objectively, the causes of China's degradation and turns the attention of the reader to faults in Chinese society which need to be combated and eliminated. There is no doubt about it—the root cause of China's troubles is that she is a weak country. She is weak because the old decadent order still prevails and because the people who run the country are still imbued with traditional ideals and have no true concept of nationalism. Even the youth who gives the impression of being overly patriotic does not grasp the essentials of progress.

In *The Philosophy of Lao Chang,* Lao She tried to show how the gentry, with its parochial interests and lack of a greater vision of the country, with its corruption and nepotism and lack of any sense of responsibility toward the common man, is the dead wood which needs clearing away before any progress can be made. Youth in *Lao Chang* is, however, so shackled and fettered that the only freedom it has is to slowly die an inner death. In *Chao Tzu-yueh,* the noisy and violent demonstrations of a revolutionary youth are shown not only not to have any significant impact on society as a whole, but, what is worse, they appear to have no great relevance to youth itself. The moment the students leave their schools and colleges they suddenly assume all the characteristics of those in authority. They become avid job-seekers and resort to bribery and corruption to achieve their end.

In *Mr. Ma and Master Ma,* too, Lao She takes the opportunity to revile student agitators for their superficiality:

> Are there any foreigners in China—foreign devils who possess big guns, aeroplanes, science, knowledge, and wealth—who see these masses of students waving paper flags, shouting righteous principles, . . . but not studying, and seeing this . . . do they laugh? This [activity] is not worth even a smile. The more you [students] fail to study the better it is [for the foreigners]. . . Those who are genuine patriots do not act in this way."[63]

In *Mr. Ma and Master Ma,* Lao She highlights the clash between the genuine seekers of the new path and those who follow the hallowed Confucian cultural synthesis. Mr. Ma is a traditionalist and Ma Wei is the new type of student, the new type of youth that China needs. What separates father and son is not the few years of difference in their ages, but two ideologies, two outlooks that are aeons apart. Ma Wei cannot but hate and despise all that his father stands for, and Mr. Ma cannot understand the psychological makeup of his son. They are two strangers living together. When ultimately Ma Wei finds it impossible to tolerate his father's actions any more, the last strand of filial piety snaps and he leaves home to seek a life of his own in the cold world outside.

Mr. Ma, when young, had attended an English language school run by a Methodist mission and later had been converted to Christianity but this shift did not change his outlook. Up to the age of 50, when he came to England, he had wasted his entire life in China waiting to get an official appointment. Mr. Ma has not only no understanding of national affairs and the nature of new forces and new ideas but also no desire to make such a venture. He is smugly self-satisfied and has an inner sense of superiority which keeps him from showing any "vulgar" curiosity about new things: he sleeps through his sea voyage, never leaving his cabin, and in London he is content to know the shortest routes between his lodging, his shop, and the Chinese restaurant of his liking.[64]

At the age of fifty he already feels that he is a venerable old man and is

ready to retire from all active life. When Mr. Evans suggests that Mr. Ma help
him read certain texts in Chinese, in return for which Mr. Evans offers to
help Mr. Ma write a book in English comparing Chinese and Western cultures,
Mr. Ma's response is:

> "I will help you, but as for my writing a book, that is not an easy mat-
> ter. Can a person who is soon going to be 50 get involved in such a
> weary job?"
> "My good friend," said Pastor Evans suddenly raising his voice by
> one note, "you are going to be 50? I am more than 60! George Bernard
> Shaw is more than 70, and is still continuing to write without relaxing!
> I ask you, have you seen one old Englishman who is not doing some
> work? If all those who reach 50 retire, to whom are they going to hand
> over the business of the world?" . . . Mr. Ma . . . said to himself, "you
> foreign devils do not understand what it is to have reverence for an old
> man, and if it was not so why would you be foreign devils?" [65]

In Mr. Ma's vocabulary the word "old" and the word "great" are closely
related and since China is an "old civilization," he suddenly feels a sense of
great pride in his "great old country." Lao She's comment on this is that
"when a race becomes old, its people are born 'old,' which means that even at
birth they are dim-sighted, deaf and racked with asthma. And if a country has
400 million such persons, who are old from birth, then this old country becomes more and more frail as time passes, till it reaches the stage when it is so
weak that it cannot even crawl." [66]
As long as Mr. Ma's brother, who owned the curio shop in London, was
living, he sent money to Mr. Ma in China and on that money Mr. Ma could
lead an idle existence, entertaining his official friends and dreaming of the day
when he himself would become an official. Now that his brother was dead
and Mr. Ma had come to England to look after the shop, one would expect a
certain change of attitude. But, no, Mr. Ma still lives in his gracious dream
world, giving away presents to his landlady and to anybody who says a few
words flattering his vanity. He pays no regard to the fact that the shop is not
doing well and that he is eating into the capital. Mr. Ma has no idea of the
business world and he has absolutely no desire to learn business techniques because "business" is vulgar (*ts'u-ch'i*) and beneath contempt.
It is for this reason that he also cannot respect the student Li Tzu-jung,
who works part-time in the curio shop. When on his very first visit to the
shop Mr. Ma sees Li working in his undershirt, his hands and arms dusty from
cleaning the shop, Mr. Ma cannot help but say to himself in disgust "*ts'u-ch'i*"
(how crude and vulgar this man is!)

In actual fact it is Li who keeps the shop running, and the Mas from bankruptcy. But in spite of everything, in spite even of his son explaining how important Li is to them, Mr. Ma cannot bring himself to have any respect for Li. Li is an honest and upright man, and at one stage, when he feels that business is slow and that it will be in the interest of the Mas for him to resign from the shop, he approaches Mr. Ma with this proposal. The confrontation between the two underlines the communication gap between the old China and the new.

> "Mr. Ma," said Li Tzu-jung . . . "we must think of some plan. Last month we simply did not see any money and have hardly sold much this month. I cannot receive a salary and just look on. In case you have some plans I, naturally, would like to help you, but if you have none, I had best search for some other job and thus save you some money. After all there is not much work here and you and Ma Wei can easily look after it . . . we should not stand on ceremony."
>
> Although what Li Tzu-jung had said was brusque and to the point, his attitude was very warm and genial; even Mr. Ma could see that his words had come from the heart but after all they were a little *ts'u-ch'i* . . .
>
> "I say, assistant Li, if your objection is that the salary is small we can discuss the matter."
>
> "Oh! My dear Mr. Ma, I object to my salary being small! Truly, I have no way of making you understand me!"[67]

This confusion, says Lao She, is due to the fact that Chinese like Mr. Ma are used to transactions which "give face" to both parties. The procedure is not very different from little children playing "blind man's buff." "Mr. Ma was really embarrassed. Actually the situation was rather simple: business was losing money and it was imperative to think of some plan of action. But Mr. Ma was a real Chinese and was not willing to think in this manner. Foreign devils think like this. Li Tzu-jung also thought in this fashion—the yellow-faced foreign devil!"[68] Although Mr. Ma finds it difficult to accept Li as his equal, calls him "assistant" instead of "mister," and generally treats him shabbily, he accepts insults from Englishmen without a murmur. When he walks down the streets of London, he is often chased by children who follow him shouting "chink, chink." Once when he went to a pub, a woman playing the accordion there was so shocked that she grew pale and screamed: "Oh, God, a chink has come."[69] All this, however, does not disturb him. On the contrary, it amuses him to live up to the Western image of China. For example when he is asked how many wives he has, he replies "five or six." Since it is popularly thought that all Chinese have many wives and concubines, some distorted sense of honor makes Mr. Ma live up to the expectation of the questioner.

As time passes Ma Wei finds it increasingly difficult to reconcile himself to the Chinese who is his father. His uncle was a hero to him and Li Tzu-jung is a hero. His uncle was adventurous enough to come abroad and establish a business and make money from the foreigners, and all that his father could do was drink away his time in anticipation of becoming an official. In the words of Ma Wei:

> "The Chinese disposition is to disregard commerce. Father simply hasn't the slightest interest in business but now that this shop is our only means of livelihood, will it do not to have any interest? He doesn't listen to me, he doesn't even listen to Li Tzu-jung. He can keep away a whole day from the shop and plant flowers for Mrs. Winter. When he goes to the shop he is likely to give away something free to a customer who praises Chinese products. In the few months that we have been here we have already spent £200 from the little money left behind by uncle. He invites somebody for dinner today, somebody for drinks tomorrow . . . some old (English) men and (English) women love him as a darling because he always speaks in accordance with their thoughts.
>
> "The other day General Kao Erh [Gore?] lectured on the affair of England sending troops to Shanghai and especially requested father to come to listen to him. Halfway through the lecture the general pointed toward my father and said, 'Hasn't the continued presence of English troops in China brought good fortune to the Chinese people? . . . Mr. Ma please tell us . . .'
>
> "Father stood up and as was expected said that English troops are welcome . . . he doesn't have even a jot of a national viewpoint." [70]

As in the previous novel, Lao She has a character in *Mr. Ma and Master Ma* who approximates the author's ideal of a truly patriotic young man. Li Tzu-jung, who is the absolute opposite of Mr. Ma, and a model after which Ma Wei wants to pattern himself, came to America as an officially sponsored student with a government fellowship. After he had spent three years in the United States and had obtained a degree in commerce, Li went to France but at this time because war broke out within China, his scholarship came to a halt. Coming, as he did, from a poor family, Li could not expect money from home so he left France for England, where he knew that it would be easier to find work. Acting as an interpreter for the Chinese workers and the police in East London, doing some translation work, and ultimately getting a job with Mr.

Ma's brother, Li managed to continue his studies. He had to live austerely on the money he made so he had never been to a Chinese restaurant even once because he was afraid that if he went once he would be tempted to go again.

To become efficient in selling Chinese curios Li read up as much as he could on Chinese porcelain, and so on, and Ma Wei is impressed when experts like Sir Simon come to the shop to ask Li's opinion about the genuineness of an article. By his skill Li had gained the healthy respect of his clients, sophisticated intellectual clients at that, and could feel a true sense of equality with them. Through Li Tzu-jung, Lao She re-emphasizes the theme he had begun in *Chao Tzu-yueh:* students must put aside their paper flags and work assiduously so that they can acquire proper expertise. Ma Wei is much impressed by the philosophy of this indefatigable Chinese young man who had imbibed, what seemed to be, the best in the West:

> During the time he was in China, Ma Wei had also demonstrated with paper flags and shouted slogans along with others, but now he perceived that England's strength and affluence was mostly due to the fact that Englishmen did not shout slogans, rather they lowered their heads and worked intensely hard. Englishmen are great lovers of liberty but it was surprising that students in college simply did not have the right to participate in a discussion concerning the college; they are great lovers of liberty but surprisingly there was peace and order everywhere. Hundreds of thousands of workers go on strike but not one shot is fired, not one person dies. Ma Wei perceived that discipline and training were the secrets of a strong country.[71]

In brief, what Lao She would have his reader learn from his own experience in England is that personal freedom implies a sense of restraint and respect for everybody else's rights, that knowledge leads to wealth, and that time is extremely valuable. Self-respect and individualism are correlated to economic independence and a sense of responsibility. A man can continue to work with dignity and contribute to society even when he is past seventy.

Money, which in the earlier novels appeared to have a corrupting influence in Chinese society and a degrading effect on social values, plays a different type of role in *Mr. Ma and Master Ma.* Economic security and individual freedom are closely connected. Sometimes it seems that the author is not very sure whether the dehumanization due to this emphasis on money and personal freedom, is after all, not a very admirable development. Mrs. Winter and her daughter often discuss what they owe each other and the sum involved is often just a few pennies. Children act independently and the parents can only watch helplessly. Mr. Evans's daughter elopes with a boy who is engaged to be married to Mrs. Winter's daughter! At times, even Mrs. Winter is envious of the apparently close relations between Mr. Ma and Ma Wei, and she particularly admires the way money plays no role at all in the relationship between father and son.

Lao She appears troubled both by the conflicts in British society and family life which arise out of ties based on money, and by the superficial unity and harmony which mark the life of the Mas. For underneath that harmony there is a greater estrangement between Mr. Ma and Ma Wei than that which exists in a normal English family. There is no communication whatsoever between Mr. Ma and his son:

> In the big city of London Ma Wei felt very solitary and lonely. Of the seven million people in London, who was there who knew him or sympathized with him? Even his own father did not understand him and actually abused him! . . . Although London was a place of so much bustle and noise, he felt very lonely and cold . . . He had no place to go.[72]

Another reason for Ma Wei's feeling of utter alienation and loneliness is unrequited love. By having Mr. Ma fall in love with Mrs. Winter and Ma Wei with her daugher Mary, Lao She created an opportunity to show how love—which, to the author, has a quality which transcends geographical, national, and racial limitations—can also fall a victim to social prejudice. The relationship between Ma Wei and Mary is rather simple. Mary looks down upon the Chinese, has nothing but contempt for them, and cannot even dream of falling in love with a Chinese. Ma Wei is aware of Mary's attitude toward Chinese, but cannot help his emotions. Li's advice to Ma Wei is: "Every time you think of her you should ask yourself—does she or does she not look upon me, a Chinese, as a man? You can, of course, give yourself a very satisfactory answer: 'She does not consider me to be a man, how then can she love me?' Your heart will then cool down a little."[73] Ma Wei understands all this, but reason is not strong enough to overcome emotion. Ultimately, Ma Wei determines to stop thinking of her, and as an act of farewell goes to Mary's room when she is not at home, and, there, kneels in front of her bed, puts his head on it and soundlessly weeps his heart out. After this day, Ma Wei reorganizes his life and turns his mind to more constructive activities, but deep down within him his love for Mary never dies.

As for Mr. Ma, his gentle behavior helps Mrs. Winter to gradually overcome her prejudices against the Chinese and respond to his love. Mrs. Winter is a lonely soul and when she learns that her daughter is getting engaged and

50

realizes that after Mary's marriage she will be left all alone, she is swept by
such a wave of desolation, that she agrees to marry Mr. Ma. For a moment,
she forgets how she has been ostracized by her friends and relatives because
she has Chinese lodgers and overlooks all the biases against the Chinese. Human warmth is sometimes worth more than all the rest of the world put together. When, however, she goes with Mr. Ma to buy an engagement ring,
and witnesses the humiliations which her husband-to-be suffers at the hands
of shopkeepers and the like, she realizes that such a marriage would never
work.

> "Society!" she tells Mr. Ma, "Society can kill love. We, English people,
> are equal politically but when it comes to social intercourse we have
> classes. The prejudices in society will kill us in three days. It is a com-
> mon occurrence for an Englishman to marry a foreign woman; people
> are suspicious but not annoyed; but an Englishwoman marrying a for-
> eign male is a different matter altogether. The English are a very proud
> race and are contemptuous of women who marry foreigners." [74]

Unrequited love is a recurrent theme in Lao She's novels, and in spite of
the pain and heartbreak there is something noble about the purity of the emotional responses. When love becomes involved with sex, as in *Chao Tzu-yueh,*
then it gets soiled and an element of prostitution comes in. Lao She gradually
expands and enlarges upon this theme till it crystallizes into a discernible philosophy.

Li Tzu-jung, who reflects so much of the author's ideal youth, believes
that conditions in China demand that "affairs of the heart" be sacrificed for
the time being so that young men can labor hard at their studies and qualify
themselves to help in the reconstruction of the motherland. While Li is in
England, his mother chooses a girl back home for him to marry. He readily
accepts this situation and his answer to Ma Wei, who wonders how such an
arrangement can lead to happiness, is:

> "I know that the correct way would be to marry someone you love, but
> if you . . . have a close look at Chinese women your ardor will be dam-
> pened. . . . love should go together with mutual help, sympathy and
> duty. However good looking she might be and however modern her
> thoughts, I cannot love a girl who cannot help me [in my work], sympa-
> thize with me, . . . having a little knowledge is the most dangerous thing
> . . . After reading one or two love stories they [Chinese students] at
> once, begin frantically preaching freedom to love. The result is the same

old story—the boy and the girl sleep together for one night, and the matter comes to an end."[75]

In *Mr. Ma and Master Ma* Lao She reflects, even more clearly than the first two novels, the dilemma of his times. Weak and impoverished China is looked upon with contempt and her citizens suffer untold humiliations in their relations with foreigners. The answer is clear. China has to strengthen herself, and to progress and prosper, so that she can gain her rightful place in the sun. Lao She wants China to be respected and to be treated as an equal. He is bitter at the wrongs she is suffering at the hands of the foreigners, but he feels that the Chinese have themselves to blame for most of their ills. The Chinese will gain a real sense of self-respect only when they become conscious of their identity as a nation. Lao She finds that the concept of nationalism does not exist in the tradition-ridden members of the older generation, but he also emphatically scores the "nationalistic" youth for having only a superficial notion of nationalism and patriotism.

To the author there are, fundamentally, only two classes in China—the corrupt, nepotistic upper class, which is coterminous with the ruling group, and the downtrodden masses, who suffer from exploitation and "squeeze." Lao She is terribly indignant at this state of affairs and feels that a radical change is necessary to modernize the nation. He is, however, suspicious of a revolutionary approach. In the politicians and militarists, who can create a revolution at the top, Lao She sees nothing but unprincipled, immoral, self-seeking criminals, who need to be wiped off the face of China for they can bring nothing but disaster to the country. The idea of a revolution from below does not at this point appear to have any appeal for him.

The only hope then is the new youth, but this youth has to be made conscious of its important role so that, instead of floundering around aimlessly, it can acquire the skills and talents in various fields of modern knowledge, which China lacked so utterly and needed so badly. Lao She is, however, conscious of the fact that youth is caught between the old traditional order and the new. At this intermediary stage the students have to develop zeal and work with the fervor of missionaries, sacrificing self in the cause of the nation.

Lao She's ideal characters are individualistic; they are loners, whose dedication is motivated by patriotism, but who suffer and sacrifice in secret and in privacy. Lao She, however, is not for individualism per se. From Yen Fu onward, Chinese intellectuals were faced with the problem of reconciling individualistic democracy, as known to the West, with a strong state which put a premium on harnessing the individual for the purposes of the state. Lao She, by denying his young people even the luxury of falling in love, seems to set aside individualism for a later stage in the development of China.

In many ways, Lao She's emphasis on the creation of a "pure" person—sincere, selfless, virtuous, working for the needs of society and conscious of a duty higher than self—is in the best tradition of Confucianism. It is not difficult to perceive that Lao She wants a "government by gentlemen," differing from the Confucian concept only in the fact that his gentlemen would be versed in Western knowledge and not in Confucian lore, but ethically the inheritors of the past. If the picture is confused it is because the author reflects the confusion in the Chinese society of the 1920s, and also the contradictions present in his own thinking.

The characters in the first three novels, who are significant examples of Lao She's thought, have positive attitudes but there is no feeling of optimism that their goodness or their actions will lead to success. These characters are born good, they have an innate sense of goodness, but the evil design underlying society as a whole creates an atmosphere of pessimism. In the vast darkness of the night the characters do not even emit a small ray of light—they stand pathetically alone, cold, and helpless.

III

THE ARTIST MATURES

Singapore Sojourn

In June 1929, shortly after he had finished writing *Mr. Ma and Master Ma* and had sent the manuscript to *Hsiao-shuo yueh-pao* for publication, Lao She left England because his teaching contract with the School of Oriental and African Studies expired at about this time.[1] From London Lao She went to the continent, where he vacationed for three months, spending most of his time in Paris. While there, he toyed with the idea of writing a sequel to *Mr. Ma and Master Ma*, using the French capital as the background for the continued story of Ma Wei. But his visit was too short to provide him with the information and insight necessary for such a venture, and he failed in his attempt to get work in Paris, which could have kept him there for a longer period.

Lao She then proceeded to Singapore. He had long wanted to visit this area, partly because of his admiration for Joseph Conrad who had drawn heavily on his experiences of the Eastern Archipelago for material for his stories, and partly because he had only enough money to buy a third-class passage to Singapore. Although he wanted to gather material in Singapore for a novel as Conrad had, his motives were far different. As Lao She explains:

> In his [Conrad's] works most of the main characters are white men and Orientals play only supplementary roles . . . I also thought of writing a similar novel but using Chinese to play the leading parts. Conrad sometimes depicts the Eastern Archipelago (Nan-yang) as poison for the white men, who cannot make nature submit to them and are swallowed by it. I wanted to write exactly the opposite of this . . . If it had not been for the Chinese, would the development of the Archipelago have been possible? The Chinese can bear the greatest hardships; they can withstand bitter pain. The Chinese leveled wild forests inhabited by poisonous snakes and fierce tigers and once sterile land is now completely cultivated.[2]

On reaching Singapore Lao She realized that he would need to spend many years in Malaya, learn Cantonese, Fukienese, and Malay languages, travel in the interior and meet the old Chinese residents, and study their lives and history before he could write his novel. So nothing came of his project but from the above quotation it is quite clear that whatever sense of deliberate apprenticeship to writers like Dickens and Conrad he may have had, Lao She is so deeply concerned with things Chinese, and a desire to see China revitalized and respected, that his productions bear small resemblance to his models. Lao She complains that it was lack of money that kept him from fulfilling his dreams. To exist he had to teach and that meant that time was not his to spend the way he wanted to; he could not travel or do research and so dropped the idea of writing a Conrad-like story.

Lao She stayed only half a year in Singapore and earned his stay there by teaching Chinese in a middle-school. The job suggests that he was in a school for overseas Chinese and so, naturally, came in contact with Chinese youth. The experience was very rewarding because Lao She was astonished at the intense earnestness with which his teenage students ("fifteen or sixteen-year-olds"), "almost all of whom came from well-to-do families" held on to revolutionary ideas. The situation heartened him and led him to the conclusion that "new ideas existed in the East, not in the West."[3] and that, "today, if you desire to understand what it is that is called revolution, you have to come to the East because it is the Eastern peoples who suffer all the oppressions known to mankind and whichever way you think about it, they must overthrow the existing order (*ko-ming*)."[4]

The impact must have been really significant because Lao She discarded a half-finished love story which he had begun on the Continent and had continued on the ship that brought him to Singapore. Though he had already written about 40,000 characters he felt that the contents were not worthy of the seriousness of the times.

From all that has been said above—and it is based on Lao She's own statements as made in *Lao-niu p'o-ch'e* (Old ox and a broken cart)[5]—it would appear that anything that Lao She wrote during his stay in Singapore would bear a mark of a heightened sense of revolution. In actual fact this is not at all the case. In Singapore, Lao She began writing a story with children as the main characters: *Hsiao-p'o ti sheng-jih* (The birthday of little P'o). The novel, which he completed on his return to China early in 1930, has hardly any social or political commentary and in no way mirrors the turbulent thought he encountered in his school. I would suggest that *Old Ox and a Broken Cart*, which was written in 1935 and which is practically the only source we have of Lao She's views on his own writings, should not be taken at its face value. It is possible that in 1935, when Lao She was turning more overtly "political" and was to become, soon after the Sino-Japanese war began, the Chairman of the Chinese Writers' Anti-Aggression Association, he tried to explain away his earlier lack of participation in politics, or said things that he had objectively thought of but had never accepted subjectively. In any case there is much in the slim volume of essays that needs to be re-evaluated by any student of Lao She.

The Birthday of Little P'o which deals with the everyday life and environment of a Cantonese boy in Singapore, does reflect the author's love for children. "This kind of book makes me feel young, feel happy," he says, adding that, "I love children, they are the brightness, a new page in history . . . we can only look in that direction . . . hope lies there."[6] In keeping with his Mencian approach, Lao She depicts Little P'o as a child possessing innate qualities of goodness.

Little P'o is not yet tainted with the prejudices and biases of the world of adults. He cannot comprehend his father's condemnation of all those who do not hail from Kwangtung, he believes that everyone belongs to "one family" (*i-chia*), he is equally friendly with Malayan, Indian, Fukienese, and Shanghainese children, and when New Year comes around he posts a greeting card to "little friends all over the world."[7] Little P'o is full of love and warmth for everyone; with the charming naiveté with which he asks about the meaning of "birth" and the difference between a girl and a boy, he also expresses his ambition to grow up and become an "Indian watchman" or a "Malayan policeman"[8] and get his children from India because, "look at the small black noses of the Indian children, their big white eyes, their red lips—how very lovable they are."[9]

Even when the hates and barriers of adults impinge upon his conscious mind, and he, for example, learns to dislike the Japanese, he has to find himself a reason. In the case of the Japanese he discovers that he does not like the shape of the islands from which they come—he had seen the map of Japan in his brother's atlas and found that it looked like "fritters of twisted dough" (*yu-t'iao*), and did not have an interesting shape.[10] The same good-heartedness which makes Little P'o love everybody also makes him go out of his way to carry parcels for old ladies, and in school take on fights with boys older than himself, when they torment anybody weak and helpless.

There is not much of a story in *Little P'o,* and the first half of the book is basically a description of Little P'o in the context of various situations—in school, at home, wandering in the streets, playing with his friends, celebrating New Year's day, celebrating his birthday, and so on. On his birthday he is taken to see the monkeys in the Botanical Gardens and to a cinema, and the excitement of the day so fires his imagination that in his dreams that night he blends fantasy and reality to find himself in a world of monkeys, wolves, and characters from the film. This venture into Little P'o's dream world forms the second half of the book.

Even when Lao She is seemingly letting his fancy roam free in describing Little P'o's dream, he cannot get too far from his pet subject—China. The undisciplined, cowardly armies of the kingdom of the monkeys, their irresponsible officers, the meaningless orders of their king, are all aspects of China. In a later book, *Mao-ch'eng chi* (Notes on Cat City), Lao She was to use a similar formula for critical analysis of Chinese society and government by describing a decadent kingdom of cats. The similarities between the two works are more than casual.

According to Lao She one other reason which motivated him to put children from different nationalities together in a friendly group was that during his stay in Singapore he did not once see a European child playing with Oriental children. "This incensed me terribly, so I had a desire to bring all the Eastern children together to one place to play [with each other]. Perhaps in the future they will go to war and stand together on the battle front!"[11] The novel fails to develop this sentiment to any reasonable degree but Lao She's intention is worthy of note.

Lao She found working conditions in Singapore rather disagreeable and it says much for his character that in spite of all the handicaps he managed to write about 40,000 characters in four months' time:

> The first half of the day was spent completely in classes and in correcting answer books. The afternoons were very hot and one could not do anything till after four o'clock. I could only write a little after dinner.
>
> Writing and driving away mosquitoes at the same time, and the disturbance caused by the rats and lizards, made me restless. Moreover, it was even more unbearable to sit alone under a light and work hard at writing in such warm evenings. The noise of insects that came in from outside; the moist, sweet evening breeze that came from the woods; the singing of the Indians on the road; the light patter made by the wooden sandals of the women . . . all these made one feel that one must go out and lie down on a lawn and watch the starry sky and never move again.[12]

Trying to write under these conditions exhausted Lao She. We will find that he has similar complaints about working in Tsinan on his return to China. He recalls with nostalgia, in 1937, the contrasting quiet and coolness of England:

> During the holidays the School (of Oriental Studies) was very tranquil, only the library was still open, but even there, the number of people reading books was not very large. The larger part of my *The Philosophy*

of Lao Chang, Chao Tzu-yueh, and *Mr. Ma and Master Ma* were written here, because it was so cool and quiet! . . . the library was on the side of a road but across from it was open space which, because of flowers and trees, resembled a park. It was very convenient to go to this little park, after finishing my studying, and sit there awhile . . . I hope that I shall have an opportunity to visit London again, and to write one or two more books in this library.[13]

Early in 1930, when *The Birthday* was only three-quarters written, Lao She left for Shanghai. There he stayed with Cheng Chen-to (Cheng Hsi-ti) long enough to finish the novel, which he then handed over to his host who was connected with the editorial staff of the magazine *Hsiao-shuo yueh-pao.* From Shanghai Lao She went on to Peiping and during his three or four-month stay in his home town, he negotiated a teacher's job at Cheeloo University in Shantung. It is possible that the fact that he had been converted to Christianity helped, for Cheeloo University was a missionary establishment.[14]

The Chinese Scene, 1930–1936

In England Lao She had become increasingly nationalistic—a fact which is abundantly reflected in his first three novels—and one can imagine the close interest with which he had followed developments in China. As he himself writes: "In London, we, a group of friends, marked a map with pins every day—when the Revolutionary Army advanced we rejoiced wildly, when it fell back we were disappointed."[15] Lao She had left China when the country lay prostrate under the trampling boots of the warlord armies and to him the re-unification of his motherland was a historic occasion—a first step in the revival of China's greatness. The picture that greeted him on his return was, however, not so rosy and, indeed, increased his pessimism.

In 1928, when the central government was established in Nanking, even the military unification of the country was far from complete. Outer Mongolia, Tibet, and Sinkiang were beyond the pale of Kuomintang jurisdiction, Manchuria had only a tenuous relationship; within China proper there were still large areas which, though nominally under the Nanking regime, were actually still controlled by the old warlords who had allied themselves with Chiang Kai-shek.

There was one other internal source of opposition which had newly arisen, and this was the Chinese Communist party. Up to 1927, the Communist party had been primarily a political organization and had been collaborating with the KMT in the unification of the country. In that year, however, for various reasons which we need not go into here, the KMT expelled the CCP members from its ranks and Chiang Kai-shek decided to suppress the Communist Party but his bloody methods of mass arrests and executions only drove the hard core underground. The CCP gradually established armed bases, soviets, in certain mountainous areas and it took Chiang Kai-shek five encirclement campaigns from 1931 to 1934 to dislodge them. In the last campaign Chiang used 700,000 troops, but the Red Army broke through the encirclement and began the historic Long March which covered 6,000 miles and took a year. At the end of the march the Communists gained a base in Shensi, from which, ultimately, they emerged to become the legal government of China.

From the success against the Communists in 1934, Chiang Kai-shek also gained control over some of the western provinces but what he lost in the process was, perhaps the possibility of unifying sentiment against the aggressive intentions of Japan.

After 1930, when the Manchurian warlord appeared to be drawing closer to Chiang Kai-shek, the Japanese Army in Manchuria, fearing that Japan's position was weakening, decided to settle the question by force. The "Mukden Incident" in September 1931 led to the creation by the Japanese of the "independent" state of Manchukuo with Henry Pu-yi—who had been a "guest" of the Japanese Legation ever since he fled the capital in 1924—as the titular emperor. To add insult to injury, the Japanese Army seized Jehol in 1933, and by 1935 had persuaded the Chinese government to withdraw its troops from Chahar as well, and to declare a demilitarized zone in Hopei.

Even at this critical stage when it was obvious that the Japanese encroachment in the north had not ended and that it was the major threat to China, Chiang Kai-shek prepared to move against the Communist "bandits" rather than against the imperialist invaders. Popular national dissent against Nanking's policies was aptly symbolized in the "kidnapping" of Chiang Kai-shek in Sian in 1936 by his own military officers, who then forced him to agree to form a united front with the Communists against Japan. Before, however, the tide of anti-Japanese feeling could be harnessed or the nation geared to defense, the Japanese Army struck and a full-scale war resulted which ended only with the collapse of Japan at the conclusion of World War II.[16]

If the KMT government could not quite solve the problem of internal unity or adequately face up to the problems of external aggression, it was even less successful in tackling the issue of economic development. It showed little concern for the agrarian sector of the economy, and the shadow of bureaucratic capitalism deepened over the modern sector.

The battle of literary theories which was fought in the 1920s ended in 1930 with the formation of the League of Left-Wing Writers headed by Lu Hsun. Though it would not be true to say that all writers developed leftist tendencies, it would not be far wrong to generalize that partly as a reaction to the arrests and executions of several "progressive" writers by the KMT, and partly as a response to the fiery leadership of Kuo Mo-jo (who in 1928 had even attacked Lu Hsun for not accepting the cause of proletarian literature), many leading writers of the day, particularly those belonging to the Shanghai group, did develop strong leftist leanings. After all the floundering around, "realism" was accepted as the most suitable brand of literature for China; tradition was completely rejected and ignored, and the translation and imitation of Western literature became the main occupation of writers. Practically all these developments took place during Lao She's absence from China.[17]

The nature of the change from 1924 to 1930 can also be seen in two statements by Lu Hsun. In 1923, he said that he began writing because he believed that "literature was the best means" to revolutionize the nation, and change the spirit of the people.[18] By the end of the 1920s Lu Hsun radically changed his stand and said: "all literature is shaped by its surroundings and though devotees of art like to claim that literature can sway the course of world affairs, *the truth is that politics comes first and art changes* accordingly."[19]

So Lao She on his return to the motherland found that if there was no place for a liberal thinker in the field of politics, where a powerful authoritarian central government denied civil liberties and majority participation, neither was there any place for a liberal writer in the field of literature, which was, to a significant extent, dominated by the authoritarian League of Left-Wing Writers. Actually, the League was established during Lao She's stay in Shanghai but he does not seem to have paid much attention to it nor had any desire to prolong his stay and make contacts necessary for future participation. Cheng Chen-to, who was very much a part of the Shanghai literary scene, must, no doubt, have given his house guest, Lao She, an insight into the latest developments and, it is also to be expected that, during his residence in Shanghai, Lao She must have met some of the local literary figures.

However, all that can be surmised from Lao She's later activities is that he still avoided politico-literary polemics, and continued to follow the path of literary development which was uniquely his own. When he left China in 1924, Lao She was a nobody, and though by the time of his return he had already acquired some name as a writer, he was still a nobody, for he had taken no sides in the literary battles, expounded no theories or ideologies and appeared to show an outsider's cold indifference to the heated clashes of the protagonists.

Didacticism vs. Creative Impulse

From the fall of 1930 Lao She began to work in Cheeloo University and for the first six months he was too preoccupied with organizing his lectures and courses to write any fiction. During this time, however, he had ample opportunity to familiarize himself with the city of Tsinan. The city still bore the marks of the Tsinan Incident of May 3, 1928, when Japanese troops, ostensibly sent to protect Japanese citizens, had clashed with units of the Northern Expedition. The memory of the horror and massacre that had accompanied the Incident was still fresh in the minds of the local residents. Lao She decided to use the Tsinan Incident in his next work of fiction and so gathered as much information as he could by talking to the people and seeing the photographs which some of them possessed. In the spring of 1931, Lao She began writing *Ta-ming hu* (Lake Ta-ming) and though the Tsinan Incident was not the main theme, it provided a part of the background for a complicated love story which also dealt with problems of national reconstruction, revolution, money, and poverty.

Lao She finished the novel by the end of the summer vacation and sent it for publication to *Hsiao-shuo yueh-pao.* Since that magazine was currently serializing his *Birthday of Little P'o,* the editors decided to hold over the publication of *Lake Ta-ming* to the beginning of 1932. Unfortunately, the Japanese military action in Shanghai which began on January 28, 1932, destroyed the printing press of the publishers and in the fire, Lao She's only manuscript of *Lake Ta-ming* was also destroyed. Some of his friends suggested that he rewrite the story but, according to Lao She, he was not completely satisfied with the novel in any case, and so decided not to do so. Later, he did write a short story— *Yueh-ya(r)* (Crescent moon)—which was based on an incident used in the novel. We shall have occasion to deal with this story at greater length later. It will suffice to say here that the story is a tragedy and depicts how a mother and her daughter, belonging to a respectable lower middle-class family, are forced by oppressive social circumstances to become prostitutes. In the original novel Lao She had driven the mother to commit suicide in Lake Ta-ming and saved the daughter from doing the same by having a kindhearted man fall in love with her and marry her.

It is possible that Lao She was not willing to rewrite *Lake Ta-ming* because by the time the manuscript was destroyed China's conditions had become even more chaotic. Manchuria had been occupied by the Japanese, and the Yangtze floods in 1931 had devastated the already poverty-stricken west. Though not a member of the League of Left-Wing Writers, Lao She had a natural sympathy for the underdog and, perhaps, unconsciously or consciously tried to prove that he was as serious a writer as the best of the left-wingers. The two things which seemed necessary to prove this were discarding humor and increasing the social realism of his novels.

Lao She made a heroic attempt to fulfill both these qualifications. We do not know anything about his lost novel, but he emphatically says that *he did not use "one sentence of humor in it,"* because he had the tragedy of the Tsinan Incident in the back of his mind.[20] Humor had to be eschewed because in the eyes of the left-wing critics it produced frivolous literature. In the early 1930s Lu Hsun attacked Lin Yutang for writing in a humorous vein and though Lao She was too insignificant a figure (in the eyes of the polemicists) to be attacked he was sensitive enough to the criticism. Several of Lao She's friends also advised him to give up humor.[21]

So in *Notes on Cat City*, the novel which followed *Lake Ta-ming*, Lao She is impelled by the need for seriousness to discard humor and use only satire. As far as the contents are concerned, *Cat City* is the most political of all his novels and at times reads like a series of editorial comments strung together with rather feeble connections. The novel is a vitriolic satire of China, and gives an unrelieved and a totally pessimistic picture of a nation in the throes of a death struggle. As Lao She explains, "the hopeless conditions of national affairs, the various military defeats and diplomatic failures" created in him a feeling of indignation and despair.[22]

This may mean that, apart from outside pressures that led him to change the style and content of his novel, he may himself have felt the need for some readjustment. As has been mentioned earlier, Lao She had only been away from China for a few months when he started feeling nostalgic for home and it was this nostalgia that was partly responsible for his turning to fiction writing. It is conceivable that not only had his nostalgia grown during the six years abroad but also that he, helped by time and distance, may have added rosier hues to the image of his motherland and glorified some of the great developments reportedly taking place there. He was indeed excited at the prospect of returning home and, as he says, he cut short his stay in Singapore to hurry back. But if things had changed in his absence they had, if anything, changed for the worse and this would, no doubt, have deepened Lao She's pessimism.

The struggle between didacticism and creative impulse marks Lao She's works right from the beginning and one notices how the author often intrudes into his London novels to give some direct advice to his readers. *Lake Ta-ming* and *Cat City* mark the stage when didacticism appears to have gained the upper hand in the struggle and creative imagination lost out. It is exceedingly fortunate that Lao She recognized that these two works were not of high literary quality, and realized that, although he might be condemned for it, he had to stand by his own vision of reality to provide consistency and meaning to his works. As he said in 1935: "Friends continually advised me to give up humor; I sincerely thank them. I also know that because of humor [my works are] often disliked. But after having experienced these two failures [*Lake Taming* and *Notes on Cat City*], only then did I realize that it is very difficult to change a dog into a cat."[23] There was no way out; Lao She had to follow his own instincts and be a loner.

The year 1931 was also important to Lao She for another, more personal reason. In this year, at the age of 33, he married Miss Hu Hsieh-ch'ing, who had been introduced to him by his old and dear friend Lo Ch'ang-p'ei. As is usual with Lao She's private life we have hardly any information of Hsieh-ch'ing except that it seems she graduated from Peking Normal College and worked as a teacher till 1949. From her photographs, she appears to be a handsome woman. She was fond of painting in the Chinese style, a hobby which she still pursues. She bore Lao She four children—three girls and one boy.[24]

Mao-ch'eng chi (*Notes on Cat City*)

After the January 28, 1932, Shanghai Incident, *Hsiao-shuo yueh-pao* ceased publication and its place was taken by *Hsien-tai* or *Les Contemporains* which became the most influential magazine of the day.[25] The editor Shih Chih-ts'un approached Lao She for a story and *Notes on Cat City* was written as a consequence.

Since *Cat City* is a political, and, to some extent, a philosophical novel dealing with a wide variety of situations, it is most difficult to give a brief summary of the story. A spaceship crashes on Mars and the only survivor is a Chinese, who has an opportunity to study life in Cat Country before he is picked up by another spaceship and brought back to Earth. The Chinese narrates the story in the first person and this technique allows the author to provide the reader with straight commentary as well as a series of interviews with local residents which help to explain the peculiar characteristics of Cat society. The narrator is employed by a wealthy landlord, who is also "a politician, a poet, and a military officer."[26] The hero becomes a friend of the landlord's son, Hsiao-Hsieh, and through him gains an intimate insight into the politics and society of Cat Country.

The main agricultural product and the main food of the country is "enchanted leaves" (*mi-yeh*), obviously a metaphor for opium, for "after eating them, even though the spirit is willing, the legs and arms do not want to move."[27] The cats are indolent, corrupt, cowardly, and without any sense of national honor. The upper strata lives in luxury by squeezing the poor but behaves abjectly before the foreigners and is ready to sell the nation for money. And the money used in all the nefarious transactions is "national spirit" (*kuo-hun*). In this decadent immoral society there are no ideals, even youth hankers after official jobs because that is the path to wealth and luxury. Schooling is a farce, the army is cowardly, the generals in the pay of the enemy, national treasures have been sold to outsiders and the country is in such a state of moral, cultural, and economic bankruptcy that when it is attacked by "dwarf soldiers" from a neighboring kingdom, who unlike the cats had "at least the concept of a 'country,' "[28] the cat nation is entirely annihilated. The narrator stays for six months more on Mars before he meets with a French spaceship which brings him back to his "great, glorious, and free China."[29]

However poor this work might be as a piece of literature, it has a wealth of information on Lao She's attitude toward various aspects of sociopolitical life in China plus the author's version of the history of China. Indeed, one of the shortcomings of the novel is the fact that the author tries to touch upon practically every problem that China is suffering from and so weakens the narrative line. An attempt to introduce several lengthy political discussions also detracts from the development of the characters in the story.

Cat City begins as an adventure story which has all the elements of a fantasy but the thin veneer of camouflage cannot be maintained for long and Cat Country, we soon realize, is China; the foreigners in it represent Westerners in China, the dwarfish soldiers who invade it are the Japanese. Under these conditions who does the narrator of the story represent? He is supposed to be a Chinese who finds himself in Cat Country on Mars and if the symbols are totally reversed he should be a Martian who has landed in China on Earth! But Lao She not only finds it difficult to divorce himself from the "I" in the novel, he actually, perhaps unconsciously, uses "I" to represent all the contradictions in his own emotional and intellectual make-up. As a complete alien, "I" is totally objective and uninvolved, and treated like all other foreigners; as one who wants to help improve the conditions in Cat Country and as one who shuns other foreigners and wants to be accepted by the cats, he is more of a Catlander than the cats themselves. Lao She seems to be fighting a battle with himself, struggling to find his own identity. We can see that there is a strong force compelling him to identify himself with China and yet he is a stranger, who can only stand outside and at best suggest action but never lead. The narrator is witness to the destruction of a great culture but, "it was not as if I was watching history with the same attitude as one watches a tragic play. In my heart I really hoped that I might be of some service to the people of Cat City."[30] The narrator's reaction to Cat City appears to reflect Lao She's feeling on his return to China:

No, I could not go to live in the foreign settlement. It is not as if the cat-people could not be trained [to become better] . . . If there were good leaders the cat-people would certainly be the most peaceful and law-abiding citizens. I could not go to sleep. A host of fresh and colorful pictures crowded into my mind: Cat City had been rebuilt into a garden city with sounds of music, sculpting, and people reading books, a city with flowers, birds."[31]

So there is hope and a dream but as the narrator proceeds to inquire into the possibilities of reform in Cat Country, hope gradually dies out and the dream is shattered.

Hsiao Hsieh, the son of the narrator's employer, is the only truly nationalistic and patriotic cat-person. He is educated, has been abroad, and is intensely aware of the fate that lies ahead for his country; he is cynical and doubts that the state of affairs can be improved, but in his heart he carries a torch of national honor and freedom, which is extinguished only by his suicide when his country is invaded and occupied. If Lao She projects himself through "I" who asks all the questions, then he also projects himself through Hsiao Hsieh who answers most of them. Both "I" and Hsiao Hsieh have the good of Cat Country in their hearts. "I" is an optimist who is driven to become a pessimist; Hsiao Hsieh is a pessimist who carries a streak of optimism within him; they are two sides of the same coin. At the end neither can help. Destruction is inevitable.

In his inquiries into the reasons for Cat Country's degradation, one of the first questions that the narrator asks is: "Is not Cat Country so impoverished and weak because the foreigners have united to make things difficult for it?" The answer is:

> When the people of a country lose their character, the country gradually loses its national character and nobody wants to cooperate with a characterless country . . . There are many other poor and weak countries on Mars but they have by no means lost their international standing because of being poor and weak. There can be many reasons for a country being weak. Natural disasters or geographical characteristics are enough to impoverish a country, but lack of character is the product of the people themselves and weakness resulting from this cannot draw sympathy from others.[32]

So it is not foreign exploitation but the weakness of national character that is the cause of Cat Country's ruination. Having accepted this as a fundamental truth, the author then goes on to probe the possibilities of ameliorating the situation through reform. "How about individual effort?" asks the narrator of Hsiao Hsieh. Hsiao Hsieh's reply is:

> It is of no use. Individual effort from such confused, simple, stupid, piti-
> able, impoverished masses, who can live happily under any circumstances?;
> from soldiers who only know how to use their clubs to steal *mi-yeh* (opi-
> um), and rape women?; from these innumerable clever, selfish, short-
> sighted, shameless, scheming politicians, who do not care for society? In-
> dividual effort?[33]

After this conversation the narrator gets ample opportunity to see for himself that Cat people have no social consciousness at all and are, indeed, exceedingly selfish and self-centered. He is forced to agree with the "foreigners" that
there was something deadly in Cat Country culture which was characterized
by "evil, disease, disorderliness, confusion, and darkness."[34] But he still hopes
that somewhere, somehow he will stumble across a relieving feature and so
continues his search by going to see the schools, the museums, the libraries,
by meeting scholars and politicians, and by trying to understand the political
ideologies of Cat Country.

Lao She allows his imagination to run wild while describing the farcical
school system in Cat City. The "new" educational system had been borrowed
from other countries, but since Cat people only tried to imitate and not emu-
late, the system had not worked and gradually deteriorated; the teachers who
had not received any salaries for years had sold school property till nothing
was left but bare walls; the students rebelled against the idea of studying and
thrashed their teachers, and demanded that they be allowed to fornicate during school hours; finally, the students received their diplomas for having graduated from college on the very first day they entered primary school. Why
would anyone want to be a teacher under these circumstances, queries the
narrator and Hsiao Hsieh explains:

> In the beginning the schools had organized different courses which pro-
> duced talent in various fields. Some studied engineering, some com-
> merce, some agriculture . . . but what were they to do after gradua-
> tion? Engineers had studied some foreign skills but we did not set up
> any foreign industries for them [to work in]; students of commerce had
> studied some foreign methods but we had only small peddlers . . .
> Such education provides no link between school and society, so what
> can the students do after graduating? There are only two ways out:
> become an official or be a teacher. It does not matter what you have

studied, you must have some connections if you want to become an official.[35]

It is Hsiao Hsieh's thesis that the salvation of the country lies only in the promotion of learning and the building up of character, and in this the students and teachers have a special role to play. He is aware of the fact that adverse economic conditions can destroy character and that a "teacher is afraid of hunger the same as a prostitute is"[36] but he points out that "there are women who would rather go hungry than turn to prostitution . . . Is it possible that an educator cannot grit his teeth and be a man of character?" Of course, the government is harsh and unjust, particularly to honest educators but "if we who administer education [Lao She appears to be speaking now directly about his own profession] really have character and the students produced also have character, is it possible that society would forever be blind to good and evil?"[37]

Lao She, in his London novels had repeatedly emphasized "character" and "education" as prerequisites for a regeneration of Chinese society, now in *Cat City* he pushes the idea a little further. While discussing the importance of the right type of teachers—teachers of character—Hsiao Hsieh makes two significant remarks. The first is that "if in the old system people could be brought up to be sincere, filial, and well mannered, how is it that the Board of New Education has not even achieved comparative success?" The second is a logical conclusion of the whole argument: "I believe that if we had ten years of education with [emphasis on] character, the shape of things in Cat Country would undergo a change."[38] But this would require the presence of a set of high-principled, dedicated, self-sacrificing teachers and students, and, unfortunately, such a group was not to be found anywhere in Cat Country.

The narrator then meets the traditional scholars, who fight each other for official patronage and waste their time in meaningless research. Obviously, they could not contribute to the betterment of Cat Country, but neither could the scholars of the new type who, because they had "been abroad for a few years" think they "know everything," whereas they are extremely superficial, and can only voice the meaningless jargon of foreign terms while vying to show how modern they are by adopting the latest foreign fashions.

A visit to the museum and the library only helped to increase the narrator's depression even further, because the museum had sold all its exhibits to foreigners (a source of government finance and a kickback for modern scholars) and the library had sold all the books. The most surprising thing was that in spite of what was happening around them the intellectuals of Cat Country were still exceedingly "proud and self-satisfied," and not one of them realized that "in the whole world their country was the most disgraced." [39]

The narrator then turns his attention to "political parties" (called political "brawls," *cheng lung* in cat language) and learns that just as "new" education had failed to take root because the system had been transplanted from abroad without a proper consideration of local conditions, political ideologies, too, were introduced without adjusting them to Cat Country's requirements. The result was that these political ideas did not work and instead of improving the situation, made it more chaotic. Tracing the history of the development of new politics Hsiao Hsieh explains:

> The first political reform was probably the demand made of the emperor to allow the people to participate in government. The emperor, naturally did not consent to this, and thereupon, the men in the political brawls got a large number of militarists to join the movement. The emperor seeing that the winds were not favorable, granted office to the leading persons in the political brawls.[40]

This took away the bite from political agitation till a new movement was begun to completely dispense with the emperor. The emperor countered this by forming a party of his own and by buying off political figures with official patronage.

The common man, according to Hsiao Hsieh, has no place in the parties and continues to suffer at the hands of the parties and the government; persons who join parties do so because this is one way of getting government jobs and making money:

> So revolution in my country has become a kind of profession. The result of all these years of politicking is manifest in two phenomena. First, in politics there is only change [rearrangement] but no reforms and this means that the more democratic thought develops the more impoverished the common people become. Second, the greater the number of political parties the more shallow the youth become.[41]

The discussion on political parties is brought to a conclusion by an analysis of "everybodyovskyism." Lao She appears to use this term to describe both the KMT revolution which was supposedly going to establish the broad socialist principles of Sun Yat-sen, and communism. He also shows considerable perspicacity in looking into the future, to a time after the Communist revolution had taken place. As in most of *Cat City,* the analysis is marred to some extent by the author's attempt, on the one hand, to be deliberately vague and, on the other, to touch on too many points in too brief a space. Everybodyovskyism came to the country because the economic question had been ignored by everybody in power for too long, and everybodyovskyism was going to solve this problem. Although this creed had been effective in other countries, it seems to lose its potency in Cat Country:

> For the true operation of this kind of system you have to (1) reform the economic system, and (2) nurture, through education, the faith that everybody lives for everybody else. Members of our "Everybodyovskyism brawl" do not, at all, have any understanding of economic problems and know, even less, of how to establish a new educational system.
>   . . .
> Now the leader of "Everybodyovsky brawl" has become an emperor. From Everybodyovsky to emperor . . . what a nightmare! . . .[42]

The last part of the above quotation, one can hardly doubt, is Lao She's reflection on the emperor-like position which Chiang Kai-shek was already assuming in 1932. Lao She appears to despair of the social and political situation in China but *Cat City* does reveal one more dimension in the author's thinking on a possible constructive approach to China's ills. In his first novel he had no solution to offer at all; in the second, he advanced the idea of character training and scholarship coupled with heroic individual action in assassinating the "evil ones"; in the third, he emphasized the need for nationalism, and for self-sacrificing youth with high moral character to prepare themselves through scholarship to reconstruct the nation but dropped the idea of anarchic assassination; now in the sixth work (the fourth was a children's story, and the fifth was never published) Lao She not only demands men of character and a proper educational system but a government that understands economics and has a true regard for the masses. This development is significant because it indicates a growing positive approach to national problems in Lao She's thinking.

As far as the KMT is concerned one wonders whether it gave Lao She any sense of personal satisfaction to find that he had very aptly described in *Cat City* the manner in which the Nanking government was to behave in the face of Japanese aggression. When Cat Country is invaded, the crafty politicians try to manipulate the situation to their advantage and the emperor shifts the capital to the interior while his armies melt away in the face of the advancing enemy.

Cat City marks the watershed between Lao She's earlier writings and his later works. None of his early novels has a fully developed theme or a fully developed character and even if one overlooks the lack of formal unity in these works, one is disturbed by the irresistible tendency which the author has to enlarge on a comic situation with what appears to be utter irrelevance. Second, in these works, Lao She also finds it difficult to adjust between didacticism and autonomous creative impulse. Sometimes the extremes of this dichotomy show up in passages where the author steps directly into the novel to make a remark full of satirical indignation, which has social implications but little bearing on the story. In novels after *Cat City* Lao She is far more successful in portraying characters and developing the themes of his stories, as well as in blending and fusing didacticism with purer creative writing. The artist has finally matured.

IV

ANATOMY OF ALIENATION

Li-hun (*Divorce*)

After *Notes on Cat City* had been published in serial form in *Hsien-tai,*
Lao She agreed to its being printed by Liang-yu Publishing House. *Hsien-tai,*
however, maintained that it held the rights for any reproduction of *Cat City*
in book form and so Lao She felt committed to provide a substitute novel for
Liang-yu. As a result, in the sweltering summer of 1933, when "several persons died of the heat in Tsinan," *Li-hun* (Divorce) was written in the record
time of seventy-odd days. It is a reflection of Lao She's self-discipline and capacity for hard work that in spite of the terrible heat (he had to "wind a cloth
around his head" to keep the perspiration from dripping on the pages[1]) he
wrote his daily average of two thousand characters from seven to nine in the
morning. Lao She was supposed to hand over the manuscript by the fifteenth
of August, but he did so a month earlier, an event he considered "the happi-
est occasion of my life."[2]

According to Lao She's own notes on *Divorce,* the author, having realized
that *Cat City* was a failure now "reverted to humor," and, incidentally, also
decided to seek salvation in writing about Peking. ("Pei-p'ing is my home
town, and the moment I think of this word, several hundred feet of pictures
of the 'Old Capital,' immediately unroll in my mind like a film.")[3] This decision of Lao She's, no doubt, contributed to the success of the novel, as also
did the fact that the subject matter had been simmering in Lao She's subcon-
scious for several years. When the author sat down to write, the story developed with ease and smoothness and he handled the theme and characters with
a deftness never before achieved.

Lao Li, who has studied banking and economics, and is a junior officer in
the Finance Bureau of the local government in Peking is the central figure in
Divorce. Li is one of those "unfortunates" who were born some time at "the
end of the Kuang Hsu period" (i.e. around 1900) and so are torn between the
old and the new.[4] He is romantic and sensitive and his ideal conception of
life often leads him to dream about an existence in which happiness and beauty
would be living experiences and not just dry abstractions. In reality, Li's
life is drab. His small-minded office colleagues and the nature of his office
work heighten the pettiness of his daily life. He is alienated and is an intro-
vert who finds it difficult to communicate with others.

Li, who comes from the country, is living alone in Peking when the story
opens. His wife and two children are still with his parents in his village home.

Li's is an arranged marriage and his wife is a village girl whose bound feet were "liberated" after the Republic was established. Li does not love his wife and finds little happiness in his surroundings.

One of Li's office associates is a man called Chang (popularly addressed as Elder Brother Chang), who is temperamentally different from Li. Chang is a gregarious, friendly person who enjoys life and finds much satisfaction both in the office and at home. In his spare time Chang works as a marriage broker and he sincerely believes that if "everybody had a satisfactory wife, the world would not at all be troubled with communism."[5] According to his way of thinking, Li's worries would disappear as soon as his family joined him and so he persuades Li to bring his wife and children to Peking.

Li does respond with some warmth to his children—little Ying and his baby sister Ling—but, on the whole, the presence of the family does not relieve Li's sense of frustration and loneliness. He finds it difficult to adjust to the fact that he is a "father and a husband" for during all the years of his marriage his wife and children had stayed with his parents and he had come to look upon his wife as "the daughter-in-law of his parents and children as the grandchildren of his parents."[6] Chang had advised Li to "teach" his wife the things Li wanted a wife to possess, but Li is embarrassed by his loud-talking country spouse and finds it impossible to communicate with her.

In spite of the fact that Li has told no one, except Chang, that he is going on leave to bring his family to Peking, the office does come to know, and on his return he is forced to invite his colleagues to a dinner in a "Western-style" restaurant to celebrate the event. He is relieved that they do not want to meet his wife and willingly accepts this expense, but he has underestimated the crookedness of Chao, the villain of the novel. Chao goes to Li's apartment and under a false pretext gets Mrs. Li and the children to accompany him to the restaurant. It galls Li to see his badly dressed wife ridiculed by Chao, but he is cowardly and though he often dreams of heroic responses, he fails to react in a "manly" fashion to Chao's baiting. The episode only deepens Li's resentment against society and family.

Chao is a perfect representative of the class of corrupt officials that Lao She attacks in all his novels. Chao has friendly relations with the wife of the office chief and thereby wields a certain amount of nefarious influence over the lives of those who work in the Bureau; he hardly ever does any official work for he is busy most of the time running private errands for the chief or his wife, and he maintains political contacts by providing women for influential persons. Mr. Wu, Mr. Ch'iu, and Mr. Sun, the other officials present at the dinner do not try to stop Chao because, not only are they afraid of him, but in this particular case, they look to him to provide some fun. Chang, though not stopping Chao, is the only one who tries to lessen the effect of Chao's attacks by turning their attention in other directions.

Soon after this dinner party two developments take place which have a strong impact on Li, and to a certain extent mark a change in his character. One is the arrest of T'ien Chen, Chang's only son, on the grounds that he is a Communist. T'ien Chen is a silly young college boy who doesn't study and wastes his father's money; he is far from being a Communist, though he sometimes uses Communist jargon. But there is no way of appealing against his arrest or getting him released because he is taken away by the secret police and no one knows where the secret police have their headquarters, or who should be approached. The incident puts the novel in the period after 1927 and most probably in the early 1930s for it is more than likely that it reflects Lao She's personal experiences in China after his return.

Chang, the good man, the popular matchmaker, the friendliest denizen of Peking, is suddenly an outcast. He loses his friends and his job but he does not care, for life suddenly becomes meaningless to him and now all he wants is the return of his son. This affair gives Li an opportunity to live up to his high ideals and, for once, to do something significant. He is the only one who not only continues to meet Chang but who tries to get the officials in the Bureau to sign a petition (nobody does) to get T'ien Chen released. Li has no friends in the upper echelons of the government and, therefore, no influence but he knows one person who can help and that is the detestable Chao. So he goes to Chao and, in a Faustian gesture, pledges himself to this devilish rascal in return for the release of T'ien Chen.

Apart from binding himself to Chao, for the latter to use or misuse his services in whatever way he thinks fit, Li also has to get Chang to part with one of his three houses and must himself pay 250 dollars in cash. The villainous Chao, however, schemes to use this opportunity to further his personal ends. He tries on the one hand to get Li dismissed from the Bureau, and on the other to acquire Chang's daughter—Chang's only other child—as his wife, with the intention of trading her away later on. Not only does Chao fail in both these plans, but he also loses his life in the bargain because Second Master Ting, Chang's servant, comes to know of the secret liaison which Chao has with the girl and very cleverly uses this knowledge to lure Chao to a lonely place and murder him. The murder takes place, of course, after T'ien Chen's release has been secured. The only person who knows the truth of what has happened to Chao is Lao Li.

With the return of his son, Chang gets his job back and regains his friends and, in spite of the suffering he has undergone, he returns to his old placidity. Li, who seems to realize that his great act of self-sacrifice was in reality more dramatic than significant, does not even attend the dinner given by Chang to celebrate the happy event of T'ien Chen's return home. Li also feels that the real hero is Second Master Ting who liquidated the evil Chao, but who is now having nightmares about being executed by the police. Li understands the nature of Ting's mental anguish, tries to allay his fears and readily gives him shelter in his own home.

The other incident which affects Li's life is his meeting with the beautiful, young, educated Mrs. Ma, who lives in the apartment next to his. Mrs. Ma had fallen in love with and married one of her teachers in high school, but a few months after the marriage her husband went off with another woman. Li's abstract dreams of a beautiful partner come true in the person of the deserted Mrs. Ma, and though they barely exchange more than formal greetings, there is a strong hint of romance between them. Li dares to hope that somehow things will work out in his favor and his dreams will be fulfilled. But when the fickle husband returns, the beautiful Mrs. Ma becomes reconciled to him and Li's faith in "the ideal woman" is shattered.

Disgusted with the corruption and nepotism of officialdom and finished with romantic love, Li decides to leave Peking and go back to the country. Peking has also had a negative effect on Mrs. Li. During her stay in this great city she has learned how to dress better and her manners have improved, but the wedge between husband and wife has widened. From the little that she has learned of modern ways, she has come to have a distorted sense of her rights. She has become a spendthrift, she has started suspecting her husband's loyalty, and she has become a nagging housewife.

The story of *Divorce,* as the title of the novel implies, can also be looked upon as a study of the problem of divorce in the China of the 1930s. The concept of free choice in marriage and the concept of divorce are both among the new ideas that had come into China with the Western impact. Most of the characters in the novel are unhappily married, and the tensions are such that their logical resolution can only lead to divorce. We have already mentioned the plight of Li and Mrs. Ma. Mr. Wu is similarly unhappy because he is wedded to a huge, ungainly woman and so is continually looking out for a concubine. Mrs. Ch'iu is an ugly college graduate and dominates her husband who, it appears, finally manages to keep a woman on the side. Mrs. Wu and Mrs. Ch'iu had always threatened to leave their husbands if they ever looked at another woman, but when faced with this situation, neither Mrs. Wu's strength nor Mrs. Ch'iu's education are of any use. They are forced to compromise and find like Mrs. Ma that society has not yet reached the stage where divorce is possible. A divorced woman loses both her economic security and her respectability.

Divorce is one of the first genuinely modern novels in Chinese literature. There is not much action in the story but the author achieves considerable success in using the psychological approach to reveal the inner make-up of the main character, Lao Li. Lao She makes no attempt to interpose himself in the story to provide political comment or advice as he did in previous works. *Divorce* transcends politics. It is not a study of the problems of society in transition and man's role in helping it move "forward"; it is a study of the problems of man, who lives in a society in the throes of change. *Divorce* thus deals with a reality which is on a higher plane than the realism that so often bogged down Chinese literature of the 1930s. Another sign of the author's growing maturity is that though he tells us he "reverted to humor" when writing *Divorce,* he manages to keep comic exaggeration, which had marked his earlier humorous writing, under fairly strict control and subordinate to the design of the whole.

In Li, the man who is in search of values that would provide a meaning to his existence, we see a whole segment of the Chinese middle class, which has lost or is losing its old values but has not yet found the new. There is a world outside Peking in the case of Li, a world full of sights and sounds, a world which has an objective unity in the eyes of an outsider, but to this generation of Chinese it is fragmented and disrupted and they are unable to put the pieces together. Li has neither the stability which derives from tradition nor the strength which is born of faith in the future and his present is like the parts of a jigsaw puzzle, which give no indication of any unified pattern.

Li is an ordinary person—a good person, but one who is a stranger to himself and to others. He lacks any strong impulse to start a revolution. He hates the prison he finds himself in but he is too weak to fight his way out of it. One half of him is a part of society, a part of the world outside, so it is also one half of his own self that is imprisoning the other half. Lao She raises the pertinent question: is the prison outside Li or inside him? and leaves the reader to find his own answer.

It was Lu Hsun who first provided Chinese literature with examples of alienation and the sense of hopelessness and futility that went with it. In his *Tsai chiu-lou shang* (In the wine shop), for example, in which the author meets an old friend, who had once been fired with ideas of revolutionizing China but was now driven by adverse circumstances to teaching the hated classics to little girls with rich parents.[7]

In *Divorce* Lao She not only goes further than Lu Hsun in dealing with alienated subjectivity but also adds many dimensions to it. For example, in Li we see not only an alienated soul but a person who is half-consciously making a search for a "homeland." One of the simplest and yet the subtlest passages in *Divorce* is the one where Li goes to dine with Mr. and Mrs. Chang. There is a certain air of tranquillity in the Chang home and a total absence of the restlessness which disturbs Li continuously. Chang, whose philosophy is that "the world cannot but be peaceful" if the question of "full stomachs and marriage" is adequately solved, finds delight and happiness in every little thing, in every minor detail, like, for example, the quality of meat cooked for dinner or the way the scallions were cut. And this makes Li wonder whether, "the kitchen fire, the smell of meat, the meowing of the kitten" do not, after all, constitute the "truth" and "life" that he is seeking.[8] After the meal is over there is a moment, but just a passing moment, when it appears that the feeling of satisfaction and comfort which a good meal has brought to Li is about to restore a friendly world to the exile, a world which his soul had missed but which his bodily sensations had reached out and touched. But the moment passes and, unlike Meursault (in *The Stranger* by Albert Camus), Li has no escape in sensuousness.

Li, the lover of books and the dreamer of dreams, is in actual life caught between the Bureau, "the monster which waits for him with its big mouth wide open" and home, where "she [his wife], the female devil, also waits for him."[9] Li hates the office but seems to be so caught in the meshes of cause and effect that chain him to existence that he is driven to go there by forces he cannot destroy:

> The nearer he approached the Yamen the less happy he felt. How had he become an official? He could not quite remember. . . When the Yamen came in sight, the big black gate looked as if it were a huge mouth exhaling cold air, and waiting every morning to swallow up a multitude of petty clerks. Swallow, swallow, swallow, till these officials, in the belly of the monster, decayed and shrivelled up and became ugly and suffocated to death . . .
>
> But, every day Lao Li had to crawl into the belly of this monster . . . and each time he crawled in he felt that his hair had turned a little greyer.[10]

Not only do the physical conditions of the office distress Li, but also the nature of the official work and the character of the officials.

> Official business! Official business, means no business at all. If there was no official business in the world, humanity would not come to any grief. Documents, documents, and more documents. Documents without heads or tails, without conclusions and without endings. Only one thing was real—a pity that it was real—money had to be squeezed from

the people. This monster ate money and vomited documents! Nobody knows where the money goes. It does come to pass that there are some people who buy mansions and cars and concubines, but documents are the only thing that everybody can see . . . This world is made for them [Li's colleagues]. At home it is [talk of] oil, salt, soya sauce, vinegar, and mahjong . . . They enter the office room and ha, ha, ha, they discuss and debate their private affairs, the quarrels of grandchildren, the wife's birthday, and the number one waitress in Ch'un-hua Restaurant. If they can come late by one minute they do so. If they can leave one minute early, they do so. Dilapidated tables, broken teacups, and endless tea drinking.[11]

In spite of his disgust for the way things are running, Li is, himself, a hard worker. This, of course, does not bring him any respect. On the contrary, others load him with their work and, at the same time, look upon him as a fool for doing it. When Li does get promoted, it is not because of his application to his duties, but because the head of the Bureau is a superstitious man who has great faith in a Taoist astrologer. Because of a coincidence, the chief thinks that Li is lucky for him and this notion, in the end, leads to Li's promotion. Nobody in the office believes Li when he says that he has no connection with the chief. Everyone knows that favors and promotions depend entirely on personal contacts!

Li is an honest and an upright man who has not even a shade of corruption in him, so he can quite objectively render judgment on all those around him:

Who was this head of the Bureau? An official and a bandit. Small Chao? A swindler and a clerk. Elder Brother Chang? A female go-between with a male character. Wu? A glutton and a boxer . . . Mr. Ch'iu? A symbol of anguish and a petty official. Could this group of "things" run an organization?[12]

And yet Li not only has to continue working with them but also has to "laugh when they laughed" and put on a "European dress for their sake."[13] Presumably, he has to undergo this torture because he has to provide for his wife and children. But even if this is so, does the end justify the means?

Li dislikes his wife; the thought of her feet which had once been bound, and the vulgar way she dresses the children in "red pants and green jackets" sends a shiver down his spine. New ideas and values often make him think of divorce but it is not easy to translate that thought into action because the old values still exert a hold over him:

"Is this life or an apology for life?" he asked himself.

All his thoughts and actions carried an explanatory note [which said]: do not fall behind modern times! At the same time he had to ask: Is this right or wrong? But what could he use as a standard of right and wrong? Is not the standard derived from the Classics? His actions, because they were in accord with his conscience had to apologize to modern ideas. His thoughts which were in keeping with the times must apologize to the past [lit., "the ghostly shadow"]. Life was, indeed, in two sections like his wife's "reformed" feet [which had been bound in keeping with the old tradition and then unbound in keeping with new ideas].[14]

The polarity between the old and the new is not an abstraction for Li. He is caught between the two, and the forces pulling him in two opposite directions are tearing at him. In the manner in which Li rationalizes his situation one can see the dilemma of the Chinese middle class in the 1930s:

Divorce is impossible, he told himself. The parents will not allow it, and how can one choose to wound the feelings of the aged ones? . . .

There is no way out. . . .

There is no way to rebuild! There is a wall in front, push it down and there are wild mountains and streams on the other side, but . . . I dare not push it over because the air [of true liberty] which hasn't yet been breathed by any man, may be poisonous. There is a wall behind, make an opening in it and there [you will find] are beds, screens, tables and chairs, fireplace, fire, tea and cigarettes, but I dare not knock that wall down either, because it is possible that the tainted air [of the traditional family life] there, may be poisoned too. Better to stand here.

And between the two walls stands a man in a dream.[15]

So, neither possessing the courage to venture forth into the unknown realms of the new nor having any faith in the old, Li, and all intellectuals like him feed on vague dreams and half-formed hopes.

"What I seek," says Li, "are some poetic ideas. Family, society, nation, world, are all so prosaic and lacking in poetic meaning . . . I am probably a little insane, and this insanity of mine, if I can understand myself is that I do not dare to be a romantic but have day dreams. I see society filled with the forces of darkness and evil, and yet hope for immediate peace and tranquillity (t'ai-p'ing); I know the fate of man, yet conjure up visions of an eternal paradise."[16] Li's "poetic dreams" are nebulous. Their importance is that they indicate the intensity of his alienation from the sordid material world around him. There is even a strong hint of Taoism in the following description: "But in his mind there was always the not very clear picture of a wheat field and a stretch of low hills under an early May sky. Or else a small stream with grassy banks studded with flowers and the sudden, unexpected, sound of a frog jumping into the water."[17]

Li often thinks that if he were to meet his "ideal woman" he might be able to live again, be able to cry and to laugh, and to apply himself to the work he loves. But like his other dreams, here also he has no well-defined ideals. So just before the story ends, anger and frustration born out of the meaninglessness of the life he leads, and the absence of any positive, concrete ideals that would inspire him to action (even the matter of helping Chang loses its significance), lead Li to complete inaction: "He did not want to go to the office. Let them do as they pleased. If they dismissed him, fine, then he would be dismissed. It did not matter . . . *Everyone was in a prison and nobody could save anybody.*"[18]

Though Li is absorbed with himself and feels alone and isolated, he is not completely oblivious of the larger problems of China. It is true that within the narrow confines of his life he is insulated from the shocking sights of hunger and poverty but even in the rare instance of his walking, inadvertently, of course, to the odorous, dirty market place near the West Gate, his sensitive intelligence is able to touch upon the most crucial of all problems:

> The stomach is everything . . . Man lives by bread alone. The root of inequality lies in the inequality of livelihood. What are poetic ideas? Stupid talk! To protect the bread of your own family it is necessary to starve others to death or to go to war . . . There were only two roads along which he could proceed: dream obscure dreams or live in reality. The latter could be divided further: live for grabbing bread for himself, or to fight for bread for everybody.[19]

This analysis remains somewhere deep within Li's mind and we notice that when he returns from the country with his family and is asked about conditions there, he says with much emotion "[the harvest was not bad] but the people are still very poor." It, therefore, does not come as a complete surprise that finally, when he is disillusioned with city life and his dreams are shattered, Li leaves his job and Peking and goes to the countryside.

It is true that Li's sudden decision to leave Peking is closely connected with his reaction to the alternative periods of discussion and silence that emanate from Mrs. Ma's room next door on the night her fickle husband returned home, and from the conclusion that a process of reconciliation was taking place. Yet it would be truer to look upon Li's resolution as a final revolt against much that had so far constituted his life. By ending the novel in the manner he has, Lao She leaves it to the reader to ponder Li's action. Though this action does not have any of the dramatic coloration of a great revolutionary deed, it does make revolt the most creative act in Li's life—an act which might put meaning into the absurdity of existence.

Li, who had often wanted to "smash the broken chair, the broken table, and the broken wastepaper basket," which constituted his office, and to "destroy the monster" (the Bureau) but never had the courage to do so, now leaves the prestigious government job, the social status that goes with it, and the great city of Peking to go and work in the country. His act of leaving cannot be construed as an act of running away. On the contrary, with this act of discarding, Li breaks the hold of the money-and-power nexus, which had held him victim. He realizes that it is fear that keeps him a prisoner in the citadel of corruption, injustice, and immorality—fear of being ridiculed by his peers, fear of not being able to provide for his family, and fear of losing touch with what is new and sophisticated. Gaining a sudden insight Li says at one point; "Anybody who is not afraid of others can perform miracles like Christ."[20] Indeed, in the act of moving out of Peking, the weak, diffident, cowardly Li rises to a great height and his action is born of strength rather than weakness. Whether he will be able to live up to his resolve is a different matter. The novel ends with Lao Chang's remark that Li is bound to return to Peking. Perhaps this reflects Lao She's lack of faith in middle-class intellectuals.

The main characters in the novels before *Divorce* were, mostly, middle-class young men who had not yet begun to earn their own livelihood. They were still outside the deadly rat-race, the demeaning competition of life, and so could still hold on to their ideals and their hopes. Li Ching-ch'un in *Chao Tzu-yueh,* and Ma Wei and Li Tzu-jung in *Mr. Ma and Master Ma,* are examples of such characters who nurse ideals of heroic proportions. In *Divorce,* however, Lao She describes what happens to men like them when they actually become a part of the cruel, corrupt world they had so wanted to change. Lao Li in *Divorce* is an older Ma Wei or Li Tzu-jung. He has studied banking and economics—new subjects to help reform China—but finds that the knowledge he had acquired at college is of no great use in his work at the Bureau of Finance. His dreams are now an escape, not a goal. Whatever new ideas he may have absorbed during his younger days, he now finds that he has to live a life of compromise because he cannot cut himself off from the old, the past.

Li is alienated from government service, from society, and from his personal family life but when he rebels he only breaks his relations with his job and with Peking and not with his wife and parents, which shows that he is not totally alienated from his family. That he would like to divorce his wife and cannot do so speaks strongly for the personal commitment he feels for his parents, whose feelings and sentiments he does not want to hurt.

A totally alienated person who can walk away from all personal commitments, for there are no longer any personal commitments that matter to him, can, perhaps, become a true revolutionary and identify himself fully with revolution. Ma Wei, when he leaves his father, is beginning to be such a person, though we can never be sure for Lao She does not seem to lay great store by middle-class romantic revolutionaries. As he depicts them, they never seem able to transcend personal considerations and, therefore, are no less self-seeking than corrupt officials. They are revolutionaries only where it comes to discarding personal obligations and commitments but have no desire for self-sacrifice. On the contrary, they believe that they have, by being revolutionaries, somehow acquired the freedom to live decadent lives.

Mrs. Ma's husband, Ma K'o-t'ung, is a good example of such a revolutionary, and in describing him Lao She expresses his distrust of such Communist intellectuals:

> Comrade Ma is a person who is not very satisfied. Although he is not a man with many ideas he is very proud of himself. He wants to become the younger brother of Marx, but his revolutionary thought and motives are all for the fulfillment of his own ends. Toward the rich he has a contempt born of pride and he thinks of dragging them down from the sky to the earth and planting his foot on their faces. Toward the poor he wants to be benevolent, an attitude also born of his pride. *He does not understand the poor at all and cannot see the significance of making revolution for them.* His best dream is that he himself has become a great revolutionary, so he always has an expression on his face which says, "look at me!" . . . He thinks that to be a revolutionary it is only necessary to run around in a car, make a few speeches, drink large amounts of beer, after which he would end up as a very exalted comrade.[21]

A few months after his marriage Comrade Ma blithely goes off with another woman because he believes, presumably as a good Communist, that "for a man to have many wives or one wife to have many husbands are both feasible, and every individual should have the freedom to follow his own course and nobody should question him."[22]

To those who are given to a Marxist interpretation of literature, Li would be an insignificant character—a little man caught in the little problems rising out of leading a little life within a little community, which forms an impediment to revolution. There is, indeed, something pathetic about the contradictions within Li's mental make-up and his inability to take decisive action. But confused, helpless men like Li, caught between the old and the new, constituted the unheroic middle class and Lao She very successfully captures its essential flavor in *Divorce*. Lao She himself had once given up a lucrative government job to suffer poverty but regain his independence, and it is highly doubtful that he considers Li's departure from Peking as an insignificant act.

From Lao She's analysis of Comrade Ma it is clear that the author is aware of the need for true revolution, and, from the novel as a whole, we find that he feels that the entire structure of society needs to be rebuilt. Also by making Second Master Ting assassinate Chao, Lao She has recognized the great potential that exists in the poor, propertyless lower classes. If there is a hero in the novel he is Second Master Ting. Lao She may not have any politics as such, but we can see that he is driven by his sense of nationalism and patriotism to conclusions that may be categorized under the broad label of "leftist thought." This, of course, in no way implies acceptance of Communist ideology; it only indicates that in a state of polarization, which had taken place in China in the 1930s, any talk of radical change would be looked upon by both sides as leftist.

Niu T'ien-tz'u chuan (*Biography of Niu T'ien-tz'u*)

At the end of March 1934 Lao She began to write the novel, *Niu T'ien-tz'u chuan* (Biography or annals of Niu T'ien-tz'u). But the teaching load and other work at the university appears to have been rather heavy, for in three months, until the school closed for summer vacation, Lao She had written only about 20,000 characters. This slow progress was not to Lao She's liking and léd him to conclude that "among the many causes [that make a piece of writing good or bad] the conditions in which the author lives are very important."[23]

After the summer holidays began in July the novel went faster but, according to Lao She, other circumstances had an adverse effect on the work. Like the previous year, the summer was extremely hot:

When you woke up in the morning the temperature in the room—in the room, mind you—was over 90°! Children refused to drink milk and were continually crying and making a noise. The elders were not willing to eat their meals and resolved only to drink water. But half-asleep, half-awake, I had to write . . . waving a fan with the left hand to drive off flies and with the right hand holding a brush and writing hastily, the

perspiration flowing down the back of my fingers to the paper . . .
Naturally, it certainly would have been a little better if I had had an
electric fan or a refrigerator but my finances were much too limited
for this kind of purchase. For a whole fifteen days I did not dare step
outdoors.[24]

Apart from the physical discomfort caused by the hot weather Lao She
was also distressed by other matters. For a long time he had been thinking of
giving up teaching and become a professional writer. In 1933 he had an opportunity to translate desire into action, and so in June of that year he decided to resign from the university. Shortly thereafter, when his friends came
to know of his decision several of them wrote to him. They advised him to
go to Shanghai and pursue his writing. Some who were teaching in other
places urged him to teach, too. Lao She was confused and unhappy. He was
afraid that if he gave up his job he might not be able to find another one. Ultimately, he made his own decision and left Tsinan for Shanghai on the nine-
teenth of August.

Before leaving Tsinan he had to finish writing *The Biography of Niu T'ien-
tz'u* and this made him complete the manuscript in a hurry. "Hot weather, a
disturbed mind, and a sense of hurry" characterized his life when he was writing
this novel, and these conditions, says Lao She, "have no great affinity with
the conditions that should prevail at the time of writing."[25]

To add to this, Lao She was writing for *Lun-yü*[26] (The Analects), a magazine of humor, and so felt obliged to emphasize humor. "When you reach
the state of selling humor by the catty," says Lao She, "it is difficult to keep
[the writing from] incurring dislike." Furthermore, because the novel was
going to be published serially and only at the rate of a few thousand characters a week, each section had to be given a certain amount of internal unity.
Lao She feels that this naturally took away from the unity of the novel as a
whole and gave it a touch of superficiality.[27]

Lao She's excessive apology is in keeping with the understatement in all
his comments on his own writing. Actually, *The Biography of Niu T'ien-tz'u*,
in spite of its flaws, is an interesting novel which provides us with Lao She's
analysis of the petty bourgeois class, in particular of "the upbringing of a
small hero of the petty bourgeois class."[28]

The story is laid in Yun-ch'eng, a small town in north China, and spans
the period from about 1905 to about 1925.[29] Mr. Niu, a well-to-do local
merchant, and his wife, both in their fifties, live a staid but comfortable existence. Their biggest grievance is that they are childless. It is, therefore, a great
joy to them when a male foundling is left at their doorstep. The child who is

adopted into the family and given the name of T'ien-tz'u (Heaven bestowed), is the hero of the novel.

The novel deals with the first twenty years of T'ien-tz'u's life and shows how environment molds his character and turns him into an ineffective middle-class intellectual. Lao She's apparent belief in the Mencian theory that man is born good and that he degenerates only if his education and upbringing are faulty underlies the story of Niu T'ien-tz'u. Lao She is aware that Western literature had introduced the element of heredity as a factor in understanding man, so he cleverly ignores that aspect by making T'ien-tz'u a foundling. "Generally speaking," the author says in *The Biography of Niu T'ien-tz'u*, "it is unlikely that heredity plays a more important role in the formation of character [*hsin:* 'moral character,' 'mind'] than upbringing."[30]

Almost from the moment T'ien-tz'u enters the Niu household he begins to suffer from a web of pressures and restrictions which reflect the attitudes and biases of the persons who come in contact with him. Mrs. Niu, who comes from a family of officials and who has always considered her husband's business rather demeaning, decides to bring up T'ien-tz'u in a style befitting the child of an official, so that he may grow up to "carry on the tradition." She believes that to attain this goal, the primary requisite in the training of a child is discipline. Since "love must not be allowed to come in the way of discipline," T'ien-tz'u is not permitted to be carried (except when being fed) and Mr. Niu's visits to the nursery are restricted. When T'ien-tz'u grows older he is not allowed to play with other children because a future official should not come in contact with vulgar humanity. In keeping with this approach Mrs. Niu engages private tutors for T'ien-tz'u so that he may avoid contact with "hooligans" in a school. Furthermore, the tutors are admonished not to spare the rod because "it is more important to teach him discipline [than to teach him how to study]. Be earnest in beating him for character cannot be perfected without beating."[31]

Mr. Niu is a henpecked husband, married to a "superior" wife, so he dare not make any plans of his own for the child. He loves the child very much and hopes that one day his son will take over the family business but he does not have the will to oppose his wife. The first stand he ever takes against his wife is when he stops one of the tutors from beating T'ien-tz'u. The teacher is so insulted that he resigns on the spot. Mrs. Niu is also insulted and, after upbraiding her husband, declares that she will no longer take the responsibility of T'ien-tz'u's education, and puts on an air of cold indifference toward the child. Mr. Niu, not wanting to aggravate her feelings any further, avoids too many meetings with his son. It takes many months for the situation to ease again.

For the first half year or so of his life T'ien-tz'u is left mostly in the company of his wet nurse, Mrs. Chi. Mrs. Chi is a poor village woman who has had to leave her own child to work for the Nius. The thought of her baby suffering at home while she has to sell her milk to bring up somebody else's child often makes her hate T'ien-tz'u. On other occasions the thought of her child makes her shower her motherly love on T'ien-tz'u. This alternate hate and love, naturally, perplexes T'ien-tz'u.

During this early period T'ien-tz'u has to suffer from physical restrictions also. He is tightly swaddled, so that he will not develop bow legs, and is kept lying flat on his back. As a result of being bandaged so tightly he develops weak legs with the toes turned inward. An act of restriction, which is meant to be good for him, maims him for the rest of his life. Similarly, being made to lie so long in one position flattens the back of his head. When the swaddling bandages are taken off and, as a further act of clemency, the child is allowed to be carried around, T'ien-tz'u comes to know Ssu Hu-tzu, the male servant in the house. The child appears to find much happiness in the arms of Hu-tzu. The bonds that develop between servant and child last throughout the novel and it can be said that if T'ien-tz'u has one true friend, that friend is Ssu Hu-tzu.

The process of alienation continues when T'ien-tz'u finally steps out of the cloistered courtyard of the Niu household and attends school. His lameness keeps him from participating in games and also earns him the scorn of his peers. Later it becomes known that he is a bastard and that makes life even more miserable for T'ien-tz'u. He learns to live by himself and his strong imagination coupled with his interest in literature make him a good storyteller, which gains him some limited recognition among the students. It appears that in some ways T'ien-tz'u is a surrogate for Lao She: T'ien-tz'u's physical restrictions represent the handicaps under which Lao She grew up; the child in the story is maimed physically, the author's spirit is crippled; T'ien-tz'u's being a bastard is in a way like Lao She's being a Manchu.

A year after he graduates from primary school T'ien-tz'u becomes involved in some trouble at school over the appointment of a new principal and as a result is expelled. Mrs. Niu is so humiliated that she falls ill and never recovers. Just before her death she gives T'ien-tz'u a packet containing her grandfather's official seal and charges her son to work hard and to continuously aspire to become an official. At this time T'ien-tz'u is about 14 years old.

Some time after his mother's death another private tutor is hired for him. Unlike his previous tutors, Mr. Chao is a man of "new" learning. He is an anarchist with romantic ideas of revolution. Because of him T'ien-tz'u becomes a writer of modern poetry and becomes involved in revolutionary student activities. This is the period following the May Fourth Movement and T'ien-tz'u writes an impassioned poem which concludes with these lines:

> Burn, burn the whole city of Yun-ch'eng
> Turn the sky red.

But when the civil war reaches Yun-ch'eng, the sky does turn red and Mr. Niu loses one of his biggest stores. T'ien-tz'u feels sorry for his aging father who falls ill from the shock of the loss. The students laugh at him for abandoning the revolution for filial piety but T'ien-tz'u is sincerely concerned for his father. When Mr. Niu recovers T'ien-tz'u once again begins his literary activities, but this time he joins a conservative literary club where everyone wears old-style clothes and writes old-style poetry.

The members of the club are mostly from the official class who maintain a superior attitude toward the merchant community and a disdainful attitude toward money. They dabble in painting, collect curios, and pay much attention to etiquette and proper decorum. T'ien-tz'u is greatly attracted to this group and even has thoughts of marrying the sister of one of his friends at the club. At this stage in the story, Yuan-ch'eng, the old-style money shop where his father had kept all his savings suddenly fails. Mr. Niu dies of the shock. T'ien-tz'u's friends from the literary club desert him and he is left alone, helpless and impoverished.

Mr. Niu's relatives, who had come making loud protestations of sorrow when Mrs. Niu died, do not even appear at Mr. Niu's funeral. They do, however, turn up later and forcibly remove everything they can lay their hands on in the house. The house itself is mortgaged. Ssu Hu-tzu is the only one who does not abandon T'ien-tz'u. They shift to a courtyard where they live among rickshaw pullers and peddlers. T'ien-tz'u discovers that the poor are big hearted and sincere but in spite of all his efforts he cannot identify himself with them and they, in turn, cannot accept him in any capacity other than that of a "Young Master."

The story ends with the reappearance on the scene of one of T'ien-tz'u's tutors, who had borrowed money from Mr. Niu. Mr. Wang now repays that money along with the interest to T'ien-tz'u, helps him sell the mortgaged house, and gets him admitted into a university at Peking.

There is no denying that *The Biography of Niu T'ien-tz'u* has weaknesses of plot and structure but since the various sections, however mechanically contrived they may appear at first sight, are meshed together in the person of T'ien-tz'u, they acquire a significant inner meaning. T'ien-tz'u is in search of his identity—a search that takes him from the revolutionary student group at

one end of society, to the conservative scholar-literati at the other extreme—
but rather than appearing disjointed the episodes acquire a unity within a
larger framework of the author's analytical vision of the hero and the hero's
society.

Lao She uses fiction to come to grips with the reality of Chinese society,
to probe the inner heart of a people living in an age of confusion. If the reader
is disappointed that the hero of the novel lacks heroic proportions it is because Lao She does not feel T'ien-tz'u is living in an age of heroes.

The novel spans more than a decade of the early Republican period but,
except for the student movement and the coming of the civil war to Yun-
ch'eng, the local inhabitants are not directly affected by the political developments in the country as a whole. Most of them lack interest in national affairs:

> [The people] could never make out clearly who was fighting whom in
> these civil wars, nor were they concerned about who won or who lost.
> They prayed only that no army should pass through Yun-ch'eng and
> that if an army did enter, it should leave as early as possible . . . If it
> was possible the best thing was to fly the Japanese flag [thus avoiding
> harassment from the warlord armies].[32]

In this town of Yun-ch'eng where "people had no concept of nationalism
or society," the new ideas of nationalism and patriotism came in with the student movement in the early 1920s. Though Lao She shows a certain amount of
contempt for the "revolutionary students," who parade in their "Western
clothes" and "leather shoes" and who "ask their fathers for money and then
proceed to stick 'Down with Capitalism' posters on their parents' door," he
does recognize the fact that student agitation opened the path for social
changes.[33]

The inhabitants of Yun-ch'eng may not have much direct involvement
with "new affairs" and may not understand or even try to understand what
the "new affairs" are; nevertheless, in many indirect ways they are affected
by the new forces. The effect on most, unfortunately, is negative and destructive. Warlord armies (symbols of new politics) and student activists
(symbols of new culture) are bad enough, for the one attacked the material
riches of the people and the other their spiritual inheritance, but the activities
of the armies and the students were open to scrutiny. The true tragedy lies in
the subtler forces of change that were silently eroding traditional society. In
The Biography of Niu T'ien-tz'u Lao She is very successful in the portrayal of
characters who, unknowingly, are caught between the old and the new and

who lose out just because they are holding on to the old values or systems.

In Mr. Niu's case, he is an easy-going, honest, old-time businessman, who at the turn of the century has three flourishing business houses. Within a decade he finds that he is losing money; within two he goes bankrupt. He is confused by the developments taking place:

> The older he grew the more attention he paid to his business, but contrary to expectations business was not as good as it was in the past . . . Why was there a deficit? Father couldn't trace the source of the trouble. The more concerned he got [about his business] the more he felt that other merchants were not following proper customary rules in doing business . . . He felt that the atmosphere in Yun-ch'eng had become more tense, merchants had become desperately competitive and nobody believed any longer in the saying that "even if the boats were many the flow of the river won't be obstructed." Everybody was using all sorts of strange and novel methods . . . Money had become very scarce and there were simply no people from the country coming to the city to buy things.[34]

Mr. Niu stands for tradition, and however high and noble the traditional principles which govern his personal and business life might be, he must meet with a tragic fate because it is tradition itself which was being swept away by the new forces of progress. The old established pattern of business operation structured on traditional lines, and the old loyalties had to give way to the new banks with their complicated impersonal paper work and to the new type of impersonal cut-throat business competition.

Lao She does not believe that the old is necessarily bad or that the new is necessarily good. He is no doubt aware that the old would, in time, be replaced by the new. His concern is not with the nature of a future society but with the complexities and problems of the one in which he lives. The positive in *The Biography of Niu T'ien-tz'u* comes out in the critical analysis the author makes of the old and the new, showing how the conflict between the two was undermining the social fabric. In the novel the victim of this conflict is T'ien-tz'u, who in many ways *is* the novel.

There is a possibility that T'ien-tz'u could have been subjected to a tension other than that between the old and the new—a tension between two aspects of the old itself as expressed in Mrs. Niu's desire that he grow up to become an official and Mr. Niu's hope that he take over the family business. By making Mr. Niu a henpecked husband and giving him a mild and easy-going temperament, Lao She has avoided the issue.

The old and the new, in the case of T'ien-tz'u, are primarily concerned with the world of education and ideas. He has old- and new-style tutors, he goes to a modern school, he joins revolutionary students' organizations and later a club that fosters classical values. Clearly intertwined with T'ien-tz'u's search for values in a confused society is the theme of his isolation and alienation. Both the old and the new drive T'ien-tz'u to withdraw to an inner world of isolation where fantasy fills the vacuum which the outer reality has created.

The physical and psychological cruelties which are inflicted on him when he is a little child, and the strict discipline with which his mother replaces expressions of love turn him into a fantasist from a very early age. This is the description of T'ien-tz'u at the age of three:

> He could not understand why grown ups were so concerned on his account. There were so many things he could not understand and he could not ask questions, for the moment he asked a question the consequences could be hard on him. So he learned to mutter to himself . . .
>
> Although he could not express himself, T'ien-tz'u felt that life was an accumulation of restrictions. As the number of things he could do increased, the number of restrictions also increased.[35]

With the appointment of the first tutor T'ien-tz'u's inquiring mind still finds no satisfaction. In a traditional approach, Mr. Wang tries to get T'ien-tz'u to memorize the primer, *San-tzu ching* (Three character classic). Since the meaning of the characters is not explained, the jumble of sounds makes no sense to the child and this effort at education is a complete failure: "On the second day they started with the book but, however hard he tried, T'ien-tz'u could not memorize *'jen chih ch'u; hsing pen shan.'** Mr. Wang, his eyes glaring, repeated these characters till his lips became numb but his disciple still could not remember them."[36]

If Lao She has no sympathy with the traditional style of primary education, he also is not satisfied with the way the new-style schools were organized. This is how he describes the "modern" school attached to the Normal College to which T'ien-tz'u is finally sent:

> What made T'ien-tz'u so lax (about going to school) was the complete disorganization in the school . . .
>
> This school was an experimental one and it seemed to experiment

---

* The opening two lines from the *San-tzu ching.*

with everything. Take for instance the principal—every year the school changed one several times and each new principal invariably introduced a new system. Yesterday the rule was that the students must enter the classroom in an orderly line. Today there is a new principal who orders that the students should quickly rush into the class. One principal emphasizes handicraft; another emphasizes music.[37]

As a result of all these changes and contradictory policies T'ien-tz'u is more confused than ever and no longer knows what to accept as true and what to reject as false. The teachers are not even worthy of respect; they revile each other in front of the students and try to organize the students into factions to back them in their politicking for promotion.

In *The Biography of Niu T'ien-tz'u* Lao She reflects once again his antipathy to politicians who use students to advance their causes:

> [the students] had to join activities outside the school too. It was as if demonstrations for the promotion of National Products, National Arts, Chinese Medicine, National Language (*kuo-yü*), and so on, depended on elementary school children. They carried the lanterns, they formed the parade, they shouted slogans, they waved flags but they had no idea what all this was about.[38]

The height of irony is that at the end of primary school, when T'ien-tz'u has concluded the first phase of this "new" education, the guest speaker at the commencement, the chairman of the local commercial club, tells his young audience: "Propriety, righteousness, integrity, and modesty are the four cardinal virtues of the nation. In all things use the reasoning of the sages to judge matters. The doctrine of Confucius is like the rules of the commercial club."[39] After T'ien-tz'u is expelled from school he continues his studies with a private tutor. Mr. Chao, his new teacher, is a young man who is a struggling writer with a personal philosophy which can be defined as a sort of romantic anarchism. He is a university graduate who has read widely but is unemployed and very poor. He makes an excellent tutor for T'ien-tz'u for he not only gives T'ien-tz'u freedom to follow his natural bent and study literature but inspires the boy to embark on literary writing.

T'ien-tz'u is greatly taken by Mr. Chao and unhesitatingly accepts his teacher's values. Mr. Chao is contemptuous of worldly goods; whenever he needs to buy anything he gets the boy to dispose of some article or other from Mr. Niu's house. When Mr. Niu learns about these goings-on he feels that Mr. Chao is teaching his son to steal but to T'ien-tz'u the selling of household articles is a "reminder of poverty" and so a good thing, because according to Mr. Chao "inspiration comes from poverty." T'ien-tz'u also learns from his teacher to live untidily and dress carelessly. But in spite of all their talk about poverty both teacher and student have the traditional scholar's arrogance, and T'ien-tz'u can say to himself: "The teacher and he were both poets and papa was a businessman—this was very obvious. It was also very obvious that poets could not take instruction from a businessman."[40] When a short article of his is published in a Tientsin newspaper T'ien-tz'u, for the first time in his life, feels a great sense of achievement and exhilaration. He feels that at last he knows what has real value in life: it is fame and not money.

After Mr. Chao leaves him, T'ien-tz'u becomes involved with the local student movement and writes revolutionary poetry. He is longing for recognition and appears to be successfully pursuing his goal when civil war reaches Yun-ch'eng. His father's illness, which followed the burning down of one of the family stores, brings T'ien-tz'u back to the world of reality. He has to decide whether to continue on the path of revolution or to attend to his aging father. It is here that Lao She brings out the theme repeated in several of his novels—that filial piety has deeper roots in Chinese society than people care to imagine. Lao Li in *Divorce* could not divorce his wife because of his regard for his aging parents. In *The Biography of Niu T'ien-tz'u* T'ien-tz'u suddenly discovers that neither the taunting of the students ("they said that he had turned the carriage around to travel on the path of filial piety") nor the admonishment of Mr. Chao ("it is not possible to stand with your feet in two different boats")[41] could keep him from devoting himself to his father.

During the course of these developments T'ien-tz'u loses faith in his new-found set of values. The revolutionary students who disappeared when the warlord armies arrived, and the irresponsible Mr. Chao are no longer attractive. Fame was elusive too; he thought of all the illiterate and poor people there were and wondered how many would read his poetry in any case.

When Mr. Niu recovers from his illness, T'ien-tz'u is once again free to go in search of his identity and of values he could live by. This time he joins the Cloud Society, a poetry club formed by members of the old scholar-official families of the town. This gentry class still lives by the traditional Confucian code of conduct and the aim of the poetry club is to promote Confucian virtues and old-style scholarship. Lao She uses this opportunity to give an elaborate description of the style of living, the behavior pattern, the family life and the mores of the dying gentry class:

> They lined their cotton garments with fine silk . . . They did not

use oil but their hair was slightly perfumed. They did not wear [Western style] leather shoes . . . their satin slippers and silk stockings had an indescribable harmony and grace . . . They were contemptuous of *pai-hua* prose and poetry, and even the novels they read were those by T'ang writers . . .

They still believed in concubines . . . They could appraise antiques and tell whether they were genuine or forgeries . . . Nearly all of them could paint landscapes . . . could write prescriptions for medicines.

When they mentioned someone, they first spoke about his official rank and career.[42]

T'ien-tz'u does not belong to this class and has been allowed to join the poetry club only because an old classmate gives him a special recommendation. He tries hard to imitate the manners of his new-found friends and cultivate their habits. He buys himself old-style clothes and puts on a grave air. He learns not to discuss money; money is a necessity but too sordid to be mentioned in this genteel company. Though T'ien-tz'u is continuously afraid that some action of his may betray him as the son of a merchant he realizes that he is living off his merchant-father's money:

He began to feel that man must have money. It was correct for his father to make money but it should not be spent the way he spent it. First you must have money and then you should spend it in the manner of the members of the poetry club—the spending should be amusing and interesting and should be devoid of the sound or smell of money. Money buys them [the gentry] materials for a poetic life.[43]

The desire to be looked upon and considered a "scholar and a man of culture" and not as one belonging to a merchant family leads T'ien-tz'u to organize a big party to celebrate his father's seventieth birthday and invite all his literati friends. The members of the club said that they would not be able to come on the day of the birthday party because they could not mix with the traders and merchants but condescended to come on the previous day. Even this was not taken as a slight by T'ien-tz'u. However, three days before the party Mr. Niu goes bankrupt and dies of the shock. T'ien-tz'u in his hour of sorrow discovers that his newly made friends had no concern for him:

The members of the Cloud Society never really had any relationship with T'ien-tz'u. They had picked him up because he was amusing and they knew that he had money. Now that he had no money why should they still notice him? They never mentioned the word "money" but news about money reached them quicker than anybody else.[44]

At the age of 19, T'ien-tz'u finds himself in the world without parents, without money, without values and—except for the poor illiterate servant Ssu Hu-tzu—without friends. He is now no different from what he was at the time when he was picked up from outside Mr. Niu's door. He was a helpless foundling then and he is a helpless orphan now. Sitting before his father's coffin in the flickering light of the candle he has an opportunity to review his life: "He understood it all: *money is everything.* The entire structure of culture stood on the foundation of money. Everybody was mercenary including the members of the Cloud Society. All were mercenary. All were speculators who ignored each other, who cheated and were false and hypocritical.[45]

Here at last, after a decade of writing, Lao She seems to come to grips with the key problem of his age. Why was China losing the coherence and homogeneity of traditional society? Why was one no longer able to relate to his fellow beings in any satisfactory manner? Lao She finds the answer in the emergence of money as a social fact. Money and the competition to make money underlay the ferment in the Chinese society which was moving from a pre-capitalist state to a capitalist one. Isolation, loneliness, and alienation were the natural result of such conditions.

Money was assuming new proportions, new power, and a new meaning in this age of transition and many could not understand the nature of the change. T'ien-tz'u is given a more than ample opportunity to witness the ugly effect of money. From the time he comes in contact with society he finds that personal relationships are invariably destroyed by money, which plays the role of a villain in the novel. In school his classmates had kept away from those who had poorer parents. Nobody from the Cloud Society had come to his father's funeral because he himself was poor. When Mrs. Niu passed away, Mr. Niu's relatives had pushed T'ien-tz'u away from the altar table and put their own children to kneel there instead. In all the clamor and confusion T'ien-tz'u felt "abandoned and lonely" but was saved from further humiliation by Ssu Hu-tzu, who took him away to a neighbor's house. When Mr. Niu came to fetch him T'ien-tz'u asked him:

"Why did they drive me out?"
"They want my money."
"Give it to them. That will end the trouble."
"No it won't. They will think the amount is too small."
"Why don't you give them more? What does money count?"[46]

In his innocence T'ien-tz'u asks a most fundamental question and gains the answer only after his father's death. Money is everything!

Money is everything because it seems to adequately replace the traditional network of kinship and social relationships. It may not integrate the social system but it provides one with status and recognition. T'ien-tz'u has had an opportunity to get a close look at another sector of society where there is no money at all. The desolation and misery and the harrowing poverty of Mrs. Chi's village is a world far removed from the one in which T'ien-tz'u lives:

> There was silence everywhere and the only sound that T'ien-tz'u heard was of a rooster crowing. There were some old people sunning themselves outside their door and smoking their long-stemmed pipes in silence. Ruins, poverty, silence, drab colorlessness marked the whole village which seemed to be waiting for a gust of wind to blow it out of existence . . .
>
> Nurse Chi's husband also came out, along with him were three children. He was over forty, tall in stature, pock-marked, and silent. The three children all had disheveled hair, and wore short jackets. Two of them had torn trousers and through the holes could be seen their emaciated legs . . .
>
> [Pa to Nurse Chi's enquiry] "The land? For our sins our few acres of land was flooded again and we did not even get a stick of firewood out of them. The rented land yielded a good harvest—about eight parts. But after paying the rent—ai!—no use even mentioning it! The few dollars you send are like gold—like gold . . . Ai! I am old and confused and cannot think of a way out."[47]

T'ien-tz'u had a dollar in his pocket and being moved by compassion brought it out and wanted to give it to the old man:

> Venerable Father's eyes became brighter and his voice louder: "Young Master you keep it! You have already brought me cakes! I cannot accept this money. I, Chi, have lived my whole like with pride . . . You keep it. I'll be a dog if I accept it."
>
> T'ien-tz'u was mystified even more. These people were poor but lovable and strong-spirited. They were not greedy like the people in the city. But they were poor. Why? Who knew why this was so?"[48]

This experience in the country could have led T'ien-tzu into a further examination of the causes of poverty but his upbringing had been successful in turning him into a petty-bourgeois urban intellectual. He can afford to ignore the poor. Even when he thinks that he has radical ideas, he is basically a romantic who writes revolutionary poetry, secure in the knowledge that his family is wealthy.

Lao She seems here to have lost all hope that the urban middle-class will provide true revolutionaries. In his previous novels, in spite of his doubts and sarcasm, Lao She appears to have thought that somehow middle-class intellectuals could become dedicated to the greater cause of the nation. Now that expectation is no more. In spite of all the humiliations he has suffered and all the losses he has borne, at the end of the story, T'ien-tz'u is still desirous of getting back into the petty-bourgeois community and continuing to study to become an official.

Money is not only a social fact but it has acquired a power of its own. Man is corrupted, disfigured, and made ugly by money. The money with which Mr. Wang helps to rehabilitate T'ien-tz'u has come from smuggled "Japanese goods" and "trading in opium" and from other "questionable quarters." With this money T'ien-tz'u would be able to attend a university in Peking. But T'ien-tz'u had not even graduated from a middle school. How can he enter a university?

> "That doesn't matter," said Mr. Wang opening his eyes wide, "it doesn't matter. Although I do not understand university affairs, I have had dealings with them and there are people who can be entrusted to do this work for me. There are places in Peking where one can buy diplomas. We can buy a School Certificate there. A few days back I got one for Colonel Sun's son. After getting the diploma you can take the entrance examination and you have only to spend a little money to pass that examination."[49]

In traditional China increasing impoverishment of the countryside coupled with the decay of moral standards among the literati and officials usually indicated that the time had come for the collapse of the dynasty. Would it be any wonder if Lao She, while painting a similar picture of society in the 1930s was anticipating the collapse of the government in power?

Lao She and Humor

Lao She was troubled about the relevance of humor in literature which was meant to have a serious social purpose. When he wrote *Notes on Cat City* he deliberately eschewed humor and took to satire in the interest of "seriousness," but he was not happy with the result. Before he reverted to humor in *Divorce*, Lao She must have given a great deal of thought to the matter and come to the conclusion that humor could serve a social purpose. But humor no longer meant just a description of the comic; it had assumed a much larger dimension.

The aim of consciously created modern Chinese literature, as has been noticed earlier, was political, i.e., it was intended to bring in new ideas that would help revolutionize society; the means adopted were wholesale translations from the West and a deliberate imitation of foreign styles and techniques. It is in this context that we must view Lao She's use of humor in his writings. Humor was a foreign commodity and Lao She seems to have chanced upon it when he read Charles Dickens and made him his first model.

Until the beginning of the twentieth century the Chinese language had words for "wit," "irony," and "satire," but no word for "humor." It appears that some time in the first decades of this century the characters *yu-mo*, transliteration of the word "humor," came to be used in Chinese. They gained greater currency and became popular after Lin Yutang started his magazine of humor, *Lun yü*, in 1932, which featured a regular *yu-mo* column. But long before this happened, Lao She had already begun writing in a humorous vein in 1924.

The absence of a Chinese equivalent for the word "humor" does not, in any way, imply that the people of China were humorless. It does, however, raise certain vital questions. Perhaps some of these questions are answered by Lin Yutang:

> The unholy awe in which Confucianism was held as the national religion . . . restricted the free expression of ideas and made the novel presentation of points of view and ideas taboo, and humor only lives on novel and original points of view. It is clear that such a conventional environment is not conducive to the production of humorous literature. If anyone were to make a collection of Chinese humor, he would have to cull it from folksongs, and the Yuan dramas and the Ming novels, all outside the pale of the classical "literature," and in the private notes and papers of the scholars (especially those of the Sung and the Ming Dynasties), when they are a little off their guard.[50]

Since Confucianism put a premium on seriousness and dignified behavior—in the words of Lu Hsun on "pulling a long face"—it is understandable that the scholar class, the propagator of Confucianism, had little provocation to coin a term for something that was not supposed to exist.

But since, also, humor had a definite place in popular Chinese literature, it would seem that *yu-mo* need not have been looked upon as an entirely foreign concept. This, however, was not the case. In 1933, Lu Hsun, in an attack on *Lun yü*, which had been founded only a year earlier, said: " 'Humor' is not one of our native products. The Chinese are not a 'humorous' people and this is not an age in which it is easy to have a sense of humor."[51] This is, indeed, surprising because of all people Lu Hsun should have known better. He had not only made a study of traditional Chinese novels and stories but had shown evidence of some humor in his own writings. *Ah Q cheng-chuan* (The true story of Ah Q)[52] is a case in point.

It appears that there was a great deal of confusion between the meaning and intent of "humor" and that of "satire." Lu Hsun favored satire because he felt that it implied the exposing of "truth,"[53] and condemned "humor" because it was frivolous. The description of Fan Chin in *Ju lin wai shih* (The scholars) by Wu Ching-tzu,[54] "refusing to use ivory chopsticks because he is in mourning, yet [given simple bamboo chopsticks] he extracted a large shrimp ball from the dish of bird's nests and popped it into his mouth,"[55] is quoted as an example of satire by Lu Hsun. He does not see the element of humor in the situation.

In 1935 Lao She wrote an article entitled "T'an yu-mo" (On humor) and in it he gives us his views on the controversial subject. "In my opinion," says Lao She, "humor is essentially an attitude of mind." A humorist is not contemptuous of those around him; he does not exaggerate his own importance, nor does he wallow in self-pity. A humorist can see "the shortcomings in the mortal world, and he makes others see them too. He not only is aware of the shortcomings of mankind, but he also accepts them. Thus, everyone has laughable traits and he, himself, is no exception." As one who had traveled abroad and seen the world outside China, Lao She feels that humor provides a writer with a kind of objectivity and a larger vision. "A humorist," he says, "looks upon worldly affairs like a traveler in a foreign land, who finds everything interesting."[56] Humor, according to Lao She, is derived from perspective, from a juxtaposition of two discordant views of a situation, but it is in no way cold or unsympathetic.

As if answering the charge that humor served no social purpose. Lao She emphasizes that a humorous writer seeks to "arouse your love, sympathy and good will—your hatred for the unreal, for false pretensions and hypocritical actions—your fellow-feelings for the weak, the poor, the oppressed, and the unhappy."[57]

How then does it differ from satire? Satire, Lao She points out:

> must use very sharp and biting speech to produce a strong sense of ridicule . . . A satirist purposely makes us unsympathetic toward the persons or situations he depicts in his writings . . . A humorist has a warm heart and a satirist a cold one, with the result that most satire is destructive . . . . It is true that satire and humor often appear together and it is

not easy to separate them, but in the main, the mental attitudes of the humorist and a satirist are clearly distinguished.[58]

Lao She does not attempt to define humor but by comparing it to the nature of irony, wit, farce, whimsicality, and satire, he shows that humor is a broad term and that it, in some ways and on certain occasions, includes one or more of the other terms within its framework. To Lao She humor is low key; it is natural and not forced.

One statement that Lao She makes about the character of a humorist is rather significant. He says that a humorist is big-hearted, he "can laugh and, moreover, can laugh at himself." Such a person does not get involved in small matters. "And in bigger matters he will definitely not invite the Manchu army to help him defeat his political enemies." In other words a humorist, says Lao She, can never be a traitor to his country, though he "looks upon all men as brothers, each one of them having some shortcomings." It is "narrow self conceit," he adds, "that is the great obstacle to the ideal of universal brotherhood (*ssu-hai hsiung-ti*)."[59]

It appears that, here, Lao She is replying directly to Lu Hsun's attack on humorists and non-leftist writers. In an article entitled "On Writing and The Choice of a Subject," Lu Hsun had referred to the Ming general, Wu San-kuei, who had invited the Manchus to invade China, and compared him with writers who thought that "all men are the same at heart."[60] This probably hurt Lao She more than the others because he was a Manchu and, therefore, sensitive to such insinuations. It is, perhaps, for this reason that his article "On Humor" is not only a defense of humor but also a not-so-subtle attack on satire and satirists, whom he considers egotistical, narrow-minded, and vicious.

Unlike Lu Hsun, who thinks humor is foreign to China and does not recognize its presence in his own works, Lao She does not overlook the fact that his humor is often tinctured with satire. On the whole, humor does provide Lao She with a liberal and a humane approach and gives his writings a depth and a universality which will make them outlast many other works of this period.

V

LO-T'O HSIANG-TZU (CAMEL HSIANG-TZU)

Lao She resigned from Cheeloo University in August 1934, and left for Shanghai hoping to settle down there as a professional writer. A short stay in Shanghai, of "ten plus some days," however, was enough to convince him that it would not be possible to make a living solely by writing.[1] It does seem rather strange that after having taken such a drastic step as giving up his job, Lao She did not think it necessary to "try out" Shanghai for a longer period! And could he not have obtained the information he needed without leaving Tsinan at all? Perhaps in Shanghai he witnessed first-hand the plight of other writers struggling to make a living, and found it distasteful.

In an article written some months later, Lao She discusses the question of payments received for short stories and has this to say:

> It is possible that 5,000 characters are better [in writing a story] than 100,000 characters . . . But for 100,000 characters one can receive three hundred to five hundred dollars, and 5,000 characters only bring nineteen dollars. This, I am afraid, is the reason one cannot always maintain a close relationship with artistry. It is very pleasant to hear about "sacrificing [oneself] for art" but nobody should die of hunger; why then is a writer called upon to starve to death?
>
> I often hear people shout: "this is not a great work." Every time I hear this statement, I think that in the mind of the critic the writer is probably some small animal that lives only on dew . . . I believe that if I am given time and provisions I can produce better works.[2]

This statement is significant not only because it may explain the reason for Lao She's withdrawal from Shanghai and return to the world of teaching, but also because it may later have been one motive for his return to mainland China after the Communist takeover: the Communist state is supposed to look after the physical needs of writers and artists and leave them free to concentrate on their creative work.

From Shanghai, Lao She went to Shantung University in Tsingtao. He stayed in Tsingtao till 1937 when the outbreak of the Sino-Japanese War forced him to leave for the south. These were crucial years for China and no sensitive Chinese intellectual could possibly avoid thinking of the problems facing the nation. The Communist annihilation campaigns by the Nationalist government had resulted in the Long March, which, no doubt, lent more than a touch of glory to the Communist party. The Central Government's apparent anxiety to destroy the Communists rather than to restrain the imperialist aims of Japan, and Nanking's policies of increasing press censorship and imprisonment of leftist thinkers, were alienating most liberal intellectuals.

Lao She, still grappling with the problem of what was destroying the Chinese social structure, came out with his most penetrating study of Chinese society in the 1930s in *Lo-t'o Hsiang-tzu* (Camel Hsiang-tzu), which was published serially in *Yü-chou-feng* (Cosmic wind) from September 1936 to May 1937. This novel is Lao She's masterpiece and, perhaps, the best work of its kind in modern Chinese literature.[3] Within a few years after its publication in China it was translated into several foreign languages including English, French, German, Italian, Japanese, Czech, and Spanish.[4]

For the first time Lao She, in this novel, uses a person from the underprivileged lower class as the main character and for the first time he appears to think that some sort of socialism may be a solution for China's ills.

Hsiang-tzu is a young man from the country, who after his parents' death comes to Peking to make good. He is honest and hardworking and possessed of a keen sense of propriety and dignity. He is endowed with great physical strength. Hsiang-tzu begins work as a rickshaw puller renting a vehicle from Liu Ssu who owns the Human Harmony (rickshaw) Shed. It is Hsiang-tzu's most ardent hope and dream that one day he will possess a rickshaw of his own and be able to live a life of freedom and independence. Since he finds that other rickshaw pullers lack this sense of purpose and are given to smoking and drinking, he avoids them. Living frugally and working hard, Hsiang-tzu saves a few cents at a time till, a few years later , he has enough money to buy himself a rickshaw. He is, indeed, a fine example of a civilized, moral human being, illiterate though he may be.

But the society in which he lives is an immoral one, in which the poor and the weak are exploited and made to suffer every kind of injustice and wrong. The first blow falls when the military authorities confiscate his rickshaw and press him into the army. Later during a night attack on his unit, when the soldiers are pulling out of camp, Hsiang-tzu escapes taking three camels with him. He sells the camels outside Peking and thus recoups some of his losses. For this adventure, he becomes known as Lo-t'o Hsiang-tzu, Camel Hsiang-tzu.

Back in Peking he starts another round of saving money to get himself another rickshaw but once again he is robbed of his possessions, this time by the secret police. Every force seems to be working against him. Hu-niu, the ugly daughter of Liu Ssu, tricks him into marrying her and though he hates her he loses his virility because of her insatiable sexual demands. Disease also takes its toll and Hsiang-tzu finds that he has lost much of the physical strength he had been so proud of. When Hu-niu dies in childbirth and he has to sell his rickshaw to pay for the funeral he loses faith in himself. Existence becomes meaningless and he has no more desire to lead a decent, clean life. Like his fellow rickshaw men he becomes lazy and quarrelsome. He also takes to smoking and drinking.

Before the novel ends Hsiang-tzu makes one last attempt to rehabilitate himself but when he discovers that Hsiao Fu-tzu, the only woman he had ever loved, had been forced by circumstances to join a house of prostitution and had committed suicide there, his spirit is finally and completely broken. The lowest point comes when he betrays the rickshaw union organizer to the secret police for sixty dollars. He becomes a part of the evil system which he had hated and fought for so long.

The story of Hsiang-tzu is a description of the process whereby a "good" man becomes "evil." The uncorrupted, good-natured Hsiang-tzu has a very limited mission—he wants to own a rickshaw—and he has the capability to achieve this end. But not only is he repeatedly thwarted in attaining his goal, he is also made to realize the futility of believing that good results will come from right action. He is destroyed by the moral sickness which pervades society. Enlarging on the theme he had touched upon in *The Biography of Niu T'ien-tz'u,* Lao She also emphasizes the corrupting role which money plays in this society. To these social factors he adds the factor of personal alienation.

A closer examination of the story of Hsiang-tzu helps to show how the author has mingled these three themes. In the beginning of the novel we note that Hsiang-tzu has no relatives and no friends but this in no way makes his heart sad or "confused." His youth (he is 18 when he comes to Peking), his robust health, his unaffected naturalness, his pride in himself and his ambition make life relatively easy and worthwhile. Hsiang-tzu does not mind living frugally and denying himself small luxuries which the other rickshaw pullers enjoy. He finds great satisfaction in his work, and in perfecting his style of running, and becoming the best rickshaw puller in town. "He did not smoke or drink or gamble. He had no weakness of any kind, and was not burdened by a family. If only he himself were willing to grit his teeth, there was nothing he could not do."[5] And grit his teeth he did for in three years he had saved enough money to buy a brand new rickshaw. His sacrifice and self-denial transformed the rickshaw from an inanimate material object to a part of his living self:

> Suddenly he remembered that this year he was 22 years old. Because his mother and father had both died early he had forgotten the date of his birth, and since coming to the city he had not once celebrated his

birthday. Well, then, he would count today, the day on which he had
bought his new rickshaw as a birthday—both his, and the rickshaw's.
That would be easy to remember, and since the rickshaw was already
his lifeblood, there was actually no reason why he should not count man
and carriage as one.[6]

After this we can readily understand the anguish of Hsiang-tzu's grief when
the soldiers seize his rickshaw. "They had forcibly taken from him his clothes,
shoes, cap, rickshaw, and even the cloth belt he tied around his waist . . . The
clothes did not matter and the bruises on his body would heal in time, but the
rickshaw—the rickshaw which he had got with years of blood and sweat—was
gone." And in his agony Hsiang-tzu weeps. " 'Why should a man be pushed
so far? Why? Why?' he shouted."[7]

Although Hsiang-tzu finds no answer to his question, the injustice he has
suffered drives him to take the first step on the downhill path of moral degradation: when he escapes from the military camp he steals three camels and
rationalizes this act of thievery by saying to himself that he "was the luckiest
man in the world and Heaven had presented him with three precious living
camels in exchange for his rickshaw."[8] The camels, however, bring him only
thirty dollars which are not sufficient to buy a new rickshaw. So he goes back
to the Human Harmony Shed and deposits the money with Liu Ssu and rents
a rickshaw. Once again he begins to labor hard to save money, keeping aloof
from the others and holding on to his ambition.

But Hsiang-tzu is not as sanguine about the future as he used to be. The
question keeps arising: "This world does not treat you more justly because
you want to better your lot. If it did, why would his rickshaw be taken away
from him?"[9] And in these moments of frustration he almost admires the other
rickshaw pullers for being able to drink and smoke and go to the whore
houses. The motivation to work hard and save money is still there and Hsiang-
tzu still wants to be independent, but now money acquires a new significance
for him and this corrodes his upright character:

Tight-fisted about spending money, Hsiang-tzu went a step further in becoming more grasping about making it . . . In the past he was not willing to take away a fare from another rickshaw puller, especially from the
old enfeebled wounded soldiers . . . Now he did not care about this. He
thought only of money—one more coin was another coin.[10]

Hsiang-tzu loses the respect that others had had for him earlier. When he
steals someone else's passenger, curses follow him; such actions cut him off

from the others and he becomes lonelier than ever before. Often he finds
work by the month with some family but most of these rich people look upon their servants as slaves and ill treat them. Hsiang-tzu still has some self-
respect, and so is unable to take such conditions for very long. Inevitably he
leaves the household of such a family and returns to Human Harmony Shed.

Liu Ssu likes Hsiang-tzu best of all the rickshaw men, because he is quiet
and hard-working. On his part, Hsiang-tzu, too, feels a sense of identifica-
tion with this place: "Of late he had considered Human Harmony Shed as his
home. Working by the month he had often changed masters; working on a
daily rental he changed customers every little while. Only here was he always
allowed to stay on, and here, there was always someone to talk to." [11]

It is on one of these occasions when Hsiang-tzu has just given up a job
with a family and is going back to Human Harmony Shed that he is swept by
a wave of desolation: "He felt as if there was not enough air for him to
breathe and he was choked by the sorrow in his breast. He felt like sitting
down and weeping bitterly. In spite of his [tall] stature, his patient disposi-
tion and his desire to better his situation, people could treat him as if he were
a pig or a dog. [12] On this evening, when he is full of sadness, loneliness, and
dejection, Hsiang-tzu is seduced by Hu-niu. Because her father has gone away
for a few days, Hu-niu has more liberty than she normally enjoys and so in-
vites Hsiang-tzu to her room and taunts him into drinking. He had never had
a drink before, the liquor weakens his will, and he ends up making love to
Hu-niu. Lao She goes into considerable detail in describing, metaphorically, of
course, the way Hsiang-tzu reaches the climax in the sex act. He hints that in
this act Hsiang-tzu regains momentary pride in his strength and that his
anger, too, spends itself.

This is the first time in his life that Hsiang-tzu has experienced drink or
sex but the action is not quite voluntary and on the following morning he is
ashamed of himself and feels sullied. He has never accompanied the others to
brothels because he is a man of principle and wants to be able to "face" his
wife when he gets married. Now Hu-niu has destroyed all that. She has robbed
him of the "clean fresh spirit" that he had brought from the country and
turned him into a man "who takes women by stealth." He feels that he has
suffered another injustice because an immoral older woman has taken advantage of him. An upright man should be worthy of his own respect and since
this act made him lose some of that respect for himself, Hsiang-tzu moves yet
a step further on his downward journey.

The act once performed, the actor cannot divorce himself from it and so
Hsiang-tzu becomes his own destroyer. Besides, there was something attractive and satisfying about the experience and Hsiang-tzu feels impelled to return

for more of the same. He is, however, saved from the vicious situation by one Mr. Ts'ao who offers him a regular job at his house. Mr. Ts'ao is an example of a really good man, a rare man in this corrupt society, who is humane and kind and sympathetic. Working for him Hsiang-tzu regains his dignity and self-respect to such an extent that he no longer "desires to calculate everything in terms of money alone." In the tranquillity of the Ts'ao household Hsiang-tzu's mind goes back to his involvement with Hu-niu and his heart is immediately disturbed:

> He came to understand that in this matter he could not, with one stroke, cut asunder his connection with Hu-niu. This kind of affair could never be washed clean . . . Without any reason he had lost his rickshaw and now without any reason he was implicated [in this affair] . . .
> The best thing was to go on working. Work well, and wait for the worst. He dare not again have the confidence in himself that he used to have . . . This life was his but he had to allow others to control it.[13]

Apart from these troubling thoughts Hsiang-tzu's life with the Ts'aos is pleasant and he continues to put by money, still with the idea of buying another rickshaw. Mr. Ts'ao exemplifies those Confucian virtues which have traditionally been valued in Chinese society. Mr. and Mrs. Ts'ao are both polite and "treat everybody as human beings." They are neat and clean and keep the house and servants the same way. They see to it that the servants have decent lodgings and wholesome food. Most important of all they have great regard for face. For example, whenever Mrs. Ts'ao sends Hsiang-tzu out to buy something, "she would always give him some money to hire a rickshaw, although she well knew that he ran faster than anybody else. This bit of money did not amount to anything but it made him conscious of human feelings, of sympathy, and made his heart happy."[14] Or she would give him some old clothes saying that he could exchange them for a few boxes of matches, knowing full well that he would keep them for himself, "as she intended he should."

Face and self-respect are closely linked in Hsiang-tzu's mind. When he stumbles on a dark night against a heap of stones left on the road by some workmen, and breaks the rickshaw shaft, Hsiang-tzu loses so much face that he offers to resign his job. "To give up his job and wages, was, in the eyes of Hsiang-tzu, no different from committing suicide. But under these circumstances, responsibility and face were more important than life itself . . ."[15] The scholarly, reasonable, modest, humane Mr. Ts'ao, "the Sage Confucius" in the eyes of Hsiang-tzu, gives him back his face by putting the blame on those who left the stones in the middle of the road.

Even in this haven of peace and propriety Hsiang-tzu cannot avoid disaster. One day when he is taking Mr. Ts'ao home the rickshaw is followed by a detective from the secret police. When Mr. Ts'ao notices this he is agitated because the policeman is shadowing him. He directs Hsiang-tzu to take him to the house of a friend, a Mr. Tso, and then sends Hsiang-tzu home with instructions to get Mrs. Ts'ao to come over to the Tso residence also. This incident has nothing to do with Hsiang-tzu but it is Hsiang-tzu who suffers from it. The detective catches Hsiang-tzu when he comes home with Mr. Ts'ao's message and ruthlessly, cold-bloodedly robs him of every penny that he owns. And that means all the money that he possesses in the world for in the piggy bank, which he hands over to the detective, are not only his entire earnings, but also the thirty dollars that he had entrusted to Liu Ssu.

In the morning after this incident somebody is sent by Mr. Ts'ao to look after the Ts'ao house, but that night Hsiang-tzu is still in charge. The thought comes to him that he should make good his losses by stealing some of Mr. Ts'ao's property: "He had been robbed of the little money which he had saved with so much difficulty. He had been robbed because of the Ts'ao family affair, why couldn't he go and steal a few things? It was on account of the Ts'ao family affair that he had lost his money, wasn't it proper that the Ts'ao family should make good the loss?"[16]

But the hold of traditional ethics is still strong and Hsiang-tzu, who is worried that he would not be able to face his master because he had not carried out his instructions properly, has not the courage to steal: "He would rather die of poverty than steal . . . If others wanted to steal they could go ahead, his good heart would not feel the shame. Though he was impoverished to this extreme, he would not let his heart be blackened by another spot."[17]

Hsiang-tzu is not moral per se, he is moral in the Confucian sense. When he had walked away from the military camp with the camels he had not looked upon the act as one of theft. No human relationships were touched or disturbed. But now there is a bond between him and Mr. Ts'ao. It is shame that bothers him, not the sense of guilt. Hsiang-tzu is worried, that even if someone else were to steal from Mr. Ts'ao's house that night, he would still be the one blamed. He is so concerned about being blamed that he wakes up the neighbor's servant—in whose room he is staying for the night—and says:

> "Lao Ch'eng have a look. This is my bedding, these are my clothes, and these are the five dollars which Mr. Ts'ao gave me. There is nothing else."

"No, there isn't. Why?" said Lao Ch'eng yawning.

"Are you awake enough to understand? My belongings are only these few things. I have not taken a blade of grass or a stick from the Ts'ao family."[18]

So once again Hsiang-tzu, financially as poor as when he had first arrived in Peking, but much poorer in spirit, goes back to the Human Harmony Shed. Human Harmony Shed was no longer home for him; it was the place where he had been seduced by the ugly Hu-niu, and where he had lost so much of his self-respect. His return is an act of surrender because only a few days earlier his involvement with Hu-niu had threatened to add to the tragedy of his existence. While working for Mr. Ts'ao, Hsiang-tzu had carried the bitter shame of his sexual misadventure in his heart but had hoped that nothing more would come of it. His only connection with the Human Harmony Shed was the thirty dollars that he had left with Liu Ssu. He could not forego that money though he wished that he would never have to face Liu Ssu or Hu-niu ever again. A few days before the Ts'ao family affair Hu-niu had come searching for him, to tell him that she was carrying his child and that he had to marry her. She had thought out a scheme which would appease her father and get his permission to marry Hsiang-tzu. To show her good will she returned the thirty dollars to him.

Hsiang-tzu is in a state of shock at this turn of events but still hopes that, now that he has "money in his hand," he may find a way out of this entanglement. But the more he ponders the matter the more he realizes that he is caught: "[It] was like the pressure of a thousand-catty flood gate—the entire pressure falling on his head . . . If he did not accept his [miserable] fate then, surely, he would lose his life . . . this is the destiny of a rickshaw puller, like that of a dog—to bear beatings and abuse."[19] Hsiang-tzu's fault is that he is "too honest" and in this exploitative society "the honest must be cheated."[20]

Here for the first time Hsiang-tzu doubts the value of being a loner: "What made him even more unhappy was that he had no place where he could go and unburden himself. He had no parents and no brothers or sisters . . . he had always been a loner. It was not not easy to find friends in the nick of time. He felt a fear that he had never felt before."[21]

Afraid, demoralized, and broke, Hsiang-tzu goes back to Human Harmony Shed like a whipped dog. At the shed he does his work in a wooden, mechanical way. His heart is dead. Both speech and anger have left him: "He did not think of anything. A day muddled through was a day gone. If there was anything to eat, he ate; anything to drink, he drank; any work to be done he did it . . . It was best for him to learn the way of the mule that pulled the grindstone."[22]

Hu-niu's scheme to win her father's approval for the marriage does not work out and she leaves the house in anger. She rents two rooms in a compound, gives some money to Hsiang-tzu to buy himself a suit of new clothes, hires a sedan chair, and gets married to him. Hsiang-tzu, still dazed, acts his part like an automaton. It is only after the marriage that he finds out that Hu-niu was not pregnant at all and had made a fool of him by putting a pillow under her waistband! So the good Hsiang-tzu finds himself cheated out of money, cheated out of his manhood, and finally cheated out of his independence.

Hu-niu has a little money of her own and is most anxious to enjoy life, so she refuses to discuss the question of Hsiang-tzu going back to work. Actually in her scheming mind she has worked out a plan for their future. She thinks that if Hsiang-tzu could go to Liu Ssu and pay his respects to him it will give her father face, and a few such visits should reconcile him to their marriage. When that happened they would have no more to worry about for they could shift back to her father's house and live in proper dignity. Of course, Hsiang-tzu would have to lose face in the process but that, to her, was a minor matter. Hsiang-tzu's character is still strong enough for him to refuse to collaborate in this plot.

Hsiang-tzu feels ashamed of the way his marriage took place; he hates his ugly wife who cheated him into marrying her; he loathes himself for having become a plaything for a woman who is draining away his vitality. He still believes that he can redeem himself to some extent if he has a rickshaw:

> "How much money have you got?" he asked Hu-niu.
> "So that's the way it is? I knew you'd ask me this question. You didn't marry a bride, you married that little bit of money. Isn't that right?"
> Hsiang-tzu swallowed several times as if he had choked over a mouthful of air. Old man Liu and the rickshaw pullers at Human Harmony Shed had all thought that he had enticed Hu-niu into the illicit relationship because he coveted [her] wealth. Now she herself had expressed the same opinion! Without any reason he had lost his own rickshaw and his money and was today crushed beneath the few dollars belonging to his old woman! . . . He hated himself for he could not put his two hands around her neck and squeeze . . . squeeze . . . squeeze . . . till the whites of her eyes showed. Choke everything to death and after that kill himself. They were not human beings and ought to die. He himself wasn't a man and should also die. Nobody should think of living.[23]

Hu-niu's reason for not wanting Hsiang-tzu to pull a rickshaw is primarily that she finds it humiliating to be the wife of a "lowly rickshaw puller." She also hopes that her father will relent and not allow her to suffer such a humiliation. But she is mistaken. Liu Ssu loses so much face because of his daughter's misbehavior that he disposes of the rickshaw shed and leaves Peking to enjoy himself in Shanghai and Tientsin. It is only when this news reaches Hu-niu that she realizes that she has lost her battle with Hsiang-tzu and at last she gives him money to buy a rickshaw.

So once again Hsiang-tzu possesses a rickshaw. Though the circumstances in which his lifelong ambition has been fulfilled are not to his liking, he does gain a certain amount of satisfaction in the achievement. Lao She now introduces another enemy of the poor: nature. In bold, strong strokes Lao She paints the picture of Peking in summer:

> The willow trees in the street looked sick, the leaves on the branches were covered with dust and were curling up, the branches were too tired even to move and hung down spiritlessly . . . Everywhere was parched, every place was too hot to touch, and everywhere was stifling. The whole city was like a fired brick kiln making it difficult for people to breathe. Dogs lay stretched on the ground with their red tongues hanging out, the nostrils of the mules and horses were extraordinarily distended, the peddlers dared not shout their wares, the tarred roads were melting. It was so hot that even the metal signs in front of the shop doors seemed about to melt. There was an extraordinary quietness about the streets.[24]

Working on this day, perspiring from head to foot and repeatedly drinking large quantities of water, dazed with the heat, Hsiang-tzu is caught in a sudden thunderstorm and falls ill. When the cloudburst takes place Hsiang-tzu has a passenger in the rickshaw who refuses to let him stop and take shelter. The portrayal of Hsiang-tzu struggling through the torrential rain with a callous, inhuman passenger sitting snugly inside the covered rickshaw is Lao She's description of man and nature combined to destroy the poor:

> Hsiang-tzu's clothes had been soaked through and through much earlier and there wasn't a dry spot on his entire body. Though covered by a straw hat his hair was completely wet. The water on the road was already higher than his feet and it was difficult to go even a step. The rain from above struck his head and back, and slantwise beat his face . . . He could not raise his head, could not open his eyes, could not breathe, and could not step forward . . . He did not know where the road was . . . Half dead and half alive, with his head held low, step by step he went

forward. The man in the rickshaw seemed to have died—without saying a word he allowed the rickshaw puller to carry on this life and death struggle.

The rain lessened a little and Hsiang-tzu straightened his back a bit and said, "Master, let us get out of the rain and go on later."

"Move on faster. What kind of nonsense is this that you want to throw me out here?" shouted the man in the rickshaw, stamping his foot.[25]

After nearly a month in bed and the expense of a doctor, Hsiang-tzu improves but his health has been permanently impaired. He would have been all right if he had had the time and money to stay at home longer and recuperate, but he could not afford to be idle and so began pulling his rickshaw before he was well enough to do so. The result was a relapse which put him back in bed for another month.

During his illness Hsiang-tzu comes to know Hsiao Fu-tzu, the motherless daughter of a drunkard neighbor and a friend of Hu-niu. Hsiao Fu-tzu is a beautiful, good-hearted woman who has to earn money as a prostitute to feed her younger brothers and maintain her useless father. A little later in the story she becomes an important figure in the life of Hsiang-tzu.

After his illness Hsiang-tzu continues to work hard, and though he no longer can hope to save any money because Hu-niu is pregnant, and her demand for delicacies has increased, he feels a certain sense of "pride and happiness" and thinks that "once there is a child [in the family], life will no longer be so empty." Hu-niu, following traditional superstitions, eats excessive amounts of rich food and does no exercise. When her time comes, the birth is difficult and the midwife cannot cope with the situation. It is obvious that they should call a doctor or go to a hospital, but they do not have enough money, and at the urging of Hu-niu, Hsiang-tzu calls a sorceress instead, to intercede with the spirits. The sorceress gives Hu-niu a charm to swallow but realizing that there is no hope for her, asks Hsiang-tzu to kneel down in front of a burning incense stick, and takes off stealthily. Hu-niu, who has been in labor for several days, gives birth to a dead child and shortly afterwards she dies, too.

Hsiang-tzu, shocked and in a daze, has to sell his rickshaw to pay for the funeral, for everything means money, a commodity so difficult to come by and also so easy to lose. And the symbolic significance of money is heightened when we see the pathetic funeral party consisting of Hsiang-tzu and the two little boys—Hsiao Fu-tzu's younger brothers—follow the coffin outside the city walls, the boys scattering paper money on the way to bribe the spirits and keep them from blocking the path against Hu-niu's soul.

After the funeral, when Hsiang-tzu has cried his fill, he sees that Hsiao Fu-tzu had helped to straighten out the rooms. She is the only person in the world who genuinely understands his suffering and anguish and he finds much solace in her company. In spite of the way she makes her living she is essentially a sincere and "pure" person. There is an unspoken bond of sympathy and love between them and Hsiang-tzu thinks of her as an ideal woman to marry. The thought of having to provide for her brothers and father if he marries her, keeps Hsiang-tzu from responding in any positive way to her unspoken but clearly indicated proposal that they should live together. "Love or no love," says the author, "the poor have to determine things on the basis of money. The seed of affection can sprout only in the homes of the rich." [26]

After selling all his household goods, which he no longer needs, Hsiang-tzu has a little over thirty dollars—the sum he had after his first rickshaw was confiscated by the military, and he sold the stolen camels. The monetary possessions are the same but the man is completely changed. Hsiang-tzu now has no more fight left in him and he not only gives up all ambition to own another rickshaw, he also no longer finds any particular joy in pulling one or showing off his style of running. Before leaving the compound he does tell Hsiao Fu-tzu to "wait—wait for me to get over my bewilderment. I will come back for you. I will definitely come back." [27]

Hsiang-tzu, though still a loner at heart, reaches the conclusion that "whether he liked it or not, the only way left for him was to become a 'real rickshaw puller' [i.e., like all others in the profession]. There was no way out but to travel along with the others." [28] So he consciously tries to identify himself with other rickshaw pullers and in the process learns to smoke and drink and gamble and visit prostitutes. The misery of existence is so great that all he can seek is a little temporary enjoyment:

> He wanted to be happy for a moment and after that to sleep so soundly that both the heavens and the earth were obliterated. Who was there who did not want it this way? Life was so cheerless, so painful and without hope. The pain of the poisonous ulcer of life would be dulled for a little while by the poisonous medication of opium, wine, and prostitutes—poison to kill poison. And one morning the miasma of these poisons would enter the heart [ending it all]. Who is there who does not know this? And then again who is there who has a better plan? [29]

An incident which reveals the extent of his moral decline is the one where Hsiang-tzu allows himself to be enticed into an affair by the mistress of the house in which he serves. From Mrs. Hsia, an ex-prostitute who is being kept as a concubine by the aging Mr. Hsia, Hsiang-tzu contracts venereal disease:

> What would normally have been a matter of extreme fear and extreme shame, he now laughingly divulged to everybody—he could not urinate!
> Everybody wrangled with each other to tell him what medicine to buy or which doctor to go to. Nobody felt this was shameful, all were sympathetic in giving advice. Moreover they, a little red-faced, recounted with great satisfaction their own experiences of a similar nature.[30]

Living in such a state of mind and body Hsiang-tzu becomes slovenly, lazy, bad-mannered, and quarrelsome. It seems that Hsiang-tzu wants to efface his past and all that was good and meaningful in it, and therefore, it is no surprise that he also completely forgets Hsiao Fu-tzu. He might have continued to the end of his days living this twilight existence but for a chance meeting with Liu Ssu. Liu Ssu, before whose looks so many had trembled, is now a very old man whom Hsiang-tzu does not even recognize when he takes him on as a passenger. Hsiang-tzu himself had changed so much that it took Liu Ssu some time before he recognized, in this broken-down, dirty rickshaw puller the sturdy, cheerful, ambitious country lad who had once worked at Human Harmony Shed. Liu Ssu enquires about Hu-niu and when he learns that she died, he says: "Falling into your bloody hands was it possible that she would not have died?" Hsiang-tzu who has been giving monosyllabic answers as if in a stupor and only just regaining consciousness, suddenly discovers himself:

> "Get down [from the rickshaw]. Get down! You are too old to stand a beating from me. Get down!"
> Liu Ssu's hands shook, and he came trembling out of the rickshaw holding on to the shafts. "Where is she buried, I ask you?"
> "It's none of your business." Hsiang-tzu picked up the shafts and went away.[31]

The psychological satisfaction which Hsiang-tzu gets in shouting at Liu Ssu and not giving the information regarding the location of Hu Niu's grave has a peculiarly Chinese connotation:

> To have gained victory over Liu Ssu was like gaining victory over everything. Although he had not boxed or kicked "the old piece of furniture," still the old man had lost his only relative . . . who could say

this wasn't retribution? If the old man did not die of anger he would, nevertheless, not be far from that state. Old man Liu had everything and Hsiang-tzu had nothing, but today Hsiang-tzu could happily pull his rickshaw while the old man could not even find his daughter's grave! Well, old man, although you have money and a temper as great as heaven, you will not be able to conquer this polished egg, this poor man who has to work all day before he can earn his two meals![32]

By standing up to Liu Ssu, Hsiang-tzu regains some of his pride and self-respect and his mind goes back to his former life when he had wanted to make something of himself. His old hopes flicker into life again—and with them comes the memory of Hsiao Fu-tzu. The only person who can help him rehabilitate himself is the saintly Mr. Ts'ao so Hsiang-tzu goes to seek his former master.

Mr. Ts'ao is, indeed, a most humane person who listens to the tearful tale of Hsiang-tzu and not only re-employs him but also gives him permission to bring Hsiao Fu-tzu along with him.

So Hsiang-tzu happily goes in search of Hsiao Fu-tzu. After several days of inquiries he finds that she had been forced by adverse economic circumstances to enter a low-class brothel, and that there she committed suicide. This is the most tragic of all blows, and it breaks Hsiang-tzu completely. Inexplicable fate or a cruel society has the last laugh and Hsiang-tzu, all goodness exhausted and all tears shed, finally sinks into the community of utterly shiftless vagabonds who form the scum of society.

Lao She concludes the novel with the remark: "Respectable, desirous of improving his lot, seeking to benefit self, with beautiful day dreams, individualistic, strong-bodied, great Hsiang-tzu [hired himself out] accompanied who knows how many funerals, not knowing when and where he would bury himself, bury this fallen, selfish, unfortunate product of a sick society, this ghost of individualism whose end was drawing near."[33]

The story of Hsiang-tzu has been so ably and deftly handled by Lao She that at no time does the reader become sentimental and shed tears for the suffering Hsiang-tzu. Hsiang-tzu is a colossal figure; he is a symbol of China's hungry, patient millions and if he had not possessed the moral strength he did, he would not have survived the pressures of a rapacious society so long. His fight against poverty, social injustice, immoral sex, and evil habits ended in defeat, but the fight was long and bitter and his failure in no way detracts from the noble effort he made. The last sentence in the novel is not, as C. T. Hsia thinks, "the author's undisguised contempt for his hero,"[34] it is a summing up of China's tragedy. The accusing finger points not at Hsiang-tzu but at the nature of society as a whole, a society that has failed to protect its poor.

The quotation, however, does indicate Lao She's reappraisal of his earlier stand on individual effort. In most of his novels up to *Camel Hsiang-tzu,* Lao She emphasized the need for the individual to work hard to improve himself so that he could improve society, and also advocated individual heroic action. In *Camel Hsiang-tzu* Lao She appears to have moved a step further in his line of thought. He has not radically altered his original stand but elaborates it a little more and changes it slightly. It would be wrong to think that he has become a Marxist revolutionary or acquired, in C. T. Hsia's words, "a surprisingly leftist point of view." It must be remembered that even when Lao She stressed the need for the individual to labor hard and acquire the skills that would be needed in reconstructing Chinese society, he denied individualism as such. He always placed the country's needs above those of the individual. In *Chao Tzu-yueh* and *Mr. Ma and Master Ma* it is more than clear that the individual once trained and perfected had to be placed at the service of the nation. Lao She had no regard for an individualism which meant the satisfaction of personal whims and desires. Even love and marriage were matters to be sacrificed to the cause of the country.

Lao She always looked upon student revolutionaries with suspicion and attacked flag-waving youth for their superficiality. Even in *Camel Hsiang-tzu* he maintains this attitude. Such a student with radical ideas, Juan Ming, is very friendly with his teacher. the socialist-minded Mr. Ts'ao:

> However, [the difference in] age and status produced a minor clash [of opinion and interest] between them: Mr. Ts'ao, looking at things from the point of view of a teacher, believed that he must teach with his whole heart and the student must study well. He could not be lax with grades, because of personal feelings. From Juan Ming's point of view, in this confused world, a student with a purpose must do some revolutionary work and for the time being, it did not matter whether one was good or bad in classroom studies. He cultivated a friendship with Mr. Ts'ao, first to hold conversations with him, and second, because he hoped that this would help him to get passing marks regardless of how badly he did in the examinations.[35]

At this point in the story, Lao She breaks in with an ironic remark of his own. "Leaders of action in a period of confusion are often worthless types—there are many instances of this in history."[36] When the examinations take place

Mr. Ts'ao finds it impossible to give a passing grade to Juan Ming. Juan Ming who has done badly in other courses, too, and has to leave college decides to take out all his anger on Mr. Ts'ao. This great revolutionary student now "edited all the lectures that Mr. Ts'ao had given in the classroom, and all he had said in his conversations regarding the problem of government and society and reported it to the party office as 'radical thought' that Mr. Ts'ao had propagated among the youth."[37] It is because of this report that Mr. Ts'ao is pursued by the secret police.

The story of Juan Ming is in keeping with Lao She's satire of student activists in earlier novels, but Mr. Ts'ao represents something new in the author's thinking. Since it is evident that Lao She identifies himself with Professor Ts'ao, it is worthwhile to examine the character of Mr. Ts'ao a little more closely. Mr. Ts'ao is an ideal man in the eyes of Hsiang-tzu because he is benevolent, kindhearted, sympathetic, soft-spoken, has a sense of justice, and a proper regard for face and the proprieties. Hsiang-tzu considers Mr. Ts'ao to be like the sage, Confucius, because "he was a scholar and very reasonable in everything."[38] The author's analysis of Mr. Ts'ao is not so effusive:

> Actually Mr. Ts'ao wasn't that lofty a character . . . He was a middle-class person. He thought of himself as a socialist and was an aesthete at the same time. He had been deeply impressed by William Morris. He had no profound views of government or art but he had one good characteristic: although he did not believe in much, he practiced his beliefs in the small affairs of his life. It was as if he realized that he did not possess a talent which could astonish others or could help him perform feats that would startle the universe. He, therefore, followed his theories in putting in order his own life and his household. Though this did not help repair society, it at least made his words and actions consistent.[39]

This is Lao She's ideal character and, no doubt, the final sentence reflects the author's own concept of what a good man could do in a corrupt and decadent society. Lao She realizes the limitation of such an attitude and hastily adds: "At times this made him [Mr. Ts'ao] ashamed of himself, at times happy with himself for he could clearly see that his household was a small green island in a vast desert and that it could only provide cool water and food to those who happened upon this place—it had no greater significance."[40]

It is remarkable that in spite of the reference to William Morris and to socialism, Lao She's concept of the "good man" is so near that of the Confucian gentleman (*chün-tzu*). Though he seems to doubt that one man's action could change society, he does seem to imply that the "regulation of self" and "the regulation of one's family"[41] is better than Juan Ming's lack of time to study or "cultivate" himself in his haste to change society.

This is hardly a "startlingly leftist point of view." The only other major occasion in the novel where leftism makes an appearance is when the grandfather of Hsiao Ma, the rickshaw puller who had once been as ambitious as Hsiang-tzu but had ended up selling hot water in his old age, talks to Hsiang-tzu:

> You thought that it would be good to work by yourself? . . . Who doesn't think so? Yet who is there who has got results [from individual efforts]? . . .
>
> For a poor man to get any good out of working independently is more difficult than [for him] to [be able to] touch Heaven. How far can a single man leap? Have you seen grasshoppers? A single one can leap surprisingly far but it attracts some child who catches it and ties it up with a thread so that it cannot even fly. But as soon as there is a host of them and in battle order, hah! In one turn they will eat away a whole crop and no one can control them.[42]

Coupled with this is the realization that the law "goodness has a good recompense and evil has an evil recompense"[43] does not apply to life on earth.

Lao She appears caught in the dilemma which faced so many Chinese intellectuals in the thirties and forties. He sees an urgent need for material welfare and, therefore, a social system which would ensure this social welfare, and at the same time feels unhappy at the destruction of Confucian values that had guaranteed an integrated social system based on proper human relationships. In a way this dilemma has been very well expressed by Fei Hsiao-tung in a lecture delivered in 1947:

> If in advancing to the present stage of technological development, the West had achieved a new order—that is an integrated social system—the problem in the East would be simpler. All we need to do is to learn to transplant the new form across the ocean . . . But the onesided emphasis [of the West] on material advancement without due consideration of a corresponding development in social relations is equally dangerous. It is, therefore, clear that the process of social change in China should not be a mere transplantation of Western culture but should imply a reorganization of social structure in conformity with the inherited spirit of harmony and integration.[44]

The confusion and disorder in Chinese society which Fei thinks is the symptom of "a process of social change without a definite aim" is effectively mirrored in *Camel Hsiang-tzu*. Lao She has no clear-cut solution to the problems facing China nor a vision of a future society but he does tend to favor a compromise between Confucianism and socialism which would produce, perhaps, a sort of Confucian socialism.

In this novel the reader gets a vivid and an intimate impression of life in China during the 1930s, and also comes to understand the interaction of character, society, and chance in the increasing poverty of the lower classes. Money, and the need for money, loom large on the horizon, but the desire for face and respectability also play a significant though a subtler role.

In the character of Mr. Ts'ao, Lao She seems to have revealed the strength and weakness of his own character which perhaps contributed to his tragic end. Mr. Ts'ao "knew how superficial his socialism was and he also understood how his love for traditional aestheticism hindered any radical action."[45] When the secret police began to follow him, Mr. Ts'ao realized that the matter had become serious. "If he had wanted to acquire fame, this was a good opportunity. To go to jail for a few days was easier than throwing a bomb, and of equal value. To go to jail was a prerequisite for becoming an important man. But he was not willing [to do so]. He was not willing to use one [low down] tactic against another to achieve false fame . . . he hated himself for not being able to become a hero; because of his conscience, he was also not willing to become an imitation hero."[46] Like Mr. Ts'ao, it appears that Lao She was not willing to play the game that others were playing around him and when the Red Guards accused him of heresy, he preferred to take his life rather than accept the humiliation of recanting all that was of any worth to him.[47]

VI

WOMEN IN A CHANGING SOCIETY

One of the most important changes marking the social revolution in China is the emancipation of women. Generalizing on the basis of the harshest criticism of the status of women in traditional society, they lived a whole life of bondage before emancipation. The situation is supposed to have changed radically within a few decades after the Republican revolution. Women gained sexual equality, the right to education on a par with men, the right to equal inheritance, the right to divorce, and the right to find gainful employment in various professions.

Lao She's novels deal mostly with men in the changing Chinese society and for some reason he avoids discussing the traditional family system. Practically all his important male characters are without any family ties: Li Ying in *The Philosophy of Lao Chang* and Hsiang-tzu in *Camel Hsiang-tzu* are both orphans; Li Ching-ch'un in *Chao Tzu-yueh* and Ma Wei in *Mr. Ma and Master Ma* have no brothers or sisters and only one living parent; Lao Li in *Divorce* is also an only child and separated from his parents. Lao She himself was an only child whose father died when he was very young. Perhaps this is the reason why he did not attempt to put his stories in the framework of an extended family system.

Whenever Lao She does touch on women he is not very sanguine about the situation. Some of his short stories published in three collections between 1934 and 1936[1] focus entirely on women and the way in which the breakdown of the Confucian value system affected their relationships with men. Invariably he uses these stories about women to show what a heavy shadow the traditional family and social system cast over his female characters' lives. Li Ching in *The Philosophy of Lao Chang* is an educated young woman who is in love with Wang Te but is forced by her guardians to become a concubine to Lao Chang. She lives with her aunt, who represents the Confucian family system and arranges the marriage. Auntie Chao has no qualms about her niece's fate and prepares the bride to leave the house with love and fondness. Lao She's comment is: "If our Confucius were living he would have praised Auntie Chao as 'a virtuous woman indeed!'" When the marriage does not work out, Auntie Chao disavows Li Ching. New education and new ideas have given Li Ching the desire for freedom but society still had no place for women outside the traditional family system. As Li Ching tells Wang Te: "Women are playthings for men."[2]

In *Chao Tzu-yueh,* Lao She makes a more poignant reference to the fate of women who had been "liberated" by the social revolution. Both Miss Wang and Miss T'an fall in love and move away from their families with their lovers. They have gained independence in the new era, but, with no economic security. This independence is extremely limited. When their love affairs do not work out, Miss Wang and Miss T'an find they have no place to go. Even the doors of their own homes are barred to them. Miss Wang is saved from an ignominious fate by a kind, generous-hearted gentleman; Miss T'an is reduced to the life of a prostitute.

In *Notes on Cat City* Lao She caricatures the new type of educated young women. They are superficial, love to dress up, imitate foreign fashions, and have lost the homely talents of cooking or sewing but have not acquired any new virtues. *Divorce* shows how the clash between old and new creates tension in the urban middle-class families and how the women still have to give in to men in the end. The right to divorce is the symbol of woman's independence and equality and yet how many can exercise this right? Mrs. Wu is incensed that her husband has taken a concubine. The situation is intolerable for her but she cannot think of divorce: "Divorce? What are you saying, Mr. Li? Isn't this enough of a humiliation? [that she has been displaced by a concubine]. How can I add divorce to it?" To Mrs. Ch'iu she explains: "It is easy to talk. Divorce? Where [and how] would I live after that?" Mrs. Ch'iu, a college graduate and confident that she could manage on her own, advocates divorce to all her friends. Faced with the same prospect, even she is ready to compromise with an untenable situation.[3]

Modern education had provided these women with modern thought but not the means to put that thought into action. Lao She feels that real happiness in married life could not come from "a few kisses and a few tender words." Women had to gain economic independence and a "healthy culture rebuilt anew."[4] Contemporary society had produced, on the one hand, women like Mrs. Wu and Mrs. Ch'iu who had one foot in the old and one in the new, and on the other, such rakes as Chao, who spent their lives seducing women and making harlots of them.

Just as Lao She reached his greatest height in sketching the character of the underprivileged Hsiang-tzu in *Camel Hsiang-tzu,* he is also at his best in delineating women from the poorer section of society. The daughter-in-law in the short story, "Liu-chia ta-yuan" (Liu's compound), Hsiao Fu-tzu in *Camel Hsiang-tzu,* and the heroine of the short story "Yueh-ya-er" (The crescent moon) are among the best examples.[5]

"Liu's Compound"

The story deals primarily with the way the daughter-in-law of the Wang family suffers at the hands of her in-laws and how this drives her to suicide. Lao She treats her as a case study representing thousands who live similar lives, and so gives her no name or individuality. It is the intensity of her pain that reaches us, revealing the harrowed soul of a person in torment, reduced to dumb automation by constant ill-treatment. "The Wang family daughter-in-law had no way out. The more aggrieved she felt, the less affable she became, and in the whole courtyard nobody loved her. She even forgot what it was to speak."[6] When she begins to have fits, the narrator is called in to get rid of the "evil spirits." His observation is: "she needs consolation and a few kind words" and not slaps in the face.

The forces that destroy her are a combination of the evil attitudes which have come down from the past, the arrogance and hypocrisy that seem to accompany the influx of new ideas, and the influence of money. Traditional family ethics teach that "a man must beat his wife; a father-in-law should discipline his daughter-in-law; the daughter should vent her temper on the sister-in-law." Since Old Wang thinks he is "cultured" (*wen-ming*), he practices this philosophy and encourages his children to follow suit. The actual task of beating the daughter-in-law falls on the son, for Old Wang, following the dictates of culture, cannot, himself, lay hands on the girl, but "after the son had beaten his wife, Old Wang was exceedingly nice to him." The son, who comes home only once or twice a month, does not want to be so harsh to his wife: "If his father had not been 'cultured' . . . he definitely would not have beaten her so often. But papa was 'cultured' and the son, naturally, wanted to be filial."[7]

Another reason for Old Wang's meanness is that he had to borrow a hundred dollars to pay the betrothal money to the girl's family. "They, father and son, would probably not be able to wipe off the debt in another year, so Old Wang took it out on the daughter-in-law . . . But it was not only because of this little bit of money. He had to practice being cultured and fully develop the demeanor of a father-in-law."[8]

On one occasion when the son is at home Old Wang, for some unknown reason, is in a kindly mood and does not urge him to beat his wife. For once, the daughter-in-law is slightly happy. The daughter, however, cannot stand her smiling face and kicks her while she is straining water from the rice causing her to spill the precious grains. This naturally results in a severe thrashing. The next day the girl hangs herself.

Suicide, a recognized way of expressing protest in traditional China, is the only escape for a woman in such circumstances for even dumb submission has limits. In spite of all the changes in Chinese society after 1900 there were still innumerable cases of women who lived this kind of miserable existence.[9]

By having the girl dress in her wedding clothes before hanging herself, Lao She symbolically points out the unity between marriage and suicide.

The girl's suicide might have created tension and heightened social consciousness, but on the contrary, it raised the social prestige of Old Wang. After the daughter-in-law's death, her family demanded a hundred dollars from Wang—fifty for the funeral and fifty for themselves. Old Wang begged the sum from his foreign employers who gave him fifty dollars as a gift and fifty as an advance against his wages. "Old Wang returned with the money, his nose touching the heavens. Such relations with foreigners made him an important figure in the locality and saved him from his landlord's displeasure over the house having been defiled by suicide: "The landlord . . . questioned the neighbors. The money had definitely come from the foreigners, besides which, everybody had respect for Old Wang. The landlord said no more to Old Wang; it was no good offending one who worked with the foreigners."[10]

The daughter who may have considered herself superior because she went to school, has no better fate than the woman she drove to death. Since she is afraid to enter the room in which the suicide had occurred, her father does not know what to do with her. He decides to marry her off: "This will bring some betrothal money . . . sell her for two or three hundred [dollars], which, apart from getting the son another wife would leave enough for a coffin for me."[11]

Hsiao Fu-tzu

Lao She enlarges on the social comment he makes in "Liu's Compound" in his treatment of Hsiao Fu-tzu, a minor character in *Camel Hsiang-tzu*. Poverty and prostitution are recurring themes in Lao She's writings and since women are not economically independent they are often driven to selling themselves in order to survive. Hsiao Fu-tzu, born into a poor family, is doomed from birth. Her father, Erh Ch'iang-tzu, is an impoverished rickshaw puller, who has a family of four to support.

Hsiao Fu-tzu is innocent and good-hearted. In spite of the dirt and ugliness which surround her she has the natural beauty of the "flowers and grasses" and like the products of the field, she is "plucked and taken to market to be sold." At nineteen she is sold to an army officer for two hundred dollars:

> Hsiao Fu-tzu's man was a military officer. Wherever he went, he established a very simple family by spending one or two hundred dollars to acquire a young girl. He would also buy a large bed of boards and two chairs, so that he could spend a few days happily. When the army moved to another place he would wash his hands of the whole affair, leaving person and bed where they were.[12]

Since his "woman" would have to pay the rent after he had gone she was not only left with nothing but in debt. Hsiao Fu-tzu returned to her family wearing a calico dress and a pair of silver-plated earrings—the only material result of her temporary marriage.

The home she returned to was more impoverished than the one she left. During her absence Erh Ch'iang-tzu had frittered away the two hundred dollars and, partly because he felt guilty over selling his daughter, he drank more and became more quarrelsome. One day, in a drunken fit, he beat his wife to death and had to sell his rickshaw to give her a proper burial. Thereafter he disappeared for days at a time leaving no food for the two little boys who had to sell bits of metal and newspaper they gathered from garbage in order to eat. "When Hsiao Fu-tzu returned they [the two boys] see [in her] a family and each clasped one of her legs; they could say nothing and could only smile at her, their tears flowing. Mother was dead and now elder sister was mother!"[13]

The suggestion that she sell her body to provide the family with food comes from her own father. "You have something ready made," he tells her in a drunken moment, "what are you waiting for before you sell it?"[14] Though it is a depraved, immoral man who says these words, Lao She does not criticize the man but the society that produced him. The cruel father and the exploited daughter are both products of an evil social system. If Erh Ch'iang-tzu could sell her once, it is just a further step in the same direction for him to ask her to sell herself. "Looking at her drunken cat of a father, and at herself, and at her two younger brothers, whom hunger had driven to look like rats, Hsiao Fu-tzu could only weep. But her tears could not move her father, they could not feed the brothers . . . Sister was a piece of meat, which she must give her brother to eat."[15]

Hsiao Fu-tzu becomes a prostitute but at heart she is still the same innocent, good-hearted girl that she has always been. She knows what she is doing and though she detests the profession, she must save her brothers from starving. Lao She condones her actions but he cannot condone her father's when he adds to her burdens by putting on a Confucian mask:

> Erh Ch'iang-tzu—it seems recently he had not been coming home much. He knew what his daughter was doing and did not have the face to enter the lane . . . what the eye does not see the heart is not vexed about . . . but when he had . . . no money . . . he pressed her for some and, on top of it, cursed and abused her, as if to let others know that it was not the fault of Erh Ch'iang-tzu—it was Hsiao Fu-tzu who naturally had no desire for face.[16]

After Hu-niu's death, Hsiao Fu-tzu hopes that Hsiang-tzu might marry her. Since Hsiang-tzu cannot afford to support the whole family, he goes away saying that he will come back for Hsiao Fu-tzu one day. When he does, he finds that she had been forced to join a brothel, where she committed suicide. The brothel keeper tells the story:

> After Little Tender Flesh [the establishment's name for her] came here she had many clients but it was unbearable for her . . . One day . . . a customer went to her room . . . stayed for about the length of time it takes to have a meal, and left . . . [later they discovered] a naked man sleeping soundly in her room. He had been drunk to begin with and Little Tender Flesh had removed her client's clothes and escaped in them. Lao Chih-kan searched everywhere. As soon as he entered the wood, he found her hanging.[17]

Like the daughter-in-law in "Liu's Compound," Hsiao Fu-tzu represents the degraded status of women and the death of all hope. As the old man Ma tells Hsiang-tzu: "We sell our sweat and our women sell their flesh."

"The Crescent Moon"

In "The Crescent Moon" Lao She displays the same genius for the fusion of creative literature and social commentary that we find in *Camel Hsiang-tzu*. There is even a parallel in the themes for the heroine of "The Crescent Moon" is a kind of female Hsiang-tzu. She wants to make good in life and achieve independence but, like Hsiang-tzu, suffers the cold isolation of self reliance and in the end is destroyed by the oppressive society in which she lives. She has some schooling and, therefore, better possibilities in life than Hsiang-tzu, but she comes from a poor home and she and her mother have a very difficult time after her father's death.

The story, which opens when the heroine is seven years old and concludes when she is in her twenties, is narrated in her own words. With this technique Lao She gives us a woman's point of view, conveys the warmth and love between mother and daughter, and shows how their relationship deteriorates under the impact of poverty.

At seven although she does not fully comprehend the significance of her father's death, she senses instinctively her mother's grief and pain. She grows up quickly because the lessons of life come sooner to those who are not sure of their next meal:

> I was only eight when I learned how to pawn things . . . I was afraid of the big red door of the pawnshop and of its high counter. The moment

I saw the door my heart would beat faster. But I had to enter. It was like crawling in because the door-sill was so high. Using all my strength I would hand up the article and shout: "Put it in pawn." Having received the money and the pawn ticket, I would hold them carefully and hurry home, knowing that mother was worried.[18]

One day she took a mirror, one of the last objects left in the house, but the pawnshop refused it because its value was too small:

I was used to that little room and had always felt that there were many things in it. It was only when I was helping mother find some article to pawn that I realized we had very few things.

"Mama, how shall we eat?" [I asked]. Crying, Mama handed me her hairpin—this was the only silver thing she possessed. I knew that she had taken it out several times earlier but, unable to part with it, had never given it to me for pawning. It was an ornament her grandmother had given her when she got married . . .
[When the child reached the pawnshop it was already closed]

I sat on the stone block outside that door, holding the silver hairpin . . . I wept for a long time and then Mama came out of the shadows and held my hand. Oh, what a warm hand. I forgot all the bitterness, even my hunger. Everything was all right as long as this warm hand of Mama's held mine.[19]

Then Mama began to wash clothes for other people. Her hands became rough and scaly and her body began to waste away. Soon after that she remarried and though the heroine found it difficult to call the man "Papa," he was good to both of them and the child could continue in school. When she was about thirteen, the year she graduated from primary school, her new father left them, for no apparent reason. The mother slipped into the life of a prostitute and though she was good to the daughter, encouraging her studies, the daughter began to dislike her for the shameful living she made:

What troubled me most was that I gradually learned to hate mother . . .

Men often came to mother's room and she no longer hid it from me. They looked at me like dogs, tongues hanging out and drooling. I could see that in their eyes I was even more capable of exciting their gluttony [than Mama].

In a short time I suddenly understood many things . . .

When I lay sleepless I thought things over very coldly: Mama deserved to be forgiven. She had to feed the two of us. But I also felt that I should refuse to eat the food she provided.[20]

But the growing girl had even bigger problems to face. Her mother was getting old and incapable of attracting clients. A man who owned a steamed-bread shop wanted to marry her, but if she married him she could not take her grown daughter with her. In her own way she still loved her daughter and wanted to stay with her and so one day she asked her daughter to join hands in the profession! "If I really loved her, Mama said, then I should help her. Otherwise she could no longer look after me. This did not seem like something Mama could say, but she said it."[21] When Erh Ch'iang-tzu in *Camel Hsiang-tzu* advises his daughter to use something which she has "ready made" to earn money the reader is shocked; when the mother tells the heroine of "The Crescent Moon" to do the same thing we are disturbed but the shock is much less. We know that the mother loves her daughter and we also know that the mother, within the limitations of her life, cannot think of another way out. Lao She turns the reader's anger from the mother to the social system, which is to blame for this state of affairs.

The heroine of "The Crescent Moon" is strong-minded enough not to accept such a situation. She moves out of the house and with the help of the kindly principal of her school, finds accommodations on the school premises. Mama marries the breadman and mother and daughter are separated for the first time: "After the event [her mother's "marriage"] I thought: the two of us, mother and daughter, are like two homeless dogs. For the sake of our mouths we had to suffer all kinds of bitterness and hardships. It was as if our bodies were nothing more than one big mouth. For this mouth we had to sell the rest of us."[22] But she no longer hates her mother and comes to understand the true nature of the tragedy.

The heroine works hard to earn her living at school but she is not there by right, only because of the charity of the principal. When a new principal takes over she naturally loses this "position." Lonely and in trouble, she thinks of visiting her mother, but "poverty has thrown up a barricade between mother and daughter," and so she hunts for a job instead. "I will depend on nobody" she says to herself, but there is no job to be found. As Lao She has repeatedly harped, education in the 1920s and 1930s did not equip women for independence: "The ability and morality which I had been taught at school were a joke. Schooling was a plaything for those who had full stomachs and time to spare."[23]

She goes to see the new principal again. Finding the principal out she talks about her problems with a handsome young man at the principal's house. That evening the young man comes to her with some money and tells her that the principal has decided to help her. He rents some rooms for her and provides her with food and clothing. She soon realizes he is doing these things on his own and not on the principal's instructions, but he is handsome and charming and she enjoys the affair until one day the man's wife comes to see her. For all her struggles she has only achieved the status of a kept woman, no better than her mother.

The heroine leaves her lover and again looks for a job. This time she does find a position as second hostess in a small restaurant. When she discovers that the job is to flirt with customers—a milder variation of prostitution, but prostitution nevertheless—she leaves. Not long afterwards, driven by hunger, she rents the rooms where she had once lived with her mother and becomes a prostitute. "These experiences taught me to recognize 'money' and 'man.' Money is more terrible than man. If man is an animal, money is his courage."[24]

Lao She focuses again on money as the increasingly important factor in human relationships and the most corrupting influence in a society which was losing its ethical values. Near the end of the story the heroine's mother comes back to the daughter and in the account of their meeting lies the gist of Lao She's entire philosophy on money, poverty, and human relations:

> After I finished crying I laughed as if I had gone mad: she [the mother] had found her daughter . . . When she was bringing me up she had no other way but prostitution; now it had gone full cycle: to look after her I had to be one!
>
> I hoped mother would comfort me . . . She was scared by hunger . . . "Will we always remain in this profession?" I asked her. She made no reply . . . There was only one thing she was not willing to say and that was that I need not continue this work.
>
> In my heart I understood very well—though it made me a little angry with her—apart from this, I could not think of another business which I could do.
>
> We, mother and daughter, had to eat and clothe ourselves and this determined everything. Mother and daughter or no mother and daughter, respectable or not respectable—money was merciless.[25]

Lao She's commentary on money appears to be that it is supposed to preserve and foster life, but, as in the case of the heroine, it can also destroy life. And money has acquired this destructive potential in Chinese society.

The heroine suffers from venereal disease several times and her rates go down. Finally she is arrested and sent to jail. "Jail is a fine place," she says. "It convinces you that there is no hope for mankind. Even in my dreams I had never seen such a disgusting place. But since I entered it I have never again thought of leaving it. In my experience the world [outside] is not much improvement over this place. I do not want to die and if there were a comparatively better place outside I could go to, I really wouldn't be like this. But death is the same in any place."[26]

Lao She's pessimism regarding the status of women in Chinese society is not limited to women from the poorer classes. We have already seen how the middle-class wives of the government officials in *Divorce* fare. In the short story "Yang-kuang" (Sunshine)[27] he deals with an upper-class woman and she too loses out in the end because she also lives in a corrupt society where men have a double standard. If lack of money destroys satisfying human relations in "The Crescent Moon," the excess of it destroys them in "Sunshine." Family status and money cannot, in themselves, improve the position of woman in society. Born and raised the daughter of a high-class family, the heroine of "Sunshine" becomes the daughter-in-law of an equally high-class family, but in all major matters, like marriage, she has no independence. Her husband, a kind of "twentieth-century Confucius or Mencius," wants to "restore the declining morality of the whole society" but at the same time he has no qualms about buying a concubine. Her own family had used money to buy daughters from poorer families and now her husband does the same thing. What was all her liberal, "modern" education worth? "It was perfectly all right for a man who preached virtue to take a concubine or visit prostitutes. As long as he did not fall in love or seek divorce, he did not violate the moral order."[28] The heroine of "Sunshine" is no angel. She has been influenced by the corrupt upper-class environment in which she was raised, but she is a woman, and as a woman she is destroyed by the hypocritical society she lives in.

By the time Lao She wrote *Camel Hsiang-tzu* he seems to have lost his earlier faith in individual action to improve society. In his maturer works he emphasizes the fact that society as a whole is the source of individual suffering, and that individual effort, whether that of Hsiang-tzu or Professor Ts'ao or the heroine of "The Crescent Moon," is bound to fail. Chinese society, in the throes of change, brought hardship, loneliness, and despair to the poor and the intellectually sensitive. Lao She repeatedly brings the reader to the conclusion that the whole social system was breaking down. There is no hope for China till the down-trodden common man can stand up again and lead a decent, dignified life. Lao She may not have had any taste for politics but he saw the need for radical change, though suspicious of violent revolution led by romantic radicals. One suspects that he was not quite sure of the proper means for achieving this end and would have welcomed any person or persons who could convince him of results.

VII

THE WAR YEARS, 1937–1949

Japan began its full-scale invasion of China before the Nanking era had suc-
ceeded in bringing the hoped-for unity and peace within the country. Strange
as it may seem, Japan's action resulted in creating a greater sense of unity and
purpose than China had known since the turn of the century. A "united
front" spirit came to pervade not only the field of political action but also
the world of literature and art. Literary factions that had been hurling vicious
abuse at each other now joined hands to save the motherland.

Even initial defeat did not seem to dampen the ardor of a people who willingly dismantled universities, industries, and offices to move them inland. A
strong will to resist the enemy stirred the nation. The army fought valiantly
and for a moment it appeared that Chiang Kai-shek was, indeed, the right man
to head the country in its hour of peril.

For a year or so, an atmosphere of enthusiasm and self-sacrificing effort—
which could perhaps be termed an "atmosphere of resistance"—prevailed in
the impoverished capital of Chungking. But as the country settled down to a
long, drawn-out war, authoritarian rule coupled with corruption, nepotism,
and embezzlement produced the evils of inflation and deprivation at one level and cynicism and demoralization at another. The intellectuals who had
voluntarily followed the government to Chungking to offer their services
without any adequate recompense now found their works censored and their
comrades jailed. During the Civil War that followed the collapse of Japan, in
more than one way it was the idealism and the spirit of sacrifice engendered
in the Communist-held areas that won the final victory over the corruption
and decadence that marked the KMT, and established the People's Republic
on October 1, 1949.

The vast migration to the interior that had taken place at the beginning of
the war affected the intellectuals in many significant ways. The war gave
those who went to the "red" areas an opportunity to participate directly in
the unique revolutionary experiment taking place under the guidance of the
Communist party. The impact on the others who had chosen to go to Chungking and the neighboring cities was different but no less critical. First, intellectuals of various shades of opinion and from various centers (for example
the *hai-p'ai* from Shanghai, and the *ching-p'ai* from Peking) were brought
closer together. Second, many who had worked in the comparative security
and isolation in the heart of big cities like Shanghai, now, perhaps for the
first time in their lives, came in contact with "reality." They not only had

to deny themselves the luxuries of metropolitan urban centers and live a hard personal life but also witnessed the tragic lives of the peasantry in the country. And finally, they were also brought nearer to the center of the authoritarian bureaucratic government which gave them ample occasion to gather evidence of its ruthless methods of suppressing undesirable opinion.

The war gave Lao She an opportunity to reveal his true attitude toward politics. As we have seen, in all his writings he had shown great scorn for flag-waving and slogan-shouting revolutionaries and patriots. He had kept away from literary factions and had studiously avoided getting involved in politico-literary polemics. But he had consistently emphasized the need for true patriotism and now, by his actions and words, he was to demonstrate that he was capable of living up to his ideals.

Lao She left Tsinan late in 1937 and went to Hankow where, in Feng Yü-hsiang's encampment, he immediately organized, along with Ho Jung and Lao Hsiang, the magazine *K'ang tao ti* (Resist to the end).[1] The goal of the magazine was to spread anti-Japanese propaganda among the masses by using popular literary forms. It published "big drum songs," plays written in the local opera style, and stories which could be recited by the traditional story-tellers. It appears that the magazine was quite successful in achieving its goal and that it attracted the attention of various groups that had been officially organized to do propaganda work. Feng Yü-hsiang, himself, sometimes contributed articles to the magazine.

In 1938, the All China Association of Writers and Artists against Aggression (Chung-hua ch'üan-kuo wen-i-chieh k'ang-ti hsieh hui) was organized in Hankow. To make sure that the association did not fall into the hands of the KMT, it was decided that it would be run by a Central Secretariat rather than by a chairman. If a chairman were appointed it was feared that the KMT might nominate one of its own officials. An even greater danger to the organization was the factionalism that existed in the literary groups. Lao She, who was one of the founder-members of the association, was chosen to head the Secretariat because he was respected by all groups. He could be trusted not to side with any one group, and at the same time help iron out any differences. As head of the Secretariat, Lao She was in fact the chairman of the association and though his work in that capacity has not been given sufficient recognition by historians in Communist China, there is ample evidence to prove that he performed this difficult task with great tact and success.[2]

Wang Yü, who met Lao She in Chungking in 1942, describes him in the following words:

Lao She did not look at all like what I had imagined he would. He had obviously lost a great deal of weight, and was much thinner . . .

The work of the Writers' Anti-Aggression Association was divided into various departments, but in actuality the one person responsible for the entire organization was Lao She. Therefore, the man who had to deal with the KMT was also Lao She, and this was not an easy matter. He had only to slip up a little and Chiang Kai-shek would have put him in jail. Under these conditions, Lao She displayed considerable ability. The association had a bigger task than just uniting the writers, for this was also the time when a large number of writers were being arrested or were simply "disappearing"—as for example Lo Pin-chi and Wei Meng-k'e . . . It was Lao She who had to obtain the release of those who had been arrested, and to find out the whereabouts of those who had "disappeared."

Many of the writers who came to Chungking would seek out Lao She to be their guarantor (*tan pao*) . . .[3]

In 1944 when four hundred friends and admirers of Lao She gathered in Chungking to congratulate him on the completion of twenty years of his literary life, Mao Tun paid him a high tribute for his work for the association. He said: "Were it not for the hard work and patience of Mr. Lao She, I fear that our great cause—the uniting of all patriotic workers in the fields of culture—could not have been established so quickly and so smoothly, nor would it have survived up to the present in the troubles and difficulties around us."[4]

Lao She himself did not distinguish the strain of the war years from the hard life he had led earlier and said: "The twenty years have not been easy. They were just like twenty years of sedan-chair carrying or rickshaw pulling."[5] The association published a magazine *K'ang-chan wen-yi* (Resistance literature), and Lao She was naturally closely involved with its production.

Life was very difficult in this period. Lao She was not well. He had stomach trouble for which he had to undergo an operation in 1943. He also suffered from anemia.[6] In 1936, he gave up teaching to devote himself entirely to the business of writing. His financial condition had improved to some extent by the sale of his writings so that he could afford to make this decision. Though the war affected all this, he preferred to continue to be a full-time writer and did not go back to teaching. Although details are scarce, it appears that his family continued to reside in Peking under the Japanese for several years after the war began. This must have been a matter of great concern to him. In the preface to *Huo-tsang* (Cremation) there is a casual reference to the fact that in November 1943 his family arrived at Pei-p'ei from Peking. Another indication that his family was indeed living in occupied Peking comes from an article about Mrs. Lao She published in 1957. It mentions that in

1944, when Lao She began the novel *Ssu-shih t'ung-t'ang* (Four generations under one roof), in which Japanese-held Peking is the backdrop, "he did not have any idea what life was like under the enemy," and his wife "described it to him."[7]

In spite of his poor health, personal preoccupations, and deep involvement with the taxing work of the association, Lao She still found time to write. One cannot help being struck by the strong character, the tenacity and self-discipline which this frail, mild man showed in the face of adversity. Lao She would get up at five in the morning so that he could write for three hours before he started his other activities. From 1938 to 1945 he wrote seven or eight plays, a long novel, and published a collection of short stories. He also wrote innumerable "big drum" songs and other propaganda pieces.

That Lao She could turn from story writing to plays and other genres shows his versatility. Though he knew that he would not be able to write great plays he, nevertheless, began to write plays because it was his contribution to the defense of his country—his act of self-sacrifice. The country needed literature that could be brought to the illiterate masses, and somebody had to produce it. Lao She was serving a cause higher than himself and higher than the government of the day, but he wrote only the things that his conscience approved of. When some friends in the army asked him to write about General Chang Tzu-chung who had been killed in the early phase of the war, he readily consented. But when a high official of the KMT offered him 300,000 yuan to write a play which would praise the KMT leaders he quietly declined the honor. This action of Lao She's becomes poignant when we realize that he was in a rather difficult financial situation. As he himself says with much bitterness:

> If a work like *Cremation* had been written before the war, I would have thrown it into the wastepaper basket. But now I do not have that type of courage. I have spent more than four months to write this book of more than 100,000 characters. I may have wasted these four months, but one does not get free food . . . It cost me 200 yuan for the paper alone. I paid 1,500 yuan to get it copied. And I ask you, having invested so much capital can I dare to easily discard the manuscript? . . . I do not make this declaration so that people may forgive me but to bring to everybody's attention the fact that the life of a writer must be improved if society still wants literature. People must not look upon the writer as an animal that does not need to eat or drink.[8]

One of the reasons why the novel *Cremation*, written in 1943, was a failure in the eyes of the author was that Lao She felt that he lacked sufficient information and background material about areas under enemy occupation to produce a successful war novel. However that may be, the writing of this novel and the earlier plays reveals Lao She's strong belief in the need for intellectuals to get involved in national affairs. It appears that there were writers who condemned literature that dealt with the war because it was not "true" literature. Obviously one can make a case for such a stand. Lao She, while discussing one of his plays, *Kuo-chia chih shang* (Country above all), which became quite popular, takes the opportunity to berate his critics and expound his own views:

> I was also very satisfied, not only because the play had been so successful, but because I felt that if anti-aggression literature could be so successful it could genuinely stop the mouths of those who insisted that literature should not be used in the service of the anti-aggression war . . . If today there are still people who consider themselves idealists and oppose war because they love peace, or if they vacillate in their attitude toward war and, therefore, express sentiments of pessimism, well then they are traitors.[9]

On another occasion he expands the theme still further:

> There are people who say that it is not worthwhile to write about war, because wars are evil and destructive. I think that this opinion is very warped. If everything concerning society can provide material for literature I do not understand why only wars must be kept out of it . . . If at this time we do not write about war or the impact of war, then we are living with our eyes closed.
>
> It is true that war is evil, but it is only we who can analyze war, be concerned about it, and express ourselves about it. And it is only by so doing that we shall understand and also let others understand how we can eliminate wars and establish peace.[10]

Here is a Lao She who appears to be quite a different person from what he was before the war. He has become a political activist, a leader in the revolutionary movement for changing China, a polemicist ready to attack his opponents. Many felt that Lao She had undergone a great transformation. He had at last discarded humor and turned serious. To Wang Yü it "seems that Lao She's ideas and ideology had shifted with the times. His speech had become more firm."[11]

Though Lao She did, indeed, change it would perhaps be quite erroneous to view it as a radical transformation of any sort. An experience like war deeply affects, and to that extent changes any sensitive person. The changes, however, often only highlight the basic philosophy of the individual and show up his true inner self. The "new" Lao She, if examined a little more closely is still the author of *Chao Tzu-yueh,* who had advised the young to work hard and prepare themselves for the day when their services would be needed by the nation. Lao She has done no more than follow his own advice. He had worked hard and had become a writer through diligence and application. Now that the nation needed writers he had offered his services.

It has been noted earlier that there was a streak of traditional morality in Lao She. In his statements on war and the need to participate in war, one detects in Lao She's opinion of himself a similarity to a traditional Chinese scholar's view of his status and role in society. There is something superior about the way in which he declares that "it is only we who can analyze war, be concerned about it, and express ourselves about it." And this is to be done not for the government but for the nation which can be looked upon as a substitute for Confucian culture. And like the gentry-scholar of old, Lao She feels that society must be responsible for the welfare of the writer.

Unlike many European writers, who even at the height of the war could still feel that suffering and pain were not the monopoly of only one side and who felt that man must struggle not against the tyranny of fascism or dictatorship as represented by Germany or Italy, but fascism and tyranny per se, so that man could be free, the Chinese writers are primarily concerned not with man as a universal entity or even with the Chinese, but with China. China had to gain freedom and develop a government that would fulfill the needs of the people. Lao She is no exception. If he is filled with a passionate desire to see his people united in the face of the enemy, he is just as passionate in his condemnation of the government that is represented by corruption, indirection, nepotism, and ingratiating attitudes.

Lao She and the Theater

Though Lao She spent the first five years of the war writing plays rather than novels and short stories, his works do not in any significant way indicate a radical change in content. He is still preoccupied with the problems of man's evil nature and the vicious role that money plays in society. It is true that somewhere in the background the Japanese become the mortal enemies of China, but the main themes of his works are more directly related to corrupt officials, lacking a sense of patriotism and nationalism and seeking to amass wealth or improve their social and official status; to superficially modernized youth who waste time in writing love poetry or seeking cheap thrills with no concern for the country; to unfortunate women who are reduced to selling their bodies to satisfy the lust of petty officials; and to the weaknesses in the Chinese character such as putting face above constructive action. He does, however, find a certain purity and strength of character among the poor which is lacking in the richer classes, a trend in his writings which became more marked from the time he wrote *Camel Hsiang-tzu*.

Lao She was among the first to use the stage as a means of reaching the masses; his plays helped to harness the theater to the war effort. He wrote his first play, *Ts'an wu* (The dispersal of the mist), in 1939, completing it in two weeks. With his usual humility, Lao She later explained that he knew nothing of playwriting and that this first attempt was poorly constructed. After he finished the play, he left the manuscript with a friend and went away to Chungking for a few months. On his return he was greeted with the news that not only had the play been published in his absence but that it had been produced and there was a small sum of 300 yuan awaiting him as his share of the profits.[12]

Traditional bureaucratic vices are depicted in this play in the person of his chief character, a Mr. Hsi, the head of a bureau in Chungking. Mr. Hsi is anxious to acquire status and also money, both of which finally lead to his betrayal by a clever and beautiful young spy and his eventual arrest as a traitor. Phrases such as "difficult times for the nation," "resist the enemy to the end," "for the country," "in my heart there is only room for the country, not the family" are uttered glibly by Hsi while he is seducing a girl or transacting a corrupt deal to cheat the government. The play reveals Lao She's concern that the old society still exists underneath the new one. The hypocritical Hsi does not wear the gown of the officials of the past; his work is in a "modern" bureau; he lives in a "modern" house with a telephone and a sofa set, but the man is nonetheless a symbol of China's past failures. Lao She continues to satirize middle-class youth in this play, believing them to be cut off from the masses, and also the pseudo-intellectuals who believe they are great revolutionaries.

There is a change here in Lao She's attitude. He is saying through this play that a hatred for the enemy, a sense of national urgency, and patriotism are only to be found among the poor. If Lao She is gradually leaning toward communism, the causes should be sought in his disillusionment with the kind of people who are running the Chungking government. This "leftism" is more like Mao Tse-tung's early response to the character of the peasantry. It has far less to do with theoretical communism than with the moral bankruptcy of the upper classes and with the desperation of the poor.

One of his female characters, Yü-ming, who is torn between taking care of her dying mother and abandoning her to fight the Japanese, finally becomes a prostitute in order to take care of her. Yü-ming is in some ways a Maoist heroine. She has experienced terrible suffering and is consumed by anger against the enemy and a thirst for revenge. Lao She has begun to write in a manner which conforms to a certain degree to the guidelines that Mao Tse-tung was to set for art and literature a few years later. He has not, however, been able to overlook the conflict between filial piety and patriotism. He indicts the evil society run by a characterless elite which exploits the destitute, but Yü-ming first fulfills her filial obligations and then goes north to join the army and settle her score with the Japanese.

Between 1938 and 1943 Lao She wrote seven or eight plays. *The Dispersal of the Mist* must have been successful enough in performance for Lao She to have been invited to write a propaganda play for the National Muslim Association for the Protection of the Country. He did so in collaboration with Sung Chih-ti. The play they wrote, *Kuo-chia chih-shang* (Country above all) was so successful that it was staged in Chungking, Kunming, Shengtu, Tali, Lanchow, Sian, Kweilin, and Hong Kong.

Of the others, two plays, *Chang Tzu-chung* (General Chang Tzu-chung), and *Ta ti lung she* (Dragon and snake over the great country), were written at the request of "some friends in the army," and the Eastern Cultural Association, respectively. Among the remaining plays, *Mien-tzu wen-t'i* (The problem of face), *Kuei-ch'ü lai-hsi* (Return), and *Shei hsien tao-la Ch'ung-ch'ing* (Who will be the first to arrive at Chungking?), are worthy of note.

The Problem of Face was written in 1940 and revised three times. The story deals with a number of government employees in a small office in the country who represent various types of officials. Secretary T'ung Ching-ming is a traditional bureaucrat who is more worried about face than office work; Yü Chien-feng, who heads a department and is subordinate to T'ung, has great regard for face but is also conscious of the importance of money and is, therefore, ready to sacrifice face if money is involved; Ch'in Chien-ch'ao, the doctor attached to Yü's office is a truly modern type, dedicated to his work and pays no heed to face.

T'ung, believing that he has lost face because Ch'in has not paid sufficient attention to his orders, connives with Yü to dismiss him. Ch'in has decided to leave the office in any case, and go to the front to serve the army because he cannot stand the intrigues of inefficient bureaucrats who have no regard for the war. Finally it is T'ung and Yü who get dismissed. T'ung because he has written a letter to a relative in the Japanese zone and is, therefore, looked upon as a traitor, and Yü because he belongs to "T'ung's party."

There are some minor characters and minor themes woven into the play. The importance of these is that they help to further highlight the nature of the times and the clash of values which are revealed in the major theme. Nurse Ou-yang Hsueh, like Doctor Ch'in, is a patriotic hard-working young girl who has no time for face in her life. T'ung's daughter, Chi-fen, is gradually wasting herself in the confines of her house because she is incapable of forgetting her status and going out to work. The couple, Fang Hsin-cheng and his wife Shan Ming-ch'in, tried to make quick money, lost their wealth, and are now living off their wits, cheating and lying, but cannot conceive of accepting any work that may lower their status. After all, Fang had once served as Head of Department (*k'o-chang*)! The office boy, Chao Ch'in, is useful to the story because he inherits some property and Lao She shows how the attitude of those around Chao changes with this incident.

The play in many ways is better structured than *The Dispersal of the Mist*. The scene where Yü and others try to make a gentleman out of Chao touches the height of comedy but in no way loses its connection with the central theme.

Like *The Dispersal of the Mist, The Problem of Face* attacks the ruling elite and shows how the harmful attitudes born of traditional ethics thwart meaningful national effort. By trying to concentrate on the single theme of face the author has made the attack with better coordination and has managed to draw attention to the allied problems of status, hierarchical relations and bureaucratic factions where loyalty to one's superior counts more than loyalty to the government or the country. Tradition is dying, but rather slowly. The strongly entrenched cultural trait of maintaining face still casts a deep shadow over the whole bureaucratic milieu. How many T'ungs and Yüs are still there, not only as a drag on the Ch'ins of new China but even as suppressors and destroyers of the Ch'ins?

Unlike *The Dispersal of the Mist,* however, *The Problem of Face* does portray two very positive characters: Doctor Ch'in and Nurse Ou-yang. They are extremely hard-working, dedicated, conscious of the needs of the country. They have no patience with *li*, the traditional ritualistic pattern of relationships; they serve the masses with greater zest than they serve their superiors whose illnesses are the consequence of laziness or lack of work. T'ung's high blood pressure increases when he plays cards or mahjong late into the night. He cannot stop doing that because he would lose face if he told his guests to go away. Chi-fen has bad dreams and is a psychiatric case only because she has no work at all and spends all her time in the house bemoaning her lot and complaining about the ill-trained servants or the lack of money. She cannot work inside or outside the house because her status forbids it.

Does Lao She see in Chiang Kai-shek's emphasis on *li, i, lien, ch'ih,* (property, righteousness, uprightness, sense of shame) a revival of Confucianism?

Is this play an attack on the KMT for allowing superficial lip-service to traditional ethics to become a camouflage behind which nepotism, corruption, and other bureaucratic abuses could flourish?[13]

T'ung, who counts several *chin-shih** among his forebears, cannot dream of sullying his hands doing business, and cannot conceive of living a life other than that of an official. The moment he realizes that he is going to lose his post he starts making preparations for suicide. Unlike Yü, he is not corrupt and Lao She could have lent some nobility to his character—that of a man holding on to past values and dying for them. But the values he holds dear are not worthy of respect and so all we get is a hollow man devoid of any ameliorating qualities, an anachronism that must be swept away to clear the path of progress. We laugh at this little man and when the end comes we cannot pity him.

If one wishes to get a good idea of the problem of face in Chinese society, perhaps no one book deals with so many aspects of it as *The Problem of Face*. It is a handbook on how to maintain face, lend face, borrow face, or destroy face. The short piece from Act II translated below gives a sample of how Lao She has dealt with the subject. Yü, Fang, Shan, Ou-yang, and Chi-fen are in T'ung's house when Chao's newly acquired wealth comes up for discussion. The couple, Fang and Shan, have been successful so far in their confidence game and have been accepted by the T'ung family and Yü as directors of an industrial company. Fang and Shan are anxious to sell shares for this non-existent enterprise, particularly to Chao. The avaricious Yü, sensing the possibility of a profit for himself, offers to handle Chao and get him to part with his money. T'ung Chi-fen, the status-conscious daughter, would like her father to participate in the Fang-Shan deal:

> Chi-fen: Papa is incapable of doing business [because he is a scholar and an official].
> Yü: I know! But I have a way to manage this affair [in such a fashion that Mr. T'ung would not lose face if he joined the venture]. In these difficult times even a professional teacher must indulge in business!
> Chi-fen: If father wants to, I would naturally not oppose him. Ah! Life has become so difficult. It would be so good if he could earn a little more without damaging our status. Ming-ch'in, it is a matter of face—please do not force [the low-placed] Chao to become a shareholder.

---

* Sometimes translated as Doctorate, *chin-shih* was the highest degree which could be attained under the Imperial Examination System.

Shan Ming-ch'in: We are all particular about giving others face but to make a living we have to struggle hard [and even accept men like Chao as a shareholder].

Ou-yang Hsueh, the nurse, is impatient with this talk.

Ou-yang Hsueh: (getting up) Miss T'ung, Mr. Yü, I am leaving.

Yü: Dinner is about to arrive. Please stay on for a little while.

Chi-fen: If you leave like this, will it not make me lose face?

Ou-yang Hsueh: It is not only a question of food! (loses control of herself) As I see it all of you who are so conscious of appearances don't want face at all!

All: What?

Ou-yang: Old Chao's money is his own, why are you making schemes about it? You gentlemen and ladies—are you worried about face or are you cheats? (leaves angrily)

Chi-fen: (after a pause when everyone is silent) Begging your pardon, I must go and rest for a while. (she is stopped from getting up by Shan Ming-ch'in) I, I never thought that I could be insulted in this manner in my own house. That I receive this insignificant nurse is excessive politeness in itself. She could . . .

Yü: Miss T'ung, this incident is of no consequence . . . Because Doctor Ch'in has received a promotion I praised him and by so doing gave the nurse a little face . . . I have my methods of dealing with them.

Shan: Miss T'ung, please don't get angry. It is undignified to get angry over people who have no rank or status. If you fall ill because of your anger, even our two faces [referring to herself and her husband] will become marked.

Yü: Miss T'ung, it is all my fault.

Chi-fen: Head of Department Yü please do not mention this matter again. I think father will definitely not be able to do business. Ours is a family which has had literary fame for generations.

[Act II]

The healthy attitude and behavior of the doctor and nurse stand out in refreshing contrast to the depressing atmosphere created by the cheating, lying, hypocritical members of the gentry. It is in this contrast that the propaganda element in the play comes out. There is something irreconcilable between the modern and the traditional. One wonders whether Chi-fen even understands what doctor Ch'in is saying to her in the following passage:

Ch'in: Miss T'ung, I cannot come very often [to see you] [Miss T'ung is his patient].

Chi-fen: Why?

Ch'in: (stands up) I am going to the front.

Chi-fen: (also stands up) Going to the front? When do you leave? When will you come back?

Ch'in: I am leaving in a few days and I don't know when I will be able to return.

Chi-fen: You are very hard-hearted! [she is secretly in love with him]

Ch'in: Indeed, I feel badly about it too. The common folk in these parts are so pitiful! Malaria and dysentery can be cured, but God knows how many die every year from them. During my stay here I have saved many lives. If, after I leave [a doctor] should come who neglects his public duties and does not want to serve the people, it will be terrible.

Chi-fen: It will be better if you do not go.

Ch'in: The brave soldiers at the front need doctors desperately. I must go. Then again the temper of "their excellencies" here make me dislike serving them.

Chi-fen: Who? Which "excellencies"?

Ch'in: Like your father, Secretary T'ung.

Chi-fen: (startled) What's wrong with him?

Ch'in: It doesn't matter. I am leaving.

Chi-fen: You cannot go! If you do not explain yourself I will immediately get seriously ill and be bedridden for at least a month.

Ch'in: It is nothing—really! Their bureaucratism has not lessened one bit because of the war and this upsets me.

Chi-fen: My father—bureaucratic? Aren't you mistaken? He does indeed have great consideration for face but definitely no bureaucratism. And, who is there who does not have consideration for face?

Ch'in: Spending the whole day in creating meaningless red tape, in meaningless talk, in meaningless affairs, all because of face! However, this doesn't matter (begins to leave).

Chi-fen thinks that Ch'in is leaving because of a minor misunderstanding with her father, suggests that a reconciliation is possible and advisable, and that Ch'in should stay on. She would, no doubt, like to marry Ch'in, but dare not think of it until he has come up in the world:

Chi-fen: Doctor Ch'in, please don't leave this place. You are such a likeable person, and if you only saw more people and entertained more often, you could certainly become head of the hospital or the head of the clinic. If you add this status to your learning and intellectual standing, you will become even more lovable! You must develop a close friendship with my father and not misunderstand him again.

Once you have established mutual affection, he will certainly help you!

[Act II]

What Lao She wants for China is men and women of education, dedication, and a sense of loyalty to the nation. This is what he always emphasized from his very first writing. The new elements are his growing concern for the common people and the feeling that the backbone of the country is in the patriotic sentiment to be found in the masses.

Some of Lao She's plays were never produced and though he labored hard on them, sometimes revising a manuscript four or five times, he felt that he never did manage to grasp the finer techniques of playwriting. The two most successful plays were both written in collaboration with other playwrights—*Country above All* with Sung Chih-ti, and *T'ao-li ch'ün-feng* (lit., "Peaches and plums in the spring wind")* with Chao Ch'ing-ko. The writers were awarded a cash prize by the government for this play, which was written in 1943 and was Lao She's last venture into playwriting during this period.

Huo-tsang (*Cremation*)

In 1943, Lao She returned to the medium he understood best—the novel and the short story. By 1943, there were many good playwrights like Ts'ao Yü, T'ien Han, and Hung Sheng, who enriched the wartime theater, and so it is understandable that Lao She felt that the time had come for him to withdraw from the scene.

In 1943 he wrote *Huo-tsang* (Cremation), a novel dealing with the Chinese resistance movement in a Japanese-held area. The author declared that the novel was a failure because he had not made a deep enough study of life in an occupied area. However that may be, *Cremation* is the first novel that has a real hero (or heroine, for the main character is a young girl, Meng-lien). In all his previous novels Lao She had anti-heros like Li in *Divorce,* and Hsiang-tzu in *Camel Hsiang-tzu,* but never a fully developed character that could be called a hero.

In the occupied city of Wench'eng, Meng-lien's father is an official who is not only collaborating with the enemy but is ready to marry his daughter

---

* A Chinese idiom which describes a successful teacher who had pupils everywhere. *Peaches and Plums in the Spring Wind* deals with a good teacher who is helped by former students when he migrates from his native Japanese-held area to the south.

to another traitor to ensure his position. Meng-lien, with all the fears and weaknesses of a young Chinese girl from a good family, revolts against her father and shows tremendous strength and courage in joining the underground to fight the enemy. When the enemy has been defeated and the traitors destroyed she joins the army to continue to serve the country.

When her father tells her about his marriage arrangements for her, she replies:

> "Papa! Ha! I still must call you Papa . . . Please find a way to let me go. The railway station is just outside the city, but I cannot escape from this courtyard. You must plan some way for me. What you are doing is a crime against the people. Even I, who am your daughter, cannot call you Papa without feeling ashamed. How much worse it must be for the others. We are no longer father and daughter because there is a high wall between us . . . I don't have the strength to bring this wall down, and you have no desire to do so."[14]

Lao She had never been able to resolve the tension between filial piety and duty to the country, because in all his works he had never been able to portray a totally evil parent. Now, however, by making the father a traitor, a symbol of the vile and hateful enemy, he can at last discard sentiment and make the daughter revolt against him and all he stands for.

Similarly, Lao She, in all his previous works, while exhorting youth to be more studious and self-sacrificing had scorned love. Love was time-consuming and distracted the young from their great task. In *Cremation* Lao She also comes to grips with the problem of love. Meng-lien loves Ting I-shan but she never uses that word and though she is completely his woman she does not stop him from fighting for the country and getting killed in the process. At the end of the novel she goes to the military commander and seeks work in the army. She "told the Brigade Commander that she was the unmarried wife of Ting I-shan! I-shan was dead and that she would honor and remember him through work."[15]

The war made it possible for Lao She to find a resolution of the tensions which had been noticeable from the time of his London novels. In *Mr. Ma and Master Ma,* Li Tzu-jung, who has been abroad for several years, willingly consents to marry a girl chosen by his mother back home. His reasons are (a) that conditions in China demand that matters of love be postponed to a date when the country is strong and free, and (b) that the so-called educated women in China have no true concept of "mutual help, sympathy, and duty" which should underlie any marriage.[16] In *Cremation,* written over a decade later, we find that Lao She recognizes the fact that love may be acceptable even before the country is liberated but that the second criterion must be the basis for this love. Meng-lien provides I-shan with help and sympathy and at the same time is conscious of her duty.

"Mutual help, sympathy, and duty" are qualities of a good wife which reflect Lao She's image of Western society and an aspect of modernization. These qualities, however, can lead to self-sacrifice in the interest of the state which is an extension of a traditional image of a good person.

Ssu-shih t'ung-t'ang (*Four generations under one roof*)

In 1946, soon after the war was over, Lao She along with Ts'ao Yü went to the United States on an invitation from the State Department. The invitation was for a year, but Lao She stayed on till the fall of 1949, returning home only after the establishment of The People's Republic of China. His unhesitating decision to go to Communist China and not Taiwan indicates that he had become a Communist at heart, or respected the Communist ideology far more than the KMT ideology, or that he was so disgusted with the KMT that he saw in the Communists the only worthwhile alternative. It was probably a combination of all these factors.

But before this trip abroad, Lao She had begun his most ambitious novel *Ssu-shih t'ung-t'ang* (Four generations under one roof). Dealing with four generations of the Ch'i family in Peking, it was to be a historical novel depicting life under the Japanese and showing how the Chinese reacted in various ways to the occupation. Lao She's intention was to write a hundred chapters— a million characters—which would be divided into three parts, each part to constitute two volumes.[17] Part I, *Huang-huo* (Bewilderment) was published in early 1946, but the remaining two parts were not finished until Lao She's stay in the United States from 1946 to 1949. *T'ou-sheng* (Ignoble life), Part II, appeared in late 1946, but the last part was never published in book form.

What made Lao She write such a novel? This question becomes particularly pertinent because in the preface to *Cremation,* which he had just finished, he explains at great length his inability to deal with life under the Japanese. One answer is that though Lao She always made excessive apologies, he did not necessarily mean them. If one were to go by his own introductions and prefaces to his works, Lao She never wrote anything worthwhile except, perhaps, *Camel Hsiang-tzu.* Another explanation could be that he felt confident that he could write about Peking because he knew the city so well and with the help of his wife, who had experienced the Japanese occupation and just arrived from Peking, he thought that he would be able to capture the mood of the times. In any case, the conjuring up of characters was not difficult for his creative genius and the rest of the writing was in many ways cerebral—Lao She projecting his theories about Chinese character, his analysis of the "good" patriotic people and the "bad" traitors and collaborators. As far as psychological tensions were concerned—for example, the dichotomy between filial piety and patriotism, should one stay on under the Japanese to serve the aging parents or leave them to die and go to join the resistance movement—here was an ideal set-up which Lao She could use to show the strength of tradition and the distress it could cause.

While in the United States Lao She helped Ida Pruitt produce an abridged translation of this novel under the title *The Yellow Storm.* Ida Pruitt recalls how Lao She would work with her by the hour, always showing much patience and never losing his humor.[18] Comparing the translation with the two available parts of the novel, one notices that though many minor incidents and characters are left out, the translation manages to capture the essential spirit of the original. Lao She's personal involvement no doubt made a significant contribution to the project. (We can, in the absence of the complete Chinese work, use the translation for our purpose here, with one departure: the widely accepted system of romanization based on the Wade-Giles system will replace the unorthodox romanization followed by Ida Pruitt in certain places.)

Of the four generations represented, the grand patriarch Ch'i is seventy-five years old at the opening of the novel. His son, T'ien-yu, is over fifty and looking after the family business. T'ien-yu's three sons, Jui-hsuan, Jui-feng, and Jui-ch'üan, form the more important element in the story. Jui-hsuan is married and has two children, a girl and a boy. Jui-feng is also married but has no children, and the youngest brother is still in college and a bachelor.

Jui-hsuan, who had "studied both Chinese and Western literature and had a considerable understanding in both," is a school teacher. His father, whose business is gradually dwindling, spends all his time at the shop, even sleeping there at night, and his mother is ailing, so the burden of running the entire household falls on his and his good wife's shoulders. He gets no help from Jui-feng, who "had some education . . . and was intolerant of his father and grandfather. He did his best to imitate the tasteful and fashionable, but he imitated too hard; he did not achieve the polish he wanted but, on the other hand, threw away his genuine inheritance. Jui-feng had the manner of a compradore or a gangster."[19] Jui-feng does not have to be encouraged by his self-indulgent wife to leave the family house and join the group of traitors who find that life can still be comfortable if they pander to the Japanese.

Jui-ch'üan is an impetuous young man who is inspired by patriotism to leave Peking and join the resistance army. Jui-hsuan supports his younger brother in this decision and is unhappy only because circumstances do not allow him to act in a similar manner. "Jui-hsuan was caught between the generations. Old Man Ch'i was a hundred percent old China; his son T'ien-yu was seventy percent old and thirty percent new; and Jui-ch'üan was seventy percent new and thirty percent old. Jui-hsuan, however, was fifty percent old and fifty percent new. He could see the problems and difficulties of both, and the beauty and reasonableness of both, and he could see the duties toward both."[20]

It is not hard to see where the author's sympathy lies. It is with the sincere, mild, courteous Jui-hsuan, the man of great strength of character, one who can suffer inwardly and stand pain and continue to live with self-respect and dignity under the most ignoble of circumstances. Jui-hsuan's father commits suicide because of the humiliations heaped upon him by the Japanese, Jui-ch'üan leaves the family to join the resistance, and Jui-feng leaves the household because he wants freedom to serve the Japanese masters and gain wealth and status. None of these paths are open to Jui-hsuan who is the sole provider for the four generations. In the manner of the traditional head of the family, he has to retain an outward calm and console everybody around him even when his heart is bursting with anguish and misery. Ultimately, he does redeem himself by working for the underground movement in Peking.

In many ways, Jui-hsuan can be compared to Chueh-hsin in Pa Chin's *Chia* (The family). *The Family* also deals with many generations under one roof—the Chinese extended family—and like Jui-hsuan, Chueh-hsin is a young man who is made to carry the responsibility of the family, and tries to reconcile the views of the older generations with those of his rebellious younger brothers. Whether or not it indicates a difference between a conservative family in Szechuan and one in Peking, the older generations are less authoritative in *Four Generations under One Roof* than in *Family*. Besides Jui-hsuan is a stronger character than Chueh-hsin. Since Pa Chin's novel is set in the late 1910s and Lao She's in the 1930s this difference could be the result of the changes brought to China by the passage of time.

Despite the title, *Four Generations under One Roof* is a story not only of the Ch'i family but of all the dozen or so families that live in the large compound in which the individual houses are located around a central open space, and which has only one exit to the main road. The most affluent resident of the compound is Kuan. He, his wife and concubine, his two daughters, and the servants (he is the only one with servants in the compound) live in comparative luxury on the wealth he had accumulated during his service with the warlords. He and his wife are corrupt, characterless opportunists, who even "sell out" their neighbors to gain favor with the Japanese. Mrs. Kuan becomes the head of the bureau looking after prostitutes and she skillfully exploits this position to squeeze money from the professional ladies as well as to force innocent girls to enter the "dark gates."

Ch'ien, the scholar-poet, leads a hermit-like existence and the doors of his courtyard seldom open. Only Old Man Ch'i goes to visit him periodically though Ch'ien does not return the courtesy. He has two sons, the elder married and the younger following the most unscholarly pursuit of bus-driver. The younger son becomes a hero when he destroys a bus load of Japanese soldiers and sacrifices his life in the process. The Kuans pass on the information to the Japanese authorities that Ch'ien is the boy's father. He is arrested and tortured till his bones are broken and he cannot stand, but nothing can bend his indomitable spirit. He crawls back from prison to find that his elder son has died of illness, and that his wife has committed suicide. Ch'ien then becomes an underground worker for the resistance.

Among the others in the compound are a rickshaw puller, a barber, a husband and wife who are opera singers, an arranger of funerals, and a "boy" from the British legation.

The story tells how during the eight years of war, life in Peking becomes harsher and harsher and how the Japanese aided by the nefarious collaborators exploit, torture, imprison, or execute without cause, the common people of Peking. Lao She's love for Peking overflows in the novel. Writing, as he does, in war-torn Chungking or far-away America, he describes with passionate detail the beauty of Peking in the various seasons and recalls the smells and sights of this fair city with a tenderness that is not matched in any of his earlier works. By so describing life as it used to be, the festivals and colors, the preparation of foods, the easy rhythm of life that blended with seasonal changes, and contrasting this with what happened during the Occupation, he graphically highlights the destruction wrought by wars on civilization and culture.

But hope lies in the fact that the spirit of the people was not crushed. In fact the people were strengthened because of the ordeal. They were weak and exhausted, they had lost many beloved ones, their clothes were ragged and their houses shabby, but there was hope. After Japan's surrender, when Ch'ien came back "home" from prison and Jui-ch'üan from the partisans, Old Man Ch'i asks Jui-hsuan, whose little daughter had died of starvation the very day Japan surrendered, to "have all the neighbors come. It's a real celebration," and there was a smile on the old man's face. In the compound, "The leaves of the locust trees stirred. A fresh wind was rising."[21]

It is worth analyzing *Four Generations*—the last novel he wrote before he declared his allegiance to Communist China—to find out whether it indicates any radical change in Lao She's thinking on revolution or revolutionary ideology.

First, we find that the author lauds the people's capacity to resist and though privation and suffering can demean human nature, and he is not blind to such a development in Peking, he is proud that, by and large, suffering strengthened the people's backbone. The war had rejuvenated them. Mild and peace-loving Peking men and women now harbor anger and a desire for

revenge in their hearts. Fourth Master Liu refuses to perform the Dragon
Dance for the Japanese; rickshaw pullers will not serve traitors like the Kuans;
the mild Mrs. Jui-hsuan, who had never left the house and had never done a
thing without consulting her husband, becomes independent enough to sign a
petition to save a neighbor from the Japanese and stern enough to ask her
little son to use his fists when molested by the Japanese children in the compound. Jui-ch'üan can kill Chao-ti, Kuan's daughter who had become a Japanese spy, with his bare hands even though he had once been in love with her
and even now had some tender feelings for her. Kao-ti, Kuan's other daughter, not only revolts against her parents but has the courage to join the Japanese secret police so that she can help the resistance workers.

Lao She, who has all along emphasized the need for character, condemns
all those who are characterless traitors and collaborators and praises the youth
and commoners who want to fight the Japanese as the ones with character.
The lack of character in the Chinese running dogs ultimately destroys them.
There is a poetic sense of retribution in their rise and fall. They are the true
representatives of the "dog eat dog" society which had been denounced by
Lu Hsun and a host of others. They report against each other to the Japanese
and the end result is that Jui-feng is executed, the Japanese confiscate the
house and property of the Kuans, Mrs. Kuan dies in prison, and Mrs. Jui-feng,
who had left her husband and married the Japanese stooge Lan, ends up as a
prostitute in Tientsin.

But revenge and the capacity to kill, however important during war, cannot be the basis on which society can be built. It is, perhaps, in the way
Ch'ien changed during the course of the war that we can get a glimpse of Lao
She's thinking. After Ch'ien was so inhumanly tortured and came home to
find that his family had practically been wiped out, his anger was so great that
he made a vow never to drink again till Peking had been liberated. "I had no
plan and thought only of revenge . . . I was like a madman urging everyone to
'kill' [the enemy]. I was angry. I hated . . . I was a one-man army." [22]

But Ch'ien soon realized that that was not enough. It became clear to him
"that I must have friends and work with them in one heart and one strength
. . . I began to understand that one man daring to die was not as effective as
many working together. Good. I cared not what the plans of others were,
what political parties they belonged to, if only they came to me. I was willing to help. *They asked me to write. Good. I would write. If they asked me
to throw a bomb, good, I would go and throw it . . . I had no political ties, I
had no thoughts of personal vengeance or of furthering a career.*" [23] Does this
not give the impression that Lao She was summing up his own attitude toward
the war during the time he was in Chungking at the end of the Anti-Aggression

League of Chinese Writers—not serving the KMT or the CCP but serving the country to get rid of the Japanese scourge?

But it is the third stage through which Ch'ien goes that is most important for our appreciation of Lao She:

> The monk, Ming Yueh, is my best friend . . . When he first knew me my heart was full of vengeance and of killing. He—in spite of the fact that Peiping was conquered—did not give up his principles. He is opposed to killing . . . He felt that war was caused by that part of mankind's nature that walks on four feet, and that it was not the fault of any one man or group . . . He did not believe in killing because he felt that revenge would only help the crime grow and could not help do away with war, yet he carried the begging bowl that I might eat . . .
>
> . . . I was to some extent influenced by him. He taught me to see further. From wanting revenge only I began to look at the whole problem of doing away with war. I saw that our *resistance was not only for revenge—an eye for an eye and a tooth for a tooth—but it was also to do away with the love of war so as to establish peace for the future.*
>
> When the war first started . . . I forgot my ideals and my poetry and went out to fight to the death with the wild beasts. While working I have found my ideals again . . . I was a man who loved peace; now I am that man again. If there is a difference, it is that before the war I often took indulgence and indolence for love of peace, and now I use determination and courage to achieve peace.[24]

Lao She in his article, "Hsien-t'an wo ti ch'i-ko hua-chü" (Random thoughts on my seven plays), had mentioned the need for artists and writers to join the war so that all wars could be eliminated. In the passage quoted above he elaborates on the same theme and tries to work it into a philosophy of sorts. It is, therefore, understandable that he is highly critical of the use of the atom bomb: "Science had reached beyond all other realms of human thought and had invented the atom bomb. Just as blundering and stupid as the Japanese, who had never thought what the world should be . . . was the creation of the atom bomb by those who had never thought what the world should be. That atomic energy was first used for war is the greatest shame of the human race."[25]

Lao She, the liberal humanist, the Confucian socialist, witnessed the horrors and the tragedy of war, and the death and destruction and economic disruption it led to. He wants to use this experience to build a new China, a new world. His cynicism born of the ineffectual nature of middle-class intellectuals is replaced by a certain faith in the common people and in the emergence of a more aggressive, more demanding new youth. Like Jui-hsuan and Ch'ien he had discovered a truth:

> A people who have not much knowledge have deep feeling . . . A man can easily get knowledge but the depth of one's being cannot be cultivated in a short time. He remembered the battles of Shanghai and Taierchuang, and the nameless heroes who fought in them. Were they not— most of them—unlettered countrymen? Most likely they could not even write the two words "country" and "nation"; but they had sacrificed their lives for their country, looking on death as a home-going. And he thought of those with knowledge, like himself—afraid of the wolf in front and the tiger behind—who dared not go forward courageously. Knowledge, it seemed, bound emotion.[26]

The conditions under which the common people lived needed to be drastically altered; the ruling elite which did not accept the responsibility of making this change ought to be destroyed and replaced. The people had tremendous reserves of energy and if properly led by a new elite that understood the correlation between "true" knowledge and "true" action, China could be once again transformed into the most cultured and civilized country in the world— powerful, yet peace-loving. Lao She, therefore, might well believe that he was needed in a new China that was being created by the Communist government, and which held forth all the promise he could have wished for.

Before we leave *Four Generations* and move on to Lao She's post-1949 life, there is one incident in the novel which must be mentioned: the suicide of Ch'i T'ien-yu. Since Lao She himself committed suicide in 1966, it is worth examining his attitude in the novel toward the problem of taking one's own life.

The most surprising element in the description of T'ien-yu's end is that Lao She does not condemn it as an act of escape or cowardice. In a novel in which he is encouraging people to develop the strength to resist Japan, suicide should have met with Lao She's disapproval. On the contrary, he gives the act an air of quiet dignity.

T'ien-yu is, in the tradition of the very best of the old-time businessmen, a mild-mannered, polite, and honest man. He is not ambitious, but he loves his work and never complains or tires of spending all his waking hours in the shop. After the Occupation his business shrinks and gradually he has to dispense with the services of his clerks whom he has always treated with complete kindness and consideration. The Japanese issue rules and regulations that make it impossible for him to carry on the business. The final blow comes when the Japanese, for a fault of their own henchmen, declare T'ien-yu to be a "profiteer."

They drag him out of the shop, make him wear a jacket with the word "profiteer" written on it, and order him to shout, "I am a profiteer," while parading him in the streets where he had been honored for his upright character and dignified behavior.

The humiliation shattered his world and there was no way for him to rebuild it:

> His mind was blank, his old father, his sick wife, his three sons, his daughter-in-law, his grandson and granddaughter, and his shop seemed all to have never existed. He saw only the moat and that loveable water, as though the water . . . beckoned to him. He nodded. His world was gone. He must go to another world. In this other world his shame could be washed away . . . Floating, floating, floating, he was floating to the great ocean where he would have freedom—cool, clean, and happy freedom, which would wash away the red letters on his breast.[27]

According to one account Lao She committed suicide by jumping into Peihai, the lake near the Imperial Palaces. Like T'ien-yu, he had been falsely accused of being a traitor and had been utterly humiliated. Like T'ien-yu his world was so shattered that he had no other way out. In spite of all his attacks on the Chinese traditional emphasis of face, it was, perhaps, his loss of face that left Lao She with no choice but to take his own life. One hopes that death brought him the "cool, clean, happy freedom" which was denied him by the authoritarian regime which he had gone to serve so enthusiastically.

EPILOGUE, 1950–1966

Lao She's return to China should in no way be interpreted as a reflection of any secret leaning toward communism. Most, if not all, of the great names in the world of literature and art had opted to serve the new regime. According to Wang Yü, "from the list prepared by the Political Consultative Conference in June 1949 [it appeared that] more or less, all the elite had been ensnared and never in the history of China has any Emperor been able to bring together so many intellectuals under him."[1] This was to a great extent the result of the failure of the KMT ideology and its policies toward the country as a whole, particularly its treatment of the intellectuals. The CCP, on the other hand, had assiduously built up an image of much reasonableness and held forth hope to the patriotic intelligentsia desirous of building the nation.

Lao She was intensely patriotic. His writings show how deeply he felt the need to radically change society, to destroy the corrupt elite, and give the common people a better chance in life. He despised the superficial urban middle-class intellectuals and the "modern" education that produced them. The country, according to Lao She, called for hard-working, dedicated, self-sacrificing youth. Love was an emotion that had to be suppressed in the larger interest of national reconstruction. Women, poor or rich, educated or uneducated, were enslaved and must be liberated. Chinese culture had to be reshaped so that a new man could emerge.

In all this he indeed approximated the Communist ideal. Add to this Lao She's growing faith in the common people, "the masses," and we have the makings of a "people's artist." As far as his personal life was concerned, Lao She had all along complained bitterly of his poverty and had repeatedly said that "society should look after the needs of the artist," so that the artist could concentrate on his creative work. Society and government are in many ways synonymous, particularly in the Chinese tradition. In Hong Kong, on his way to Peking, he also mentioned the fact that the "KMT government did not 'respect' literary men," implying, obviously, his desire to be respected.[2]

In certain significant ways Lao She's expectations of the new government were immediately justified. Back in his beloved Peking, he was put on the government payroll, and found an old-style house where he could grow his flowers and do his writing without worrying about finances. If he had wanted respect he was given more than his fill. Among the offices he occupied, sooner or later, the following are worthy of mention: People's Representative from Peking City to the National People's Congress; Member of the Chinese People's Political Consultative Conference; Member of the Peking City People's Council; Vice-Chairman of the Federation of Writers and Artists; Chairman

148

of the Peking Writers Union; and Deputy Director of the Peking Russia-China Friendship Association. He was also connected with the organization set up to propagate the standard dialect, with the Federation of Afro-Asian Writers, and the Committee for Looking After Foreign Guests.

But when all is said and done, Lao She was a liberal humanist and if he had certain convictions or had come to certain conclusions about his country and his people, they were the results of his own personal experience, and not the product of any ready-made ideology. He was, in a manner of speaking, an elitist who believed that he had an important role to play and though his sympathies were for the downtrodden, he had never accepted a simplistic formula for a good society. Indeed, he himself points out the fact that he avoided the so-called radical schools of literature because they appeared, to him, hollow and slogan-ridden.

How did such a person fit himself into the Communist scheme of things? Lao She went enthusiastically and voluntarily to a China where politics was not only in command of all spheres of individual and social activity, but had become the very essence of literature. New literature was to have a class character, it was to be for and about the heroic workers, peasants, and soldiers; it was to serve the great cause of building a true socialist society. It appears that stringent guidelines alone could not change the writers into true Maoist thinkers and so, to gain conformity, the party had to periodically organize rectification campaigns which attacked, humiliated, and often destroyed well-known writers. If famous leftist writers like Hu Feng and Ting Ling could be demolished, one need not add that scores of others, who were never closely attached to the party, also came in for severe criticism and thought reform. As time passed the circle of those attacked became larger and larger and in the last campaign for purification—The Great Proletarian Cultural Revolution (GPCR)—Lao She was beaten by the Red Guards. As a result he committed suicide.

Yet during the sixteen years that he lived in Communist China, Lao She continued to produce. In fact, he was perhaps the only writer belonging to the older generation who was so prolific. Mao Tun, Kuo Mo-jo, Pa Chin, Shen Ts'ung-wen, and others had hardly a noteworthy output—some just faded away! In spite of his public duties and his illness (he had leg trouble, which kept him from moving about much), Lao She wrote continuously. Had Lao She indeed become, in the words of Cyril Birch, "a master craftsman"? Lacking "a message" or a "line," was his production similar to that of a "plumber or an engineer"?[3]

The answer, one suspects, is far more complex. Until 1949 Lao She had shown himself to be a man of tremendous character—a true scholar in the traditional sense who, if we follow Mencius' definition [Mencius, III, ii, 2], could not be corrupted by riches and position, who was not swayed by poverty, and who stood steadfast in the face of power and violence. It is true that he had camouflaged his writings so that the real meaning was partially hidden, but no one would ever dispute the fact that his works exposed corruption and nepotism and denounced the government of the day.

It appears that in the beginning Lao She was more than happy to serve the new government. It stood for practically everything that he had stood for, and since it needed all the help it could get to stabilize the country, and bring it peace and order and dignity, Lao She was happy to make his contribution.

We should also remember that unlike those who were party members or very closely allied to the party, Lao She had no bones to pick with the policies being formulated. He was an outsider wanting to belong. There is no reason whatsoever not to accept the fact that Lao She was truly in favor of what was happening in the country after the Communist takeover. If in 1937, he could sacrifice his true medium of expression—fiction—to write propaganda plays (which he knew would not be successful) because he wanted to help the country, why should he not make a similar sacrifice now? Indeed, we find that Lao She, no doubt realizing the need for the new government to make propaganda, reverted to playwriting—with considerable success this time. His wartime training stood him in good stead.

As time passed Lao She began to feel the suffocation born of endless controls and though he did not stop writing, we can see glimpses of irony and satire that make the study of this period so interesting. In a preface written in 1950 to a collection of his short stories, Lao She says:

> I myself was born in poverty, and, therefore, I have a deep sympathetic feeling toward those who suffer. Although my work has kept me in the field of intellectuals, my friends are not found only among teachers and professors. Boxers, singers, rickshaw pullers are also my friends. And when I have social intercourse with the poor, I do not only sit with them in a teahouse and secretly record their actions and their conversations. I have never done such things . . . I only want to make friends. They help me and I help them. They come to wish me happiness on my birthday, and I go to do the same when there is a marriage or a birth in their homes.[4]

This is not the first time that Lao She has mentioned his childhood poverty and his natural inclination to make friends among the lower strata of society, and, therefore, one cannot consider this statement as one in which he is trying to score points with the Communist government. Lao She may have overemphasized his impoverished background but he has done so consistently and, in fact, it cannot be denied that most of the other great writers did come from more affluent homes.

He goes on to say that in his younger days he had studied classical prose writing in the style of the *t'ung-ch'eng-p'ai,** and poetry in the style of Lu Fang-weng and Wu Mei-ts'un. The May Fourth Movement changed all that and he became "madly happy" with *pai-hua.* There was an upsurge of romanticism following the May Fourth Movement, but "one could not completely ignore the great affairs of the nation."[5] Lao She also refers to the Russian Revolution and Marxism and indicates that these things also affected him. He had never said this earlier and one feels uneasy and wonders whether Lao She's memory is not discovering details which had never really existed! But we can rest easy because, a little further on, he tells us with remarkable frankness of how he reacted, on his return from England, to the literary world in the China of the thirties:

> On returning home I found that literary polemics had already shifted from the subject of literary revolution to that of revolutionary literature. In the field of creative literature there was the rise of popular literature based on a well-worked-out theory. I am not one of those who ventures to discuss theory lightly. So I continued to write actively and did not participate in the polemics.[6]

Lao She was not taking sides because he trusted his own insights and if there were any theories which were going to guide him they would be the product of his understanding.

Lao She goes on to say that he expressed indignant sorrow on behalf of the miserable poor but he never tried to lead them on the path of revolution. Why?

First, I saw that in the revolutionary literature of the day, the contents

---

* T'ungcheng School of Prose Writers was founded by Fang Pao (1668–1747) who hailed from T'ungcheng County in Anhui province. According to Ch'en Shou-yi, the guiding principle of the school in reviving classical (*ku-wen*) prose was that "the writings of the Chou and Ch'in dynasties and before contained everything in the way of basic principles of writings. Writers of the Han and Sung dynasties were not without faults although they had watched every single step they had taken." Ch'en Shou-yi, *Chinese Literature* (New York, The Ronald Press Company, 1961), pp. 571–572.

often lacked a quality of wholeness; characters were not moving, but there were large numbers of radical slogans . . . Second, I knew only a little bit about the theory of revolution which I had picked up from books in a confused manner. I dared not use this little bit of theory to write about the reality of revolution. Third, my literary training had, after all, come from what I had read of Western classical literature. Therefore, I could never forget that one should pay respect to characters, language, thought, the unities, background, scenery, and so on, and not solely emphasize thought in a biased way.[7]

Having made his stand clear, Lao She concludes the preface with words of praise for the People's Revolution and Mao Tse-tung, and an expression of hope that he will continue to study creative writing and produce according to the directions of Mao Tse-tung.

In 1952, when Lao She had already written a few plays, he wrote an article, "Mao chu-hsi kei-la wo hsin ti wen-i sheng-ming" (Chairman Mao gave me a new literary life), for the *People's Daily* in a series commemorating Mao's Yenan Forum on Art and Literature.[8] After confessing vigorously to his shortcomings—the shortcomings of a petty bourgeois writer who had a "sense of righteousness" but no understanding of or enthusiasm for "the revolutionary struggle"—he tells us how Mao's lectures on literature and art, which Lao She read for the first time on his return to China in 1949, made him doubt his past work and gave him a clearer picture of what literature was all about. Though he was "bewildered on learning Chairman Mao's principle of subordination of literature and art to politics,"[9] he, however, began to follow the new precepts assiduously and this is reflected in his post-1949 plays. We shall have occasion to analyze some of these plays later in this chapter.

The two important points that Lao She makes in this essay are that on the one hand, he is grateful to Mao Tse-tung for having provided him with an opportunity to serve the country, which he loved so dearly; on the other hand, he was "a man hailing from the old society [and] I would only be trying to fool myself and other people if I were to pretend to change into a present-day thinker overnight."[10] This apology also forms the main theme of the concluding paragraph, which looks like an abject and humiliating self-criticism, but should be seen as a necessary ritualistic formula:

I am still far from being a writer schooled in the thoughts of Chairman Mao Tse-tung, but I shall forever try to advance step by step in accordance to Chairman Mao's instructions, as well as to rectify all my faults in thought and life. Only thus shall I be prevented from being impeded by the burdens of the 'old writer,' enabled to accept all criticisms

with all modesty, and given a new lease of life in literature and art.
I am grateful to Chairman Mao.
Long live Chairman Mao.[11]

Lao She's expression of loyalty to the new regime and his ardent desire to serve it disturbed many of his friends who could not believe that Lao She was capable of such sycophantic sentiments. If we remember that although Lao She had no ideology to propagate, he had in all his pre-1949 writings incessantly harped on the need for the "old society" to be destroyed and a "new society" to be created, then his hymns of praise become understandable. As long as he believed that the Communist party (or Mao Tse-tung) was trying to do away with the evils of the old society, evils which Lao She had attacked so passionately in his novels and plays, he wholeheartedly supported Mao.

It must also be remembered that he was not after personal fame or riches. As soon as he started to receive enough in the way of royalties, he voluntarily gave up his government stipend. On one occasion he was given the opportunity to go to Peitaiho, a health resort, to relax and recuperate. He declined to go because he felt that, "the country is not yet rich enough and all must tighten their belts and help in the reconstruction."[12] Lao She never fought for position or power and though he had been given a few offices they were without much influence. His modesty and selflessness cannot be denied by his worst critics.

Gradually one notices a change in Lao She's attitude toward the new regime. To support the regime in its national construction efforts was one thing; to have to suppress all one's thought and feeling was quite another. In Lao She's plays we find his new attitudes emerging. His public statement uses the same camouflage which had once helped him to avoid arrest by the KMT. However, even this careful man could not but heave a sigh of relief at the time of the Hundred Flowers Campaign in 1957, when the intellectuals were given a brief opportunity to air their grievances. Referring to the years that had elapsed since the founding of the People's Republic he said, "such a long winter—it was too much to suffer from." Describing the atmosphere engendered by the Hundred Flowers period, he wrote a letter in which he said: "As I write this letter, the baby is reciting a poem, the brick-layer is singing . . . the carpenter is singing . . . and in the western room young Miss Chou is listening to a broadcast of new poetry read in a clear voice. Can all this be called the blooming of the Hundred Flowers? If it is so, then although this year's autumn has come a little late, it is specially lovable."[13]

Since Lao She was not showing the change in his writings which the party demanded, his plays came in for increasing criticism. *Ch'ing-nien t'u-chi-tui* (The young shock troop) was publicly attacked by Hsia-shun, and the play was taken off the stage. Lao She carried on patiently but stubbornly. He could not be frightened into submission. In the Thirteenth Session of the Enlarged Conference of the Writers' Union, he finally spoke out:

> I know that there are people who do not respect me. They say that to have made me the Vice-Chairman of the Writers' Union is to have raised me too high. I say it is not at all high.
>
> I am not a person who wants to clamber upwards. I am incapable of recommending myself to the leaders and asking them to make me a Vice-Chairman. I have my good point—I do not boast.
>
> If I am not made the Vice-Chairman, I am not going to revolt. If I am called upon to be a member of the Standing Committee or even a common member of the Union—even that is all right.[14]

Lao She wrote about the changes taking place around him, selecting aspects which he agreed with and rejecting others which he could not accept. He totally rejected class struggle as a theme for his writings. As a writer he still rose to great heights when dealing with or describing the old society. He said that this was because he understood the old society and that the new was beyond his full comprehension. Could it not be that he had found it difficult to reconcile himself to what was new in the new society? He had once sought the renovation of society and he had been enthused by the first steps taken by the Communist party but as time passed he must have realized that his vision was far from being fulfilled.

Lung hsu kou (Dragon beard ditch), written in 1950, deals with the life of the poor who live along the side of a big sewage canal in Peking, and shows what a change took place after the Communist government came to power. Before the Liberation, the tenants living in shacks had no drinking water. They suffered from smells from the putrifying matter in the canal, and from the flies and mosquitoes, their dwellings collapsed when it rained, they suffered from malaria, their children drowned in the canal, and they were exploited by the local thugs. They were unwanted by society. After the Liberation, the government cleans up the canal, gets rid of the bullies, provides work for the unemployed, and gives the residents a new lease on life.

Lao She is lyrical about the government's new concern for the poor. He does not care whether the people are real participants in the political processes of the country or not. All he wants is a good government. From his first novel onward that was all that he had ever demanded: a government that would have the people's interest at heart. He had never recommended a parliamentary government or a Communist government! Like a commoner in traditional China, he only seemed aware that governments could be good or bad. And here at last was a good government. The government and the people never had any connection. They stood on two opposing sides, or on two different levels: above and below. This dichotomy comes out even in the play:

> The People's Government is truly great.
> It's truly great for it mended the ditch
> And took great pains for us though we were not rich.[15]

If one were to substitute the word "emperor" for "government" in the following lines, it would make not a whit of difference:

> When the Government saw it [the ditch] their very heart sank.
> A first rate government, loving all poor men.[16]

It is in the same strain that Ting Szu says in the play: "The Government have played fair by us, and we must play fair by them isn't that right?" And Old Chao's answer is simple but categorical: "That's it."

In 1955, we find that Lao She is able to revert to a type of writing he does best—writing which exposes the weaknesses and vices of society. In that year, Lo Jui-ch'ing, the then Minister for Security, brought to the notice of the People's Congress a case regarding one Li Wen-ming, an imposter who had infiltrated the party posing as a wounded hero and not only had managed to remain undetected for a long time, but had received honors and preferential treatment from cadres and party members. Lao She immediately fashioned a play out of this material.

Hsi-wang Ch'ang-an (Looking westward to Ch'ang-an)[17] shows up two weaknesses of the Communist government. First, by creating heroes, the Communist party was establishing an elite that was above criticism, and which had an open door to the highest echelons of the government. Second, and as a corollary to the first point, the cadres and party members who were ambitious tried to ingratiate themselves with such heroes. By implication, such officials of the party and government would, no doubt, expect similar servility from those below them or from the common people over whom they rule.

Lao She was the first and perhaps the only writer to put cadres and party members on the stage and ridicule them. It was, and still is, impossible to represent the Liberation Army or the Communist party in a work of literature and not give the representatives superhuman qualities. Lao She satirizes the ruling elite by revealing how, under the cloak of empty slogans, a new type of corruption had come to exist. In the play Li Wan-ch'eng, the imposter "party member," "hero," and "cadre," uses the correct political jargon to hide behind and, with a certain amount of discreet name-dropping, manages to rise higher and higher. Nobody dares challenge the words of a hero and so Li, with comparative ease, works his way into the central administration. The play ends with the security police discovering Li's true identity—a landlord's son and member of the KMT—and arresting him.

In this play Lao She laughs at the myth of the hero as fostered by the Communist party. Obviously, he is not any happier with the way the new bureaucracy is working than he was with it under the Kuomintang.

Looking Westward to Ch'ang-an pleased many critics and writers, particularly, one suspects, those who did not like the policies of the Communist government. Referring to the play, Wang Yü says that Lao She used material from real life to expose the local leaders:

> He entered deeply into the bottom of their shameless souls, and put these characters on the stage making the audience laugh with happiness. At this time to write satirical plays was to brave danger . . . There were people who decried satirical plays as a backward phenomenon . . . [and argued] that one could not represent members of the party, or dramatize the Liberation Army . . . Lao She pushed this aside and fearlessly wrote the play. Lao She points out that "the obstacles and corruption in our lives, if they find a suitable soil to exist in, will start growing and developing." . . . This was indeed the true Lao She who had never been tempted by personal fame or position.[18]

There was criticism too, and some critics went so far as to say that this play "tranquilized the counterrevolutionaries (*su-fan*)." Lao She, as he usually did, apologized that his "living experience" was not sufficient and that for him to write about the new society was like looking "at a cat and trying to draw a tiger."[19]

As is now well known, the brooding resentment which the intellectuals nourished against the regime came out in a torrent in the period of the Hundred Flowers Campaign in 1957. At about this time Lao She wrote, what may be aptly termed, his greatest play, *Ch'a-kuan* (Teahouse).

He was now nearly sixty years old, but he still had the youthfulness of spirit and mental vitality to break new paths. In *Teahouse* he ignores practically every rule which is supposed to make a good play and yet manages to produce a unique masterpiece. Perhaps it would be correct to say that *Teahouse* is not a drama in the accepted sense of the word—it has no unity of time, it lacks a central plot, and it has no story to tell. The three acts of the play (there are no scenes) are set in 1898, 1917, and 1945 respectively, and each one of them represents a phase in the development of Chinese society over a span of fifty years. The teahouse and the manager of the teahouse provide a sense of unity and continuity to the play.

As the play unfolds the audience is given a glimpse of history, the nature of the social and political changes that mark the last years of the Manchu rule, the decline of China into warlordism, and the end of the Nationalist period. With a Lao-she-esque abandon the stage is crowded with nearly seventy characters who come from all walks of Peking life. There are fortune-tellers, marriage-brokers, reciters of stories, Manchus, eunuchs, spies, students, teachers, members of secret societies, soldiers, peddlers, and officials.

The author, with a few deft touches, brings to life a whole panorama like a traditional Chinese painting scroll, and each act of the play can, indeed, be looked upon as an artistically worked out vignette. In his desire to touch upon as many aspects of social development as possible, Lao She has recourse to subtle references, hints, and understatements. To cover fifty years of change and development in a short play is obviously impossible. Lao She makes use of every device he can, including realistic stage properties. In each act the teahouse presents a different setting, changing with the times. The beams on which patrons hang their bird and cricket cages in 1898 disappear by 1917; the tables acquire tablecloths, and the benches give way to chairs; scrolls depicting the "eight drunk immortals" or the "god of wealth" are replaced with pictures of fashion models advertising cigarettes; and electric lights take over from old-style lamps. Similarly the costumes of the cast change from act to act and we come to see how fashion changed over the decades.

Teahouse is Lao She's appraisal of the Chinese Revolution. It is his commentary on state and society, and we come to know as much about what he believes from what is said in the play as we do from what is left unsaid but subtly hinted at. Writing in Communist China, soon after the intellectuals had been suppressed in the 1957 Anti-rightist campaign, Lao She obviously cannot give his judgment of the current scene. That he is generally reluctant to discuss political ideologies is apparent in the way the play is structured.

The first act has a few oblique references to K'ang Yu-wei and T'an Ssu-t'ung, and these only go to show that the majority of the people are not much aware of the Reform Movement or the imperial reasons behind its suppression. If a man like Fourth Master Ch'ang feels that the "Manchu government must go" it is not because of his appreciation of K'ang or T'an, but because he sees in the rising tide of human suffering and the repressive measures of the government the end of a dynastic cycle.

The second act is laid in 1917. If it had been 1919 Lao She would have had to bring in student agitation and the May Fourth movement, so he cleverly avoids this issue. Once again his emphasis is on the inhumanity of the times. The ruthlessness of the warlords, as brought out by the increasing numbers of refugees, the increased impoverishment of the people, the exactions of the soldiers, and the continued uncontrolled activities of the spies, all point to the fact that there is still a crying need for change that would bring back a good government.

The last act deals with Peking soon after the defeat of Japan. Lao She is able to attack the perfidious nature of the Nationalist government without having to refer to the Communist party or the Liberation Army because they were not on the scene. Peking as represented in the teahouse is a total shambles, inflation is reducing to a state of desperation even those who had survived the worst of the past fifty years, the government is looting its own people, the local commanders are vicious corruptors of morals and debauchees who symbolize the lowest level which human nature can sink to. Once again the author's message is clear: the government must change.

Lao She does not introduce any foreigners in the play but he effectively reveals the growing presence of the foreign powers. In Act I, Lao She touches upon two aspects of this foreign presence. First, there are persons like Mr. Ma who "eat foreign rice, believe in foreign religion, speak a foreign language, and if there is any matter [he wants to discuss] he goes directly to the . . . district magistrate . . . even the officials are afraid of provoking him!"[20] If Mr. Ma has so much social power and prestige because of his association with the foreigners, one can easily imagine what awful power the foreigners themselves must be wielding. Second, we notice how many foreign articles are coming into common use. Liu Ma-tzu, the marriage broker, is proud of his imported snuff and his foreign watch, and of his clothes which are made of foreign material. Liu represents the community of people who have no sense of nationalism and so Lao She sarcastically makes him declare: "Foreign things are really smart. If I were to wear clothes made of the local cloth I would look like a country bumpkin. Who would respect me then?"[21]

In Act II, the encroachments made by the foreigners have a more deadly significance. The governments are run by the warlords but the warlords are manipulated by the foreigners who encourage them to fight each other.

In the last act Lao She identifies the foreigner as the United States and shows how in 1945 America was omnipresent on the Chinese scene. While

American jeeps have become a hazard on the Peking streets, Chinese girls are becoming "jeep girls" who serve the American soldiers, the KMT currency is looked upon as trash and everybody wants to possess U.S. dollars, and the peddler chants: "American needles, American thread, American toothpaste, American medicine. I also have lipstick, shaving cream, nylon stockings. The box is small but the goods are all there. The only thing I don't sell is the atom bomb." [22] And this is the year of China's glory—the year Japan is defeated.

Although Lao She tries to round off his picture of the Chinese scene by referring to the foreigners, he in no way seems to imply that they are the target of his attack. They are an evil which has to be destroyed but the anger and indignation which he arouses in the audience is directed against the government. The governments change but the callousness and the corruption of the ruling class remain the continuing factors. It matters little that the imperial system has given way to the republican, or that the warlords have been replaced by the KMT. Lao She, the critic of an inhuman and unjust society, provides no political solutions, recommends no ideologies, but like a censor of the past, exposes the evil he sees and rouses public indignation. The Mandate of Heaven has obviously been withdrawn from the government in power and Lao She only helps to bring this fact home. There must, inevitably, be a *ko-ming,* and if one translates this as "revolution" or renders it literally as "depriving the ruler of the divine mandate," it is of no consequence.

It is extremely significant that *Teahouse* falls far short of true "revolutionary literature," in the Maoist sense of the phrase. It lacks all reference to revolution and gives one no feeling of optimism. On the contrary, the growing atmosphere of pessimism culminates at the end of the last act in the ritualistic funeral ceremony in which Wang Li-fa (the manager of the teahouse), Fourth Master Ch'ang (the nationalistic, patriotic Manchu), and Ch'in Chung-yi (landlord of the teahouse and the man who tried to "save China by developing industry") take part. Who would not shed a tear at seeing these three old and worthy citizens of China who had spent half a century trying to do the right thing and hoping that one day life would improve, now impoverished and bowed with age and with the humiliations they had suffered, standing in the middle of the stage throwing paper money over their white heads and performing their own funeral service? Soon after this last meeting Wang Li-fa, indeed, hangs himself as if to show that the funeral service was not a jest.

Lao She's humor and the fact that he had originally been inspired by Dickens has led many to compare him to Dickens and even refer to him as the "Dickens of China." This is misleading. To understand Lao She it is necessary to remember that though all his life he wrote literature that exposed social abuse and relentlessly attacked the evils of bureaucracy, he is quite different from Dickens, the social reformer. Dickens attacked social ills in a narrower framework, hoping to draw attention to spheres of life where reform was needed. Thus Dickens is worried about debtor's prisons, about homes for orphans, about conditions of work in factories and mills, about slums, and so on. These things can be remedied by laws enacted by parliament and by a heightened sense of social responsibility.

Lao She's worry is for the nation as a whole and his concern is with government in the broad meaning of the term. The streak of pessimism which comes out in practically every one of Lao She's writings contrasts strongly with the optimism which Dickens reveals in his. And, of course, Lao She has no faith in charity and never tries to conclude his works with happy endings as Dickens does.

The vast gloom and suffocating pessimism of *Teahouse* follow the tragic vein of his earlier writings, particularly the very first novels that he ever wrote. But underlying Lao She's pessimism, it must immediately be added, is a basic optimism. By showing how the good people are crushed by an evil ruling class, he stresses the underlying hope that given a better government they can make China a great country. The strength of the nation lies in its common people and they are basically good. Good people only need to be led by a good government for the miracle to take place. This echo of the Confucian ideal, is indeed, the implied moral.

When the Communist government took over, Lao She, no doubt, felt that the long awaited change had at last come and he hurried back to be a part of the miracle. As time passed his earlier enthusiasm seems to have been dampened to some extent. Lao She exulted in and praised the government when it was good to the people; but he found it hard to accept a government above criticism. As a literatus following the censorial role it was for him to decide what was to be praised and what to be decried. The modern concept of freedom of speech added to the traditional role of censor gave Lao She a certain birthright which he felt he could not be denied.

In *Teahouse* Lao She expresses, in a most effective manner, his resentment against being gagged. In the first act we see long strips of paper with the characters *mo-t'an kuo shih* (do not discuss national [state] affairs) pasted on the walls of the teahouse. In each subsequent act, other things change, but these strips of paper are continuously there. The only difference where these signs are concerned, is that their number increases and the size of the characters becomes larger. Times change, traditions die, old fashions give place to new, Imperial China turns into a Republic, the warlords are displaced by the KMT, but the admonishment "*mo-t'an kuo-shih*" is always there.

No official censor in Communist China could possibly object to Lao She putting up these slogans on the walls of the teahouse. After all they only helped to reveal the extent of suppression exercised by the reactionary governments of the past! One wonders, however, how many sitting among the audience in 1958, watching this play, the year following the Hundred Flowers and the rectification campaigns, would have missed reading a secret message in these four characters?

Those who opted to live under the Communist regime hoped, like Lao She, that at last they would be granted the basic freedoms denied to them over the decades. They had been hounded by the KMT secret police, had been censored and forced into silence, yet never during the Chungking days had the government been successful in wholly suppressing expressions of disapproval. Now, on the contrary, under the Communist regime, when the people thought they would regain their lost freedom, the restrictions were throttling them completely.

All his life Lao She had been preoccupied with the problems of society as reflected in the nature of human suffering, in social injustice, in the destruction of good people by the forces of evil born of corruption and callousness. The underlying theme was always that a government run by rapacious officers who exploit the poor and innocent gave an opportunity to the wicked to exercise brutality and savagery and hold the country in thralldom. He was never interested in political theories and ideologies per se. He was in a manner of speaking above politics but never unconcerned with politics. Lao She did not uphold one type of government against another. All he tried to do was to point out that regardless of what type of government came into power it would be judged by the manner in which it ameliorated the living conditions of the vast masses and gave an opportunity to the intellectuals to contribute to the development of the country in a healthy, free atmosphere. In some ways this stand has strong overtones of the literati ruling class ideals.

The Communist government was a good government as far as the first point is concerned but deficient with regard to the second. Why must one be wholly for a government or wholly against it? Lao She baffles the simple-minded critics who look upon Chinese writers as "pro-Communist" or as "anti-Communist." He is a patriotic, nationalistic Chinese and he loves the new government because it has achieved so much for China. If he is critical of it, it is because he has hopes for it. And *mo-t'an kuo-shih* is, perhaps, Lao She's greatest indictment of the Communist government.

One other way in which Lao She reviles the Communist government for not differentiating between criticism voiced by the intellectuals who loved China and that which came from China's enemies, is by introducing a Manchu character in the play. Fourth Master Ch'ang, a Manchu bannerman, is one of the most positive of the characters in *Teahouse*. However important the benefits he personally receives from being a bannerman may be, they do not keep him from having strong nationalistic feelings and from reacting rather passionately to the increasing degradation of society that he sees around him. This leads him to remark: "As I see it, the Ch'ing dynasty is about to end."[23] This comment, which he makes to a friend of his, is overheard by one of the spies in the teahouse and Ch'ang is arrested. He protests, "I love the Ch'ing dynasty and [I said this only because] I am worried that it will collapse."[24] There is, however, no appeal against the action of a spy. The height of irony is that while he is being handcuffed, he reveals that he himself is a Manchu, implying thereby that he has no reason to be an enemy of the dynasty. The spy's retort is that this only makes him doubly guilty!

In using Manchu characters in the play, Lao She seems to have also, at last, unburdened himself of a weight that he had carried hidden in his heart all his life. Though he himself was a Manchu he had never before used any Manchu figures in any of his writings. The camouflage that was necessary after 1911 for a Manchu to avoid being attacked, kept Lao She from ever standing up for his much-maligned community. Now in this play he introduces two Manchu characters representing two different types of people. Like Ch'ang, Second Master Sung is also a good man but a weak one. He is ready to humble himself in front of petty officials and spies because he does not want any trouble.

By 1917 both Sung and Ch'ang have been reduced to poverty. In spite of all his excessive humility, Sung, who is the more educated of the two, is no better off than Ch'ang who has to scrape for a living by peddling vegetables. When the two meet in Act II, it is after a lapse of several years and this gives Lao She the occasion to reveal something of what the Manchus had to suffer:

> Ch'ang: . . . *Erh Yeh,* how are you?
> Sung: How am I: I would like to shed a flood of tears! Haven't you seen what clothes I'm wearing? Do I still look like a human being?
> Ch'ang: Second Brother, is it possible that you who can read and calculate cannot find some work to do?
> Sung: Is there anyone who would deliberately go hungry? But who wants us bannermen? When one thinks of it the Great Ch'ing dynasty was not necessarily good but once we got the Republic I began to starve.[25]

It is Ch'ang, however, who represents the best of the Manchus. "Not long after I was released from jail," he recounts, "it was in the *keng-tzu* year (1900) that

I joined the Boxers whose slogan was: support the Ch'ing, and destroy the foreigners. We fought a few battles with the foreigners . . . In the end the Ch'ing dynasty came to an end—as it deserved to. I am a Manchu but I must speak honestly. Now I get up at five in the morning and go around with a load of fresh vegetables which I manage to sell by ten o'clock. I make my living by depending on my own strength and my body has become more energetic. If ever the foreigners dare to make war again I, with the surname of Ch'ang, am still prepared to go and fight them. I am a Manchu and the Manchus are also *Chung-kuo-jen* (Chinese)."[26]

It seems to have been most important to Lao She to say, loud and clear, that not all Manchus were traitors and, indeed, in an age when there was no shortage of Han traitors, there were still Manchus who were ready to sacrifice their lives for China. Lao She told Ida Pruitt, when she was visiting Peking in the 1950s, that "Mao Tse-tung himself has told me that not all Manchus were a total blight on China."[27]

Teahouse was both praised and criticized. It was praised primarily for having so effectively revealed the history of the past and for giving the audience the flavor of the social conditions that had existed in the three eras of the play. The criticisms ranged from the charge that the play could not be easily put on the stage for it had too many characters, or that it had no proper development of characters, to (more importantly) the judgment that it lacked positive elements and political orientation (*hung-hsien:* lit., "red line").[28]

Though Lao She did not stop writing after *Teahouse,* it will suffice for our purpose to consider this play as the last great work in which he could manage to express himself without having to introduce Communist slogans and to force himself to emphasize revolution. Gradually *Teahouse* and even his earlier plays came in for stronger criticism. It was said that he "presumed on his old age to despise others" (*i-lao mai-lao*) and Feng Hsueh-feng once called him "backward" (*lo-huo*).[29]

It is difficult to believe that in the decade-and-a-half that Lao She lived under communism, he could not comprehend the nature of the new changes and write about them. It is, however, not difficult to understand why he would use this as an apology whenever criticized for writing the way he did.

In 1966, just before his death, Lao She was interviewed by a visiting foreign couple, Roma and Stuart Gelder, who have set down Lao She's replies at length, in their book.[30] In spite of the fact that Lao She's comments, like those of any Chinese in Communist China talking to a foreigner, are guarded and follow the official line, they are worth quoting because they provide us, in however diluted a fashion, with Lao She's defense of himself:

"Tell me," he [Lao She] said, "about Piccadilly and Leicester Square and Hyde Park and St. James' and the Green Park. Are they still the same? Peking is beautiful, but I shall always think of London in spring as one of the most attractive cities in the world. And the people—I received great kindness in England. It's a pity we don't get on better. They don't understand China very well nowadays. But that will change in time."

"How have you changed after all this time? How is the revolution with you now?" [asked Gelder] . . . "But apart from one or two plays, a few stories and essays, you have written little about it."

"That is because although I am in sympathy with it, I am not a part of it. Therefore, I cannot really comprehend it, and without comprehension it is impossible to write anything of value . . . I have no inner experience of the situation."

"But you wrote *Rickshaw Boy* with such understanding that it could be imagined you had pulled a rickshaw yourself."

"Yes, but that was a world which one identified oneself with. The relationships were sharper, more clearly defined. There was privilege and poverty. There was exploitation and there were the exploited . . . This was a simple situation to write about—the contrast between riches and poverty . . . In those days you were with those who accepted this human condition as the natural order of things or you were against them. *This was what the revolution was about* and if you believed that all men were brothers you had no choice. *You were a revolutionary and supported those who had the will and the courage to change the state of affairs.*

"This did not mean we were all Marxist revolutionaries. We weren't scientific reformers. Mao Tse-tung wasn't a Communist when we all joined together in the May 4th Movement. He couldn't be. No one in China knew about Communism. But to him as to all of us the situation was intolerable.

" . . . The first stage of the Liberation was patriotism. The second was patriotism and revolution in the civil war, in which our own native forces of reaction, still supported by Imperialism had to be overthrown . . . Now the revolution is in a new phase, *not so much to change conditions as to change ways of thinking.*

"I can understand why Mao Tse-tung wishes to destroy the old bourgeois concepts of life *but I cannot write about this struggle because I am not a Marxist, and, therefore, I cannot feel and think as a Peking student in May 1966 who sees the situation in a Marxist way.*

" . . . We old ones can't apologize for what we are. We can only explain why we are and wave the young ones on their way to the future."[31]

A few weeks later Lao She was visited by the Red Guards and though we do not know the details of what transpired it is not difficult to visualize that the sixty-nine-year-old Lao She was possibly beaten up, definitely humiliated, and this led to his committing suicide. Why did he commit suicide? Was it because *humiliation* betrayed his traditional self-image—self-respect depending on the respect accorded by others? Or was it because suicide, still in the framework of the Chinese tradition, was a form of indictment of the authorities from whom one could get no justice? Or, again, was it just that he felt old and tired and cornered and isolated and had reached a stage when he could take it no longer? These sentiments are not necessarily mutually exclusive, though we do notice that unlike the suicide of Ch'i T'ien-yu in *Four Generations under One Roof,* where humiliation is the keynote, Wang Li-fa in *Teahouse* takes his life because everything that mattered is taken away from him and he has no hope or faith left in society or government. Wang Li-fa's act of suicide takes on the dimensions of a religious ritual—by performing the funeral ceremony beforehand, he cuts himself loose from all ties with the world and death becomes a release from the ugliness and sordidness of life.

The Gelders wrote to a Communist friend, an acquaintance of twenty-two years, asking about Lao She's death. In reply they were told:

> "With regard to Lao She, I don't know the facts. But if Lao She really should have done this [committed suicide], what would it indicate? Inability to stand the test of a revolutionary storm . . . If the rupture with traditional ideas is so painful to a person that he lays hands on himself, if the grip of the past is so strong that he chooses this road, whether he is an old acquaintance or not, does one blame the revolution, which if it does not dismantle the past has no meaning.
>
> "In general suicide in China today is never publicized. In fact it is regarded as a disgrace—at best cowardice, and at worst a desperate kind of counter-revolutionary gesture."[32]

But the most recent version of Lao She's suicide to come from China might perhaps be set down without judgment. The event could well have been described by Lao She's own pen and seems as inevitable as any of his tragic final chapters.

According to this report, after a day of interrogation by the Red Guards Lao She was allowed to leave but was ordered to return the next day for further examination. When he reached his home, he found the courtyard strewn with all his possessions, his house looted, his paintings and sculpture wrecked, and his manuscripts, the work of a lifetime, in shreds. He did not enter his house but instead turned and walked toward the nearby canal, and there he drowned himself.

NOTES

I. *Growing Up, 1898–1924*

1. There is some controversy both about the date and place of Lao She's birth. Joseph Schyns, *1500 Modern Chinese Novels and Plays* (Peiping, 1948; reprinted in Hong Kong, 1966), p. 84, mentions Lao She's date of birth as 1897. Ting Yi, *A Short History of Modern Chinese Literature* (Peking, 1959), p. 172; and the note "About the Author" at the end of Lao She, *Dragon Beard Ditch,* tr. Liao Hung-ying (Peking, 1956), gives the date 1899. C. T. Hsia, in *A History of Modern Chinese Fiction, 1917–1957* (New Haven, 1961), p. 166, gives it as 1898 but provides no clue as to how he reached this date.

   I have calculated 1898 to be Lao She's year of birth from his article "Tiao-nien Lo Ch'ang-p'ei hsien sheng," *Chung-kuo yü-wen,* no. 1:23 (1959), in which he says that Mr. Lo was a year younger than he—Mr. Lo was born in 1899. In Lao She, *Lao-niu p'o-ch'e* (first published in *Yü-chou feng* in 1935; Hong Kong edition, 1961), p. 3, Lao She mentions that he left for England in 1924 when he was 27 *sui.* This also points to 1898 as his year of birth.

   Joseph Schyns, Ting Yi, and C. T. Hsia all agree that Lao She was born in Peking but Hsu Chien-wen in "Lao She ti ch'eng-ming yü mo-lo," *Chung-yang jih-pao* (Taipei, Oct. 22, 1966), p. 4, makes an emphatic statement that Lao She was born in Shantung.

   There is a dismaying lack of information about Lao She's family background, his childhood, and his youth. Lao She appears to have fought shy of writing about himself.

2. Shu Chun-ch'eng, "Yi shu-fu," *Chung-yang jih-pao* (Taipei, Oct. 13, 1966), p. 4; see also Zbigniew Slupski, *The Evolution of a Modern Chinese Writer* (Prague, 1966), p. 81.

3. It is difficult to comprehend what "impoverishment" means in this context. Lao She first studied with a private tutor and then went to school and this can hardly be called a state of impoverishment but he repeatedly emphasizes his childhood poverty and later financial difficulties; in 1935 at the age of 37 he said that "I have been poor since childhood" (Lao She, *Lao-niu p'o-ch'e,* p. 5).

4. See Lo Ch'ang-p'ei, "Wo yü Lao She" in Lo Ch'ang-p'ei, *Chung-kuo-jen yü Chung-kuo-wen* (Hong Kong, 1966), pp. 96–101.

5. Lao She, "Tiao-nien Lo Ch'ang-p'ei hsien-sheng," pp. 23–24.

6. Ibid., p. 23.

7. Y. C. Wang, *Chinese Intellectuals and the West, 1872–1949* (Chapel Hill, 1966), pp. 231, 232.

8.   For example, see ibid., pp. 241-242, for the story of Miss Chiu Chin's execution in 1907.

9.   Ibid., p. 233. Yehonala was the name of the Manchu clan to which the Dowager Empress belonged.

10. See Li Chien-nung, *The Political History of China, 1840-1928* (Stanford, 1956), p. 192. These are among the mildest sentiments expressed by Chou Jung. At one place in the book the author says that if the Manchus "sucked" the Han clean after they had urinated and "licked" them clean after they had excreted, the Manchus thereby would not be able to compensate by one-thousandth for the harm they had inflicted on the Han; see *Chou Jung chuan* (Taipei, 1953), p. 69. The book became a best seller and went into more than twenty printings, according to Y. C. Wang, p. 239.

11. Li Chien-nung, p. 207.

12. Ibid.

13. Ibid., p. 209.

14. Ibid., p. 212.

15. P. H. Kent, *The Passing of the Manchus* (London, 1929), pp. 42-43.
     An interesting insight into the superior status of the Manchus and the superiority complex of the Han is given by Princess Der Ling in her autobiographical work, *Kowtow*. She recollects that when she was a child and used to play with the son of a Han magistrate [her own father was of the first rank and higher in status], the "amahs" of the two children discussed the possibility of marriage between them. Der Ling's amah thought the marriage unlikely as the boy's father was not of the same rank as Der Ling's father, but the boy's amah made a crushing reply: "come to think of it, our master wouldn't hear of the match at all . . . because your master is only a Manchu." When Der Ling went weeping to her father to inquire as to what was wrong with being a Manchu, he tried to give the child the history of the Manchus concluding with the statement, "remember this, however: Manchus have no reason of being ashamed of being Manchus! They were a great people, and they still are; but they are not Chinese. The Chinese hate us, yet we are their masters! Perhaps we will not always be, but . . . well I'll tell you the whole story when you are old enough to understand." And this was even before 1900. See Princess Der Ling, *Kowtow* (New York, 1929), pp. 42-43, 49.

16. Kent, p. 76.

17. Ibid., p. 131. See also J. C. Keyte, *The Passing of the Dragon* (London, New York, etc., 1913), pp. 42-46.

18. Kent, p. 207.

19. Aisin-gioro Pu Yi, *From Emperor to Citizen* (Peking, 1965), II, 423.

20. Ssu-yü Teng and John K. Fairbank, *China's Response to the West* (Cambridge, Mass., 1961), pp. 267–268 (italics added).

21. Lao She, *Lao-niu p'o-ch'e,* p. 2.

22. Lo Ch'ang-p'ei, p. 97. For a translation of Lao She's official rank see H. S. Brunnert and V. V. Hagelstrom, *Present-Day Political Organization of China* (Taipei, n.d.), p. 409.

23. Lo Ch'ang-p'ei, p. 97. Similar adjectives have been frequently used by the Maoists in their attacks on the followers of Liu Shao-ch'i during the Great Cultural Revolution, 1966–1968.

24. Ibid., pp. 97–98.

25. Lao She, "A Vision," tr. Gladys Yang, *Chinese Literature,* no. 6:81–82 (1962).

26. Lao She, *Lao-niu p'o-ch'e,* pp. 2, 53.

27. Yao Nai-lin, *Chung-kuo wen-hsueh-chia chuan-chi* (Shanghai, 1937), pp. 215–216; Fang Ch'ing, *Hsien-tai wen-t'an pai-hsiang* (Hong Kong, 1953), pp. 43–44.

28. Lao She, *Lao Chang ti che-hsueh* (Shanghai, 1949), p. 157.
    Lao She's nephew, who is currently residing in Taiwan, says that Lao She was converted *after his return* to China and that one day, when his mother was asleep Lao She broke the wooden statue of Sakyamuni and threw away the vessels of worship which were in the house. When his mother awoke and discovered what had happened she was very angry, and Lao She received a beating and was turned out of the house. Later Lao She recanted and became a Buddhist again. Lao She's nephew did not know his uncle personally, and has only repeated hearsay stories in an article written in 1966 after the death of Lao She. The first reference above comes from an article published in 1937 and seems far more plausible. See Shu Chun-ch'eng, "Yi Shu-fu."

29. Reginald F. Johnston, *Twilight in the Forbidden City* (London, 1934), gives a detailed account of the relations between the emperor and the Republican government.

30. Ch'ien Tuan-sheng, *The Government and Politics of China* (Cambridge, Mass., 1967), p. 76.

31. Lao She, "Tiao-nien Lo Ch'ang-p'ei hsien-sheng."

32. See Lao She, *Lao-niu p'o-ch'e,* p. 20.

33.   Quoted in Lai Ming, *A History of Chinese Literature* (New York, 1964), p. 351.

34.   *Selected Works of Lu Hsun* (Peking, 1956), I, 3. (Italics added.)

35.   See *Hsin ch'ing-nien,* vol. 2, no. 5 (January 1917).

36.   Hu Shih also suggested three ways of collecting materials: "(1) enlarge the area from
      which material is to be collected . . . At present, the poor man's society, male and
      female factory workers, rickshaw pullers . . . small shop owners and peddlers every-
      where, and all conditions of suffering have no place in literature [as they should].
      Moreover, now that new and old civilizations have come into contact, problems like
      family catastrophes, tragedies in marriage, the position of women, the unfitness of
      present education, etc., can all supply literature with material; (2) stress actual ob-
      servation and personal experience; (3) use broad and keen imagination to supplement
      observation and experience."

37.   Lau Shaw, *Rickshaw Boy,* translation of *Lo-t'o Hsiang-tzu* by Evan King (New York,
      1945).

38.   The May Fourth Movement is named for an incident which took place on May 4,
      1919. The incident was a violent student demonstration against the terms of the
      Versailles peace talks, terms which the students considered a "sell-out" because the
      Chinese government ceded the German possessions in the province of Shantung to
      Japan. In the weeks that followed the incident, public sentiment in the whole coun-
      try sided with the students against the pro-Japanese government. There were sym-
      pathetic strikes by merchants and workers, and ultimately, the government sur-
      rendered by dismissing the pro-Japanese ministers and releasing the students who
      had been arrested in the incident. See Chow Tse-tsung, *The May Fourth Movement*
      (Cambridge, Mass., 1964), pp. 84–116.

39.   See William Ayers, "The Society for Literary Studies, 1921–1930," *Papers on China*
      7:34–79 (Cambridge, Mass., East Asian Research Center, Harvard University, 1953).

40.   In 1924 Sun Yat-sen admonished the students saying: "Having absorbed the idea of
      liberty, the students can find no place to practice it except in their schools. Insur-
      rections and strikes follow, under the guise of fighting for 'liberty' . . . This is abuse
      of freedom." See Y. C. Wang, p. 334.

II. *The First Novels: 1924–1929*

1.   Lao She, *Lao-niu p'o-ch'e,* p. 3.

2.   Wang Yao, *Chung-kuo hsin wen-hsueh shih kao* (Shanghai, 1953), p. 231.

3.   Lao She is himself conscious of this shortcoming in his early works. See Lao She,
     Lao-niu p'o-ch'e, p. 6.

4. For example *Lao Chang ti che-hsueh* was reprinted 12 times up to 1949. See Slupski, p. 105.

5. Lao She, *Lao-niu p'o-ch'e*, p. 4.

6. Ibid., p. 5.

7. Lo Ch'ang-p'ei, p. 97.

8. Lao She, *Lao Chang ti che-hsueh*, p. 49.

9. Ibid., p. 48.

10. Ibid., p. 86.

11. Ibid., p. 50.

12. Ibid., p. 230.

13. Ibid., p. 58.

14. Ibid., pp. 134–135.

15. Ibid. See chap. 29, pp. 169–174.

16. Ibid., p. 15.

17. Ibid., p. 17.

18. Ibid., pp. 43–44.

19. Ibid., p. 178.

20. Ibid., p. 196.

21. Ibid., p. 202.

22. Ibid., p. 202–203.

23. Ibid., p. 245.

24. Lao She wrote this novel as a hobby, and took a year to finish it. Just about this time Hsu Ti-shan, a well known literary figure and a member of the Society for Literary Studies, was visiting London. Lao She tells us that he showed the novel to him and that Hsu made no criticism, only smiled after reading it, and suggested that Lao She send it back home for publication. Thereupon, Lao She, without even registering the parcel, sent the book to Cheng Chen-to, who was one of the founder

members of the Society for Literary Studies and later editor of *Hsiao-shuo yueh-pao* (Short story monthly). Lo Ch'ang-p'ei says that Lao She sent the novel to him and that he showed it to Lu Hsun before it was published in the prestigious *Hsiao-shuo yueh-pao*. Lo adds that Lu Hsun appreciated the vividness of the local color but felt that the technique could bear discussion. Lao She, *Lao-niu p'o-ch'e*, p. 7, and Lo Ch'ang-p'ei, p. 119.

25. Lao She, *Lao-niu p'o-ch'e*, p. 9.

26. Ibid.

27. Lao She, *Chao Tzu-yueh* (Shanghai, 1949), p. 41. The last paragraph of the translation is taken from C. T. Hsia, *A History of Modern Chinese Fiction*, p. 171.

28. Ibid., p. 42.

29. Ibid., p. 67.

30. Ibid., pp. 70–71.

31. Ibid., p. 113.

32. Ibid.

33. Ibid., p. 48.

34. Ibid., pp. 97–98.

35. Ibid., p. 97.

36. Ibid., p. 26.

37. Ibid., pp. 205–206.

38. Ibid., p. 205.

39. Ibid.

40. Ibid.

41. Mao Tse-tung, "On the People's Democratic Dictatorship," in *Selected Works of Mao Tse-tung*, 4 vols. (Peking, 1961), IV, 411–423.

42. Lao She, *Chao Tzu-yueh*, p. 215.

43. Ibid., p. 218.

44. Ibid., p. 140.

45. Ibid., pp. 178–179.

46. Ibid., p. 199.

47. Lao She, *Lao Chang ti che-hsueh,* pp. 186–187.

48. Lao She, *Chao Tzu-yueh,* p. 137.

49. Lao She, *Lao-niu p'o-ch'e,* pp. 18–19.

50. Ibid., p. 16.

51. Lao She, *Erh Ma,* p. 9.

52. Ibid., p. 12.

53. Ibid., p. 8.

54. *Selected Works of Lu Hsun,* I, 415.

55. Lao She, *Erh Ma,* p. 70.

56. Ibid., pp. 72–73.

57. Ibid., p. 211.

58. Ibid., p. 210.

59. Ibid., p. 10.

60. Ibid., pp. 164–165.

61. Ibid., pp. 177–178.

62. Ibid., p. 178.

63. Ibid., p. 133.

64. Mr. Ma's character comes out in the story as a whole but there are specific passages in which his laziness, ignorance, and so on, are highlighted. For example, see p. 75, and pp. 130–131.

65. Ibid., p. 120.

66. Ibid., p. 34.

67. Ibid., pp. 109–110.

68. Ibid.

69. Ibid., p. 80.

70. Ibid., pp. 75–76.

71. Ibid., p. 134.

72. Ibid., p. 203.

73. Ibid., p. 116.

74. Ibid., p. 190.

75. Ibid., pp. 184–185.

III. *The Artist Matures*

1. See Lao She, *Lao-niu p'o-ch'e,* pp. 16, 22.

2. Ibid., p. 24.

3. Ibid., p. 30.

4. Ibid., p. 32.

5. The book contains a collection of the following 14 essays which were first published in 1935:
    (i)   How I Wrote *Lao Chang ti che-hsueh.*
    (ii)   How I Wrote *Chao Tzu-yueh.*
    (iii) How I Wrote *Erh Ma.*
    (iv)   How I Wrote *Hsiao P'o ti sheng-jih.*
    (v)   How I Wrote *Ta-Ming hu.*
    (vi)   How I Wrote *Mao-ch'eng chi.*
    (vii) How I Wrote *Li-hun.*
    (viii) How I Wrote Short Stories.
    (ix)   How I Wrote *Niu T'ien-tz'u chuan.*
    (x)   On Humor.
    (xi)   Description of the Scene.
    (xii) Description of Characters.
    (xiii) Use of Facts.
    (xiv) Language and Style.
    Lao-niu p'o-ch'e is practically the only source of information on Lao She's early

writing career but it is written in a defensive manner and is full of self-deprecation. Many of the statements made in it by the author need careful appraisal and should not be accepted uncritically.

6. Lao She, *Lao-niu p'o-ch'e,* p. 29.

7. Lao She, *Hsiao P'o ti sheng-jih* (Hong Kong, 1966), p. 20.

8. Ibid., p. 6.

9. Ibid., p. 18.

10. Ibid., p. 11.

11. Lao She, *Lao-niu p'o-ch'e,* p. 28.

12. Ibid., pp. 26–27.

13. Lao She, "Tung-fang hsueh-yuan," *Hsi-feng,* no. 7: 15 (March 1937).

14. I learned from Mr. Gerald F. Winfield (author of *China: The Land and the People* [New York, 1957]), who was connected with Cheeloo University and also knew Lao She, that Lao She's being a Christian definitely helped him to get the job with this university. He also mentioned that Lao She was a practicing Christian in the early 1930s.

15. Lao She, *Lao-niu p'o-ch'e,* p. 20.

16. For a history of this period see O. Edmund Clubb, *Twentieth Century China* (New York, 1964), chaps. 5 and 6.

17. See Nym Wales, "The Modern Chinese Literary Movement," in Edgar Snow, ed., *Living China* (New York, 1937). Nym Wales gives a list prepared by Mao Tun in 1935 of the writers who had suffered at the hands of the KMT. It appears that about forty writers were executed by the government by 1936. Also see Yi-tsi M. Feuerwerker, "Tradition and Experiment in Modern Chinese Literature," in Albert Feuerwerker, ed., *Modern China,* pp. 169–183.

18. *Selected Works of Lu Hsun,* I, 3.

19. Ibid., III, 45. (Italics added.) This quote is from a talk given by Lu Hsun on May 22, 1929, to the Chinese Literature Society of Yenching University.

20. Lao She, *Lao-niu p'o-ch'e,* p. 33.

21. Ibid., p. 43.

22. Ibid., p. 42.

23. Ibid., p. 43.

24. See sketch of Hu Hsieh-ch'ing by a staff reporter in *Kuang-ming jih-pao* (Peking, Mar. 8, 1957), p. 2.

25. See Hsia, pp. 134–135, and Lao She, *Lao-niu p'o-ch'e,* p. 39.

26. Lao She, *Mao-ch'eng chi* (Shanghai, 1949), p. 26.

27. Ibid., p. 27.

28. Ibid., p. 190.

29. Ibid., p. 192.

30. Ibid., p. 71.

31. Ibid., p. 72.

32. Ibid., p. 70.

33. Ibid., p. 76.

34. Ibid., p. 96.

35. Ibid., pp. 110–112.

36. Ibid., p. 114.

37. Ibid., p. 115.

38. Ibid.

39. Ibid., p. 127.

40. Ibid., pp. 138–139. In 1932, when Lao She wrote this novel, it was difficult to attack the government and escape punishment. It seems that Lao She could get away with his satirization, partly because he uses symbols like "emperor" and partly because he attacks all the political parties in the same broad way as he does the government.

41. Ibid., p. 140.

42. Ibid., pp. 141–142.

IV. *Anatomy of Alienation*

1. See Lao She's preface to *Li-hun* (Hong Kong [no date of publication but preface is dated May 1947]), pp. 1-2.

2. Lao She, *Lao-niu p'o-ch'e*, p. 49.

3. Ibid., p. 48.

4. Lao She, *Li-hun*, p. 5.

5. Ibid., p. 4.

6. Ibid., pp. 53-54.

7. *Selected Works of Lu Hsun*, I, 174-187.

8. Lao She, *Li-hun*, p. 13.

9. Ibid., p. 60.

10. Ibid., pp. 60-61.

11. Ibid., p. 61.

12. Ibid., p. 160.

13. Ibid., p. 62.

14. Ibid., pp. 34-35.

15. Ibid., pp. 33-34.

16. Ibid., p. 22.

17. Ibid., p. 241.

18. Ibid., p. 243 (italics added).

19. Ibid., p. 38.

20. Ibid., p. 191.

21. Ibid., pp. 278-279 (italics added).

22. Ibid., p. 279.

23.   See Lao She, *Lao-niu p'o-ch'e,* p. 65.

24.   Ibid., p. 66.

25.   Ibid., p. 67.

26.   The magazine was founded in 1932 by Lin Yutang. See Hsia, p. 132.

27.   Lao She, *Lao-niu p'o-ch'e,* p. 68.

28.   Lao She, *Niu T'ien-tz'u chuan* (Shanghai, 1947), p. 201.

29.   These dates have been arrived at from the context of the story. For example we are told in Chapter 20 that T'ien-tz'u is eighteen when co-education begins in Yun-ch'eng. This would be in the early 1920s. Eighteen years earlier when T'ien-tz'u was taken into the Niu family it must have been about 1905.

30.   Lao She, *Niu-T'ien-tz'u chuan,* p. 8.

31.   Ibid., p. 75.

32.   Ibid., p. 163.

33.   Ibid., p. 161.

34.   Ibid., p. 155.

35.   Ibid., p. 49.

36.   Ibid., p. 78.

37.   Ibid., p. 97.

38.   Ibid., p. 99.

39.   Ibid., p. 105.

40.   Ibid., p. 153.

41.   Ibid., p. 167.

42.   Ibid., pp. 168–169.

43.   Ibid., p. 172.

44.   Ibid., p. 179.

45.   Ibid. (italics added).

46.   Ibid., p. 131.

47.   Ibid., pp. 139-142.

48.   Ibid., pp. 142-143.

49.   Ibid., p. 199.

50.   Lin Yutang, *My Country and My People* (New York, 1935), p. 68.

51.   *Selected Works of Lu Hsun,* III, 226.

52.   For the English translation see "The True Story of Ah Q" in *Selected Works of Lu Hsun,* I, 76-135.

53.   See *Selected Works of Lu Hsun,* IV, 169, 183.

54.   Wu Ching-tzu, *Ju-lin Wai-shih* (The informal history of the forest of scholars) a Ch'ing novel satirizing the classical examination system. English translation by Yang Hsien-yi and Gladys Yang entitled *The Scholars* (Peking, Foreign Languages Press, 1957).

55.   *Selected Works of Lu Hsun,* IV, 168.

56.   Lao She, "T'an yu-mo" (On humor) in *Lao-niu p'o-ch'e,* p. 80.

57.   Ibid., p. 72.

58.   Ibid., pp. 74-75.

59.   Ibid., p. 80.

60.   See *Selected Works of Lu Hsun,* III, 239-241.

V. *Lo-T'o Hsiang-tzu (Camel Hsiang Tzu)*

1.   Lao She, Preface, *Ying-hai chi* (Shanghai, 1937), p. 1.

2.   Lao She, *Lao-niu p'o-ch'e,* pp. 61-62.

3.   Cyril Birch, "Lao She: The Humorist in His Humor," p. 52, agrees with Hsia, p. 187, that this is the "finest modern Chinese novel."

4.   Lao She, Preface, *Lo-t'o Hsiang-tzu* (Shanghai, 1950), p. 1. The English translation,

Rickshaw Boy (New York, 1945), was made by Evan King, but the translator introduced many changes which distorted the original. The most important one was that Lao She's tragic ending became a happy one in King's translation. Lao She in the "Preface" expresses his dismay at the violence done to his work by Evan King.

5.   Lao She, *Lo-t'o Hsiang-tzu*, p. 9.

6.   Ibid., p. 12.

7.   Ibid., p. 19.

8.   Ibid., p. 30.

9.   Ibid., p. 50.

10.   Ibid., p. 52.

11.   Ibid., p. 45.

12.   Ibid., p. 61.

13.   Ibid., pp. 75–76.

14.   Ibid., p. 77.

15.   Ibid., p. 84.

16.   Ibid., p. 147.

17.   Ibid.

18.   Ibid., p. 148.

19.   Ibid., p. 108.

20.   Ibid., p. 112.

21.   Ibid., p. 113.

22.   Ibid., p. 157.

23.   Ibid., p. 186.

24.   Ibid., pp. 221–222.

25.   Ibid., p. 227.

26. Ibid., p. 249.

27. Ibid., p. 251.

28. Ibid., p. 258.

29. Ibid., p. 264.

30. Ibid., p. 262.

31. Ibid., p. 269.

32. Ibid., p. 270.

33. Ibid., p. 308.

34. C. T. Hsia, p. 185.

35. Lao She, *Lo-t'o Hsiang-tzu,* p. 142.

36. Ibid., p. 143.

37. Ibid., p. 144.

38. Ibid., p. 77.

39. Ibid., p. 78.

40. Ibid.

41. This is a basic Confucian philosophy and is best expressed in the passage in *Ta Hsueh* (The great learning) which says that "From the emperor down to the common people, all, without exception, must consider cultivation of the individual character as the root. If the root is in disorder, it is impossible for the branches to be in order." (See deBary, I, 115.)

42. Lao She, *Lo-t'o Hsiang-tzu,* pp. 284–285.

43. Ibid., p. 284.

44. Fei Hsiao-tung, *China's Gentry* (Chicago, 1953), p. 142.

45. Lao She, *Lo-t'o Hsiang-tzu,* p. 144.

46. Ibid., p. 145.

47. This parallel between Lao She and Mr. Ts'ao has been very well worked out in Stuart and Roma Gelder, *Memories for a Chinese Granddaughter* (New York, 1968), pp. 192–194.

VI. *Women in a Changing Society*

1. The collections entitled *Kan chi, Ying hai chi,* and *Ko tsao chi* were first published in 1934, 1935, and 1936 respectively.

2. Lao She, *Lao Chang ti che-hsueh,* pp. 202, 186.

3. Lao She, *Li-hun,* pp. 166, 167, 272–273.

4. Ibid., p. 160.

5. See Lao She, *Kan chi* (Hong Kong, n.d.), pp. 140–158; and Lao She, *Ying hai chi* (Shanghai, 1937), pp. 195–242.

6. Lao She, *Kan chi,* pp. 147–148.

7. Ibid., pp. 148, 147, 154.

8. Ibid., p. 145.

9. Descriptions of the brutal treatment often meted out to the females in the family are available in scores of books written by visitors to China before 1949. For example see Jack Belden, *China Shakes the World* (New York, 1949), p. 307. That these conditions continued for some time into the post-Communist period is well expressed by Fang Yen, "Making the Marriage Law Work," in *China in Transition* (Peking, 1957), pp. 308–317. Fang says:
     "But the old customs, deeply rooted for thousands of years could not be overcome by legislation alone . . . Many marriages are still on a buy-and-sell basis . . .
     "Even such barbarous customs as child marriages, 'wait-for-husband brides' (grown women engaged to infants), keeping slave girls, renting of wives and abducting of widows had not completely disappeared. Young village women were still committing suicide . . .
     "In Chengyu . . . seven out of ten family grievances involved the beating of wives, who under the buy-and-sell system were regarded as chattels by their husbands and parents-in-law."

10. Lao She, *Kan chi,* pp. 156, 158.

11. Ibid., p. 157.

12.   Lao She, *Lo-t'o Hsiang-tzu*, pp. 158, 156.

13.   Ibid., p. 158.

14.   Ibid., p. 159.

15.   Ibid., p. 158.

16.   Ibid., p. 162.

17.   Ibid., pp. 210–211.

18.   Lao She, *Ying hai chi*, p. 199.

19.   Ibid., p. 200.

20.   Ibid., pp. 207–208.

21.   Ibid., p. 208.

22.   Ibid., p. 210.

23.   Ibid., p. 216.

24.   Ibid., p. 232.

25.   Ibid., p. 235.

26.   Ibid., p. 241.

27.   Ibid., pp. 243–292.

28.   Ibid., p. 285.

VII. *The War Years, 1937–1949*

1.   See Lao She's Preface to *Huo-tsang* (Shanghai, 1949), and Chi Lin, ed., *Chung-kuo tso-chia chien-ying* (Hong Kong, 1958), p. 102.

2.   See Lao She, "Wei-la t'uan-chieh," *Wen-i pao,* no. 20:7 (August 1957); Chi Lin, pp. 103–104; Chu Fu-sung, "Wartime Chinese Literature," in *China: After Seven Years of War* (New York, 1945), pp. 125–147; Wang Yü, "Chi Lao She hsien-sheng," *Chang-wang Fortnightly* (Sept. 1, 1970), pp. 20–23. For Communist China's appraisal of the Writers Anti-Aggression Association, see Wang Yao and Ting Yi.

3. Wang Yü, p. 20. This translation is not literal but captures the essential spirit of the original.

4. Quoted in Slupski, pp. 90–91.

5. Chu Fu-sung, p. 125.

6. It is for this reason that he entitled his collection of short stories published in 1944 *Anaemic Stories (P'in-hsueh chi)*.

7. See article on Hu Hsieh ch'ing (Lao She's wife), published in *Kuang-ming jih-pao* (Mar. 8, 1957).

8. Lao She, Preface to *Huo-tsang*, p. 6.

9. Lao She, "Hsien-t'an wo ti ch'i ko hua-chü," *K'ang-chan wen-i* 8.1:27 (Chungking, Nov. 15, 1942), p. 27.

10. Lao She, Preface to *Huo-tsang*, pp. 3–4.

11. Wang Yü, p. 20.

12. Lao She, "Hsien-t'an," p. 27.

13. See Mary C. Wright, "From Revolution to Restoration: The Transformation of Kuomintang Ideology," *Far Eastern Quarterly* 14.4:515–532 (August 1955).

14. Lao She, *Huo-tsang*, p. 110.

15. Ibid., p. 225.

16. See Chapter 2, "The First Novels, 1924–1929."

17. Lao She, Preface to *Huang-huo*, which is pt. 1 of *Ssu-shih t'ung-t'ang* (Shanghai, Fourth Printing, 1949), p. 1.

18. This information was obtained from Ida Pruitt by the author in an interview in 1969.

19. Lau Shaw, *The Yellow Storm*, p. 33.

20. Ibid., pp. 37–38.

21. Ibid., p. 533.

22. Ibid., p. 449.

23. Ibid. (Italics added.)

24. Ibid., p. 450 (italics added).

25. Ibid., p. 512.

26. Ibid., p. 194.

27. Ibid., pp. 334–335.

VIII. *Epilogue: 1950–1966*

1. Wang Yü, "Chi Lao She hsien-sheng," p. 22.

2. Piao Yu-ming, "Tsai 'k'un-tzu' hsia 'tai-ping yen-nien' ti Lao She," *Ta kung pao* (Hong Kong, January 1962), pp. 15–21.

3. Birch, p. 59.

4. Lao She, Preface, *Lao She hsuan-chi,* pp. 8–9.

5. Ibid., p. 10.

6. Ibid., p. 11.

7. Ibid., p. 12.

8. Lao She, "Mao chu-hsi kei-la wo hsin ti wen-i sheng-ming," *Jen-min jih-pao* (May 21, 1952); and abridged translation is available in *Current Background,* no. 203 (Hong Kong, U.S. Consulate General, Aug. 15, 1952).

9. *Current Background,* no. 203:39.

10. Ibid.

11. Ibid., p. 40.

12. Wang Yü, p. 22.

13. Ibid.

14. Ibid., p. 23.

15. Lao She, *Dragon Beard Ditch,* p. 90.

16. Ibid., p. 91.

17. Lao She, *Hsi-wang Ch'ang-an, Jen-min wen-hsueh* (January 1956), p. 36.

18. Wang Yü, p. 22.

19. Huang Sha, "Lao She ti hsieh-tso sheng-huo," *Hsin kuan-ch'a,* no. 7:26 (Apr. 1, 1956).

20. Lao She, *Ch'a-kuan* (Peking, 1958), p. 8.

21. Ibid., p. 11.

22. Ibid., p. 58.

23. Ibid., p. 14.

24. Ibid., p. 18.

25. Ibid., p. 30.

26. Ibid., p. 31.

27. I am grateful for this information to Wilma Fairbank, who kindly permitted me to see Ida Pruitt's letter to her dated October 26, 1966. In this letter, written on hearing of the tragic death of Lao She, Ida Pruitt recounted her last meeting with him.

28. See the article "Tso t'an Lao She ti *Ch'a-kuan*" in *Wen-i pao,* no. 1: 19–23 (January 1958).

29. Shu Wen, "Lao She ti ch'a-kuan," *Ming pao* (Oct. 26, 1966).

30. Stuart and Roma Gelder, *Memories for a Chinese Grand-Daughter* (New York, 1968), pp. 182–195.

31. Ibid., pp. 184–186 (italics added).

32. Ibid., pp. 194–195.

BIBLIOGRAPHY

Aisin-gioro Pu Yu. *From Emperor to Citizen,* tr. W. J. F. Jenner. 2 vols. Peking, Foreign Languages Press, vol. 1 (1964), vol. 2 (1965).

Ayers, William. "The Society for Literary Studies, 1921–1930," *Papers on China* 7: 34–79. Cambridge, Mass., East Asian Research Center, Harvard University, 1953.

Belden, Jack. *China Shakes the World.* New York, Harper & Bros., 1949.

Birch, Cyril. "Lao She: The Humorist in His Humor," *The China Quarterly* 8: 45–62 (October–December 1961).

Brunnert, H. S. and V. V. Hagelstrom. *Present-Day Political Organization of China,* tr. A. Beltchenko and E. E. Moran. Shanghai, Kelly and Walsh, 1912. Reproduced in Taipei, n.d.

Chi Lin 李林 , ed. *Chung-kuo tso-chia chien-ying* 中国作家剪影 (Pen portraits of Chinese writers). Hong Kong, Wen-hsueh ch'u-pan she 文学出版社 , 1958.

Ch'ien Tuan-sheng. *The Government and Politics of China.* Cambridge, Mass., Harvard University Press, 1967.

Chou Jung chuan 鄒容傳 (The biography of Chou Jung). Taipei, 1953.

Chow Tse-tsung. *The May Fourth Movement.* Cambridge, Mass., Harvard University Press, 1960.

Chu Fu-sung. "Wartime Chinese Literature," in *China: After Seven Years of War.* New York, Macmillan & Co., 1945.

Clubb, O. Edmund. *Twentieth Century China.* New York, Columbia University Press, 1964.

deBary, Wm. Theodore, Chan Wing-tsit and Burton Watson. *Sources of Chinese Tradition.* New York, Columbia University Press, 1960.

Der Ling, Princess. *Kowtow.* New York, Dodd, Mead & Co., 1929.

Fang Ch'ing 方青 *Hsien-tai wen-t'an pai-hsiang* 現代文壇百象 (Sketches of contemporary Chinese writers). Hong Kong, 1953.

Fang Yen. "Making the Marriage Law Work," in China Reconstructs, ed., *China in Transition.* Peking, 1957, pp. 308–317.

Fei Hsiao-tung. *China's Gentry.* Chicago, The University of Chicago Press, 1953.

188

Feuerwerker, Yi-tsi M. "Tradition and Experiment in Modern Chinese Literature," in Albert Feuerwerker, ed., *Modern China*. Englewood Cliffs,
Prentice Hall, 1964.

Gelder, Stuart and Roma. *Memories for a Chinese Grand-Daughter*. New York.
Stein and Day, 1968.

Harvey, W. J. "Chance and Design in Bleak House," in John Gross and Gabriel
Pearson, eds., *Dickens and the Twentieth Century*. London, Routledge &
Kegan Paul, 1962.

Hsia, C. T., *A History of Modern Chinese Fiction, 1917–1957*. New Haven,
Yale University Press, 1961.

Hsin Ch'ing-nien 新青年 (New youth), vol. 2, no. 5.(January 1917).

Hsu Chien-wen 徐鑑文 "Lao She ti ch'eng-ming yü mo-lo" 老舍的成名
與沒落 (The rise and fall of Lao She), *Chung-yang jih-pao*
中央日報 (Central daily news, Taipei; Oct. 22, 1966), p. 4.

Hu Shih. *The Chinese Renaissance*. New York, Paragon, 1963.

Huang Sha 黃沙 "Lao She ti hsieh tso sheng-huo" 老舍的寫作生
活 (Lao She's writing life), *Hsin kuan-ch'a* 新覌察 (New observer),
no. 7 (Apr. 1, 1956).

Johnston, Reginald F. *Twilight in the Forbidden City*. London, Victor Gol-
lancz, 1934.

Kent, P. H. *The Passing of the Manchus*. London, E. Arnold, 1912.

Keyte, J. C. *The Passing of the Dragon*. London, New York (etc.), Hodder &
Stoughton, 1913.

Lai Ming. *A History of Chinese Literature*. New York, Capricorn Books,
1964.

Lao She. "Tung-fang hsueh-yuan" 東方學院 (School of Oriental studies), *Hsi-feng* 西風 (West wind), no. 7: 10–15 (March 1937).

——— *Ying-hai chi* 櫻海集 (Cherries and the ocean). Shanghai, T'ao-k'ang-te
陶亢德, 1937.

——— "Hsien-t'an wo ti ch'i ko hua-chü 閒談我的七個話劇

(Random thoughts on my seven plays), *K'ang-chan wen-i* 抗戰文艾 (Resistance literature), vol. 8, no. 1 (Chungking, Nov. 15, 1942).

——— *Ko tsao chi* 蛤藻集 (Clams and seaweed). Shanghai, K'ai-ming shu-tien 開明書店, 1947.

——— *Niu T'ien-tz'u chuan* 牛天賜傳 (Biography of Niu T'ien-tz'u). Shanghai, Hsin-feng ch'u-pan kung-ssu 新豐出版公司, 1947).

——— *Chao Tzu-yueh* 趙子曰. Shanghai, Ch'en-kuang ch'u-pan kung-ssu 晨光出版公司, 1949.

——— *Huo-tsang* 火葬 (Cremation). Shanghai, Ch'en-kuang ch'u-pan kung-ssu, 1949.

——— *Lao Chang ti che-hsueh* 老張的哲學 (The philosophy of Lao Chang). Shanghai, Ch'en-kuang ch'u-pan kung-ssu, 1949).

——— *Mao-ch'eng chi* 貓城記 (Notes on Cat City). Shanghai, Ch'en-kuang ch'u-pan kung-ssu, 1949.

——— *Ssu-shih t'ung-t'ang* 四世同堂 (Four generations under one roof).
    Pt. 1: *Huang-huo* 惶惑 (Bewilderment). Shanghai, Ch'en-kuang ch'u-pan kung-ssu, 1949.
    Pt. 2: *T'ou-sheng* 偷生 (Ignoble life). Shangha, Ch'en-kuang ch'u-pan kung-ssu, 1949.
    Translated as *The Yellow Storm,* by Ida Pruitt. N.Y., Harcourt Brace & Co., 1951.

——— *Lo-t'o Hsiang-tzu* 駱駝祥子 (Camel Hsiang-tzu). Shanghai, Ch'en-kuang ch'u-pan kung-ssu, 1950. Translated as *Rickshaw Boy,* by Evan King. New York, Reynal-Hitchcock, 1945.

——— *Lao She hsuan-chi* 老舍選集 (Selected works of Lao She). Peking, K'ai-ming shu-tien, 1951.

——— "Mao chu-hsi kei-la wo hsin ti wen-i sheng-ming" 毛主席給了我新的文艾生命 (Chairman Mao gave me a new literary life), *Jen-min jih-pao* 人民日報 (People's daily; May 21, 1952).

——— *Dragon Beard Ditch,* tr. Liao Hung-ying. Peking, Foreign Languages Press, 1956.

——— "Hsi-wang Ch'ang-an" 西望長安 (Looking westward to Ch'angan), *Jen-min wen-hsüeh* 人民文学 (People's literature; January 1956).

——— "Wei-la t'uan-chieh" 为了團結 (For the sake of unity), *Wen-i pao* 文艾报, no. 20 (August 1957).

——— *Ch'a-kuan* 茶館 (Teahouse). Peking, Chung-kuo hsi-chü ch'u-pan she 中国戏剧出版社 , 1958.

——— "Tiao-nien Lo Ch'ang-p'ei hsien sheng" 悼念羅常培先生 (In memory of Lo Ch'ang-p'ei), *Chung-kuo yü-wen* 中國語文 (Chinese language and literature), no. 1: 23 (1959).

——— *Lao-niu p'o-ch'e* 老牛破車 (Old ox and a broken cart). Hong Kong, Yüchou shu-tien 宇宙書店 , 1961.

——— "A Vision," translation of *Wei-shen* 微神 by Gladys Yang, *Chinese Literature,* no. 6: 77–88 (1962).

——— *Erh Ma* 二馬 (Mr. Ma and Master Ma). Hong Kong, Ts'ui-wen shu-tien 萃文書店 1963.
Title changed by publisher to *Ma hsien-sheng yü Ma Wei* 馬先生與馬威 (Mr. Ma and Ma Wei).

——— *Hsiao P'o ti sheng-jih* 小坡的生日 (The birthday of Little P'o). Hong Kong, Ta Fang ch'u-pan she 大方出版社,1966.

——— *Kan chi* 趕集 (Collection of hurriedly written stories). Hong Kong, Liang-yu t'u-shu kung-ssu 良友圖書公司 , n.d.

——— *Li-hun* 離婚 (Divorce). Hong Kong, Chi-pen ch'u-pan she 基本出版社 , n.d.

——— *Ts'an wu* 殘霧 (The dispersal of the mist), in *Lao She hsi-chü chi* 老舍戏剧集 (Collected plays of Lao She). Shanghai, Ch'en-kuang ch'u-pan kung-ssu, n.d.

Li Chien-nung. *The Political History of China, 1840–1928.* Stanford, Stanford University Press, 1956.

Lin Yutang. *My Country and My People.* New York, Reynal and Hitchcock, 1935.

Lo Ch'ang-p'ei 羅常培 . "Wo yü Lao She" 我與老舍 (Lao She and I), in Lo Ch'ang-p'ei, *Chung-kuo-jen yü Chung-kuo-wen* 中國人與中國文 (Chinese people and Chinese literature). First published in Chungking in 1943, reprinted by Lung-men shu-tien 龍門書店 , Hong Kong, 1966.

Lu Hsun, Selected Works of. 4 vols. Peking, Foreign Languages Press, 1956–1960.

Mao Tse-tung. "On the People's Democratic Dictatorship," in *Selected Works of Mao Tse-tung.* 4 vols. Peking, Foreign Languages Press, 1961, IV, 411–423.

Ning En-ch'eng 寧恩丞. "Lao She tsai ying-kuo" 老舍在英国 (Lao She in England), *Ming-pao yueh-k'an* 明报月刊 (Dawn monthly), pt. 2, pp. 53–59 (June 1970).

Paauw, Douglas S. "The Kuomintang and Economic Stagnation 1928–1937," in Albert Feuerwerker, ed., *Modern China.* Englewood Cliffs, Prentice Hall, 1964.

Piao Yu-ming 表有明. "Tsai 'k'un-tzu' hsia 'tai-ping yen-nien' ti Lao She" 在棍子'下帶病延年'的老舍 (Ailing and aging Lao She under the "cudgels" of the Communists), *Ta kung pao* 大公报 ("L'Impartial"; Hong Kong, January 1962), pp. 15–21.

Roy, David T. "Kuo Mo-jo: The Pre-Marxist Phase, 1892–1924," *Papers on China* 12: 69–146. Cambridge, Mass., East Asian Research Center, Harvard University, 1958.

Schyns, Joseph, et al. *1500 Modern Chinese Novels and Plays.* Peiping, Catholic University Press, 1948. Reprinted by Lung Men Bookstore, Hong Kong, 1966.

Shibagaki Yoshitarō 柴垣芳太郎. "Ro Sha no nenpu," 老舍の年譜 (A chronological personal history of Lao She), *Akadimia* アカデミア, no. 12: 207–224.

Shu Chun-ch'eng 舒俊塝, "Yi shu-fu," 憶叔父 (Remembering uncle), *Chung-yang jih-pao* (Oct. 13, 1966), p. 4.

Shu Wen 舒文. "Lao She ti *Ch'a-kuan*" 老舍的茶馆 (Lao She's Teahouse), *Ming pao* (Oct. 26, 1966).

Slupski, Zbigniew. *The Evolution of a Modern Chinese Writer.* Prague, Oriental Institute in Academia, 1966.

192

Teng Ssu-yü and John K. Fairbank. *China's Response to the West.* Cambridge, Mass., Harvard University Press, 1961.

Ting Yi. *A Short History of Modern Chinese Literature.* Peking, Foreign Languages Press, 1959.

"Tso-t'an Lao She ti *Ch'a-kuan*" 座談老舍的茶館 (A discussion of Lao She's *Teahouse*), a transcript of a discussion between Chiao Chü-yin, Chao Shao-hou, Ch'en Pai-ch'en, Hsia Ch'un, Lin Mo-han, Wang Yao, Chang Hen-shui, Li Chien-wu, Chang Kuang-nien, published by *Wen-i pao* 文藝報 (Literary gazette), no. 1: 19–23 (January 1958).

Wales, Nym. "The Modern Chinese Literary Movement," in Edgar Snow, ed., *Living China.* New York, Reynal and Hitchcock, 1937.

Wang Yao 王瑤. *Chung-kuo hsin wen-hsueh shih kao* 中國新文學史稿 (A draft history of modern Chinese literature). Shanghai, 1953.

Wang, Y. C. *Chinese Intellectuals and the West, 1872–1949.* Chapel Hill, University of North Carolina Press, 1966.

Wang Yü 王翊. "Chi Lao She hsien-sheng" 記老舍先生 (In memory of Lao She), Chan-wang pan-yueh k'an 展望半月刊 (Chan-wang fortnightly; Sept. 1, 1970), pp. 20–23.

Wen I-wen 溫以文. "Hu Hsieh-ch'ing" 胡絜青, *Kuang-ming jih-pao* 光明日报 (Kuang-ming daily; Mar. 8, 1957).

Wright, Mary C. "From Revolution to Restoration: The Transformation of the Kuomintang Ideology," *Far Eastern Quarterly* 14.4:515–532 (August 1955).

Yao Nai-lin 姚乃麟 *Chung-kuo wen-hsueh-chia chuan chi* 中國文學家傳記 (Biographical notes on Chinese writers). Shanghai, 1937.

INDEX

198

HARVARD EAST ASIAN MONOGRAPHS

18. Frank H. H. King (ed.) and Prescott Clarke, *A Research Guide to China-Coast Newspapers, 1822–1911*

19. Ellis Joffe, *Party and Army: Professionalism and Political Control in the Chinese Officer Corps, 1949–1964*

20. Toshio G. Tsukahira, *Feudal Control in Tokugawa Japan: The Sankin Kōtai System*

21. Kwang-Ching Liu, ed., *American Missionaries in China: Papers from Harvard Seminars*

22. George Moseley, *A Sino-Soviet Cultural Frontier: The Ili Kazakh Autonomous Chou*

23. Carl F. Nathan, *Plague Prevention and Politics in Manchuria, 1910–1931*

24. Adrian Arthur Bennett, *John Fryer: The Introduction of Western Science and Technology into Nineteenth-Century China*

25. Donald J. Friedman, *The Road from Isolation: The Campaign of the American Committee for Non-Participation in Japanese Aggression, 1938–1941*

26. Edward Le Fevour, *Western Enterprise in Late Ch'ing China: A Selective Survey of Jardine, Matheson and Company's Operations, 1842–1895*

27. Charles Neuhauser, *Third World Politics: China and the Afro-Asian People's Solidarity Organization, 1957–1967*

28. Kungtu C. Sun, assisted by Ralph W. Huenemann, *The Economic Development of Manchuria in the First Half of the Twentieth Century*

29. Shahid Javed Burki, *A Study of Chinese Communes, 1965*

30. John Carter Vincent, *The Extraterritorial System in China: Final Phase*

31. Madeleine Chi, *China Diplomacy, 1914–1918*

32. Clifton Jackson Phillips, *Protestant America and the Pagan World: The First Half Century of the American Board of Commissioners for Foreign Missions, 1810–1860*

33. James Pusey, *Wu Han: Attacking the Present through the Past*

DEMCO 38-297